고등학생을 위한 문법 연습의 길잡이

문제로 미스터하는 고등영문법

MASTER

문제로 마스터하는 고등영문법

지은이	NE능률 영어교육연구소
선임연구원	김지현
외주연구원	정향, 이유진
영문교열	Patrick Ferraro, Caitlin Schmitt
디자인	안훈정, 오솔길
맥편집	김미진

43rd SINCE1980
Let's grow together
NE능률이
미래를
창조합니다.
건강한 배움의 고객가치를 제공하겠다는 꿈을 실현하기 위해
40년이 넘는 시간 동안 열심히 달려왔습니다.
앞으로도 끊임없는 연구와 노력을 통해
당연한 것을 멈추지 않고
고객, 기업, 직원 모두가 함께 성장하는 NE능률이 되겠습니다.
NE 능률

There are no great limits to growth because there are no limits of human intelligence, imagination, and wonder.

인간의 지성, 상상력, 호기심에는 한계가 없기에 성장에도 한계가 없다.

★★★★

Ronald Reagan

이 책의 구성과 특징

핵심만 담은 문법 설명 ★

문법 설명에서 군더더기를 모두 걷어 냈습니다.
핵심 설명만 간결하게 담아서 쉽게 이해할 수 있게 했습니다.

자세하게 나뉜 문법 point

문법 항목을 아주 자세하게 구분하였습니다.
각 point별로 학습 내용을 파악하기가 더 쉬울 것입니다.

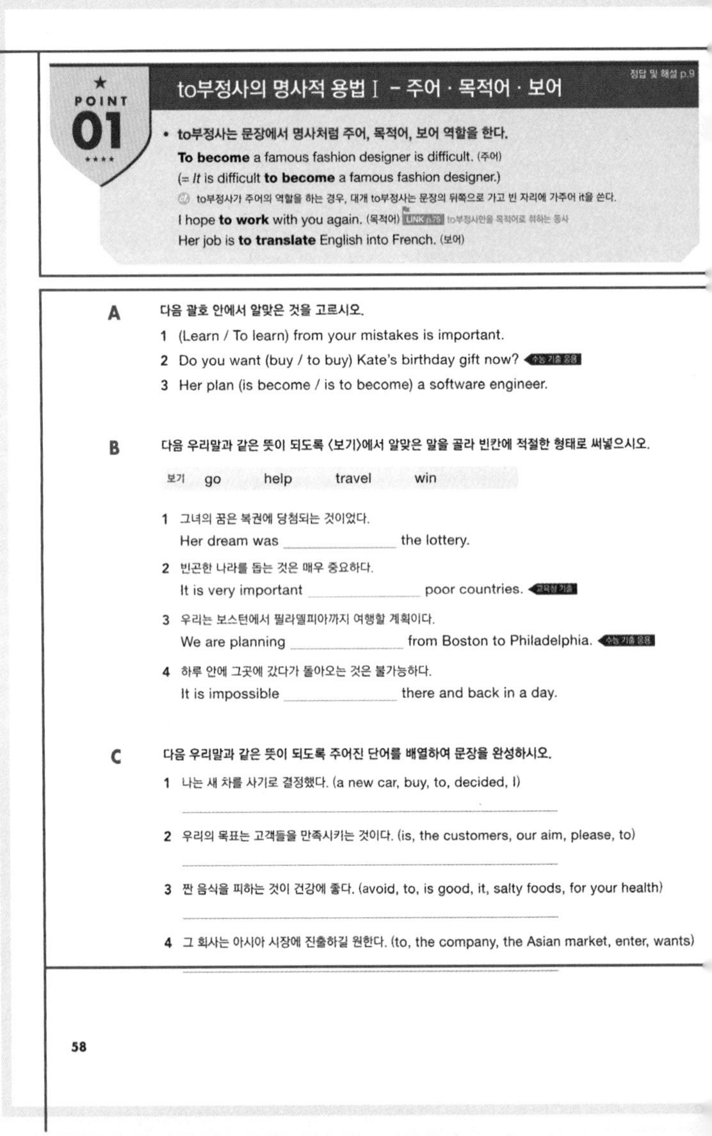

POINT 01

to부정사의 명사적 용법 I - 주어 · 목적어 · 보어

정답 및 해설 p.9

- **to부정사는 문장에서 명사처럼 주어, 목적어, 보어 역할을 한다.**

To become a famous fashion designer is difficult. (주어)
(= *It* is difficult **to become** a famous fashion designer.)
cf. to부정사가 주어의 역할을 하는 경우, 대개 to부정사는 문장의 뒤쪽으로 가고 빈 자리에 가주어 it을 쓴다.
I hope **to work** with you again. (목적어) LINK p.78 to부정사만을 목적어로 취하는 동사
Her job is **to translate** English into French. (보어)

A 다음 괄호 안에서 알맞은 것을 고르시오.

1 (Learn / To learn) from your mistakes is important.
2 Do you want (buy / to buy) Kate's birthday gift now? 수능 기출 응용
3 Her plan (is become / is to become) a software engineer.

B 다음 우리말과 같은 뜻이 되도록 <보기>에서 알맞은 말을 골라 빈칸에 적절한 형태로 써넣으시오.

보기 go help travel win

1 그녀의 꿈은 복권에 당첨되는 것이었다.
Her dream was ______________ the lottery.
2 빈곤한 나라를 돕는 것은 매우 중요하다.
It is very important ______________ poor countries. 교육청 기출
3 우리는 보스턴에서 필라델피아까지 여행할 계획이다.
We are planning ______________ from Boston to Philadelphia. 수능 기출 응용
4 하루 안에 그곳에 갔다가 돌아오는 것은 불가능하다.
It is impossible ______________ there and back in a day.

C 다음 우리말과 같은 뜻이 되도록 주어진 단어를 배열하여 문장을 완성하시오.

1 나는 새 차를 사기로 결정했다. (a new car, buy, to, decided, I)
2 우리의 목표는 고객들을 만족시키는 것이다. (is, the customers, our aim, please, to)
3 짠 음식을 피하는 것이 건강에 좋다. (avoid, to, is good, it, salty foods, for your health)
4 그 회사는 아시아 시장에 진출하길 원한다. (to, the company, the Asian market, enter, wants)

58

학생들이 스스로 많이 써 볼 수 있는 주관식 문제 구성

전체적으로 주관식 위주의 문제 구성을 지향했습니다.
간단한 체크 형식의 문제를 지양하고 학생들의 작문 실력 향상을 도울 수 있는 문제들로 구성하였습니다.

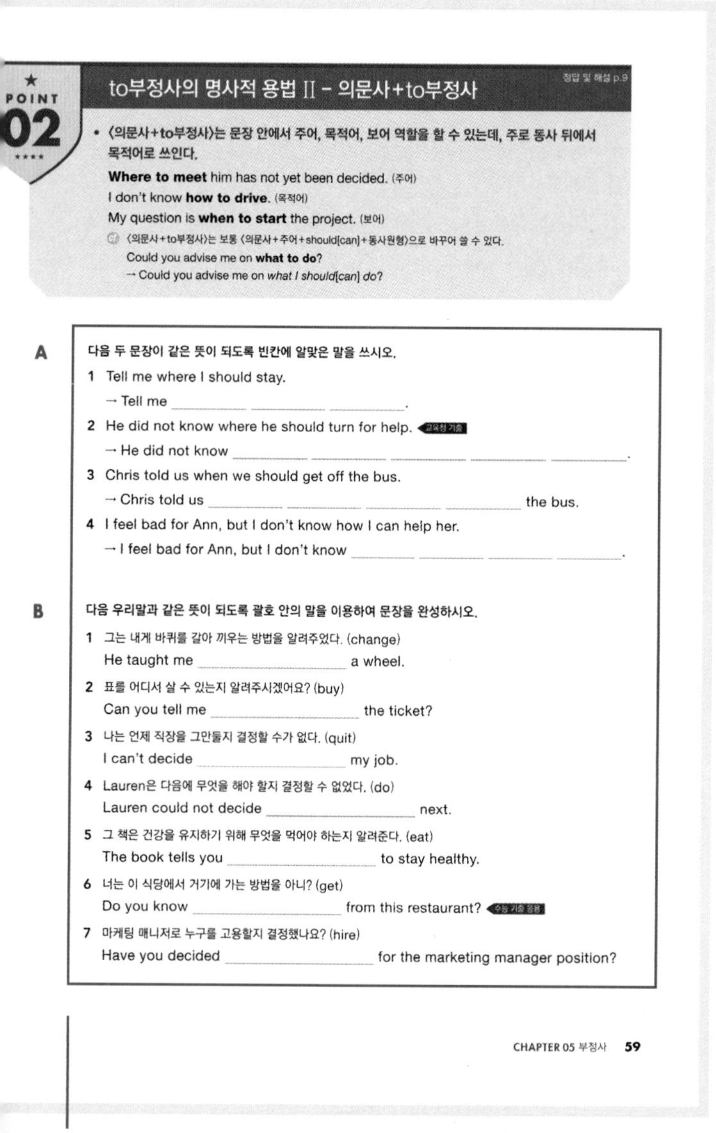

★ POINT 02 ★★★★

to부정사의 명사적 용법 II - 의문사+to부정사

정답 및 해설 p.9

- 〈의문사+to부정사〉는 문장 안에서 주어, 목적어, 보어 역할을 할 수 있는데, 주로 동사 뒤에서 목적어로 쓰인다.

Where to meet him has not yet been decided. (주어)
I don't know **how to drive**. (목적어)
My question is **when to start** the project. (보어)
〈의문사+to부정사〉는 보통 〈의문사+주어+should[can]+동사원형〉으로 바꾸어 쓸 수 있다.
Could you advise me on **what to do**?
→ Could you advise me on *what I should[can] do*?

A 다음 두 문장이 같은 뜻이 되도록 빈칸에 알맞은 말을 쓰시오.

1 Tell me where I should stay.
→ Tell me ________ ________ ________.

2 He did not know where he should turn for help. 교과서 기출
→ He did not know ________ ________ ________ ________ ________.

3 Chris told us when we should get off the bus.
→ Chris told us ________ ________ ________ ________ the bus.

4 I feel bad for Ann, but I don't know how I can help her.
→ I feel bad for Ann, but I don't know ________ ________ ________ ________.

B 다음 우리말과 같은 뜻이 되도록 괄호 안의 말을 이용하여 문장을 완성하시오.

1 그는 내게 바퀴를 갈아 끼우는 방법을 알려주었다. (change)
He taught me ________________ a wheel.

2 표를 어디서 살 수 있는지 알려주시겠어요? (buy)
Can you tell me ________________ the ticket?

3 나는 언제 직장을 그만둘지 결정할 수가 없다. (quit)
I can't decide ________________ my job.

4 Lauren은 다음에 무엇을 해야 할지 결정할 수 없었다. (do)
Lauren could not decide ________________ next.

5 그 책은 건강을 유지하기 위해 무엇을 먹어야 하는지 알려준다. (eat)
The book tells you ________________ to stay healthy.

6 너는 이 식당에서 거기에 가는 방법을 아니? (get)
Do you know ________________ from this restaurant? 수능 기출 응용

7 마케팅 매니저로 누구를 고용할지 결정했나요? (hire)
Have you decided ________________ for the marketing manager position?

CHAPTER 05 부정사 59

★

문법 항목별로 많은 문제 수록

세분화된 문법 항목별로 많은 문제를 수록하였습니다.
많은 연습 문제를 풀다 보면 어느새 고등영문법을
마스터하게 될 것입니다.

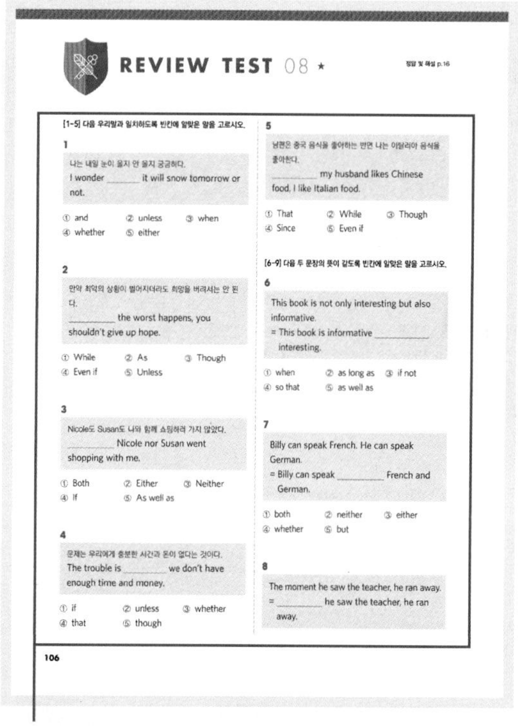

REVIEW TEST 08 ★

정답 및 해설 p.16

[1-5] 다음 우리말과 일치하도록 빈칸에 알맞은 말을 고르시오.

1
나는 내일 눈이 올지 안 올지 궁금하다.
I wonder ______ it will snow tomorrow or not.
① and ② unless ③ when ④ whether ⑤ either

2
만약 최악의 상황이 벌어지더라도 희망을 버려서는 안 된다.
________ the worst happens, you shouldn't give up hope.
① While ② As ③ Though ④ Even if ⑤ Unless

3
Nicole도 Susan도 나와 함께 쇼핑하러 가지 않았다.
________ Nicole nor Susan went shopping with me.
① Both ② Either ③ Neither ④ If ⑤ As well as

4
문제는 우리에게 충분한 시간과 돈이 없다는 것이다.
The trouble is ________ we don't have enough time and money.
① if ② unless ③ whether ④ that ⑤ though

5
남편은 중국 음식을 좋아하는 반면 나는 이탈리아 음식을 좋아한다.
________ my husband likes Chinese food, I like Italian food.
① That ② While ③ Though ④ Since ⑤ Even if

[6-9] 다음 두 문장의 뜻이 같도록 빈칸에 알맞은 말을 고르시오.

6
This book is not only interesting but also informative.
= This book is informative ________ interesting.
① when ② as long as ③ if not ④ so that ⑤ as well as

7
Billy can speak French. He can speak German.
= Billy can speak ________ French and German.
① both ② neither ③ either ④ whether ⑤ but

8
The moment he saw the teacher, he ran away.
= ________ he saw the teacher, he ran away.

106

★

통합적인 문제를 다룬 Review Test

세분화된 문법 항목별로 배운 내용들을 복습해
볼 수 있도록 Review Test에 다양한 문제들을
담았습니다. 통합적인 문제들을 통해 각 Chapter의
학습 내용을 정리할 수 있습니다.

목차

CHAPTER 01 문장의 이해

CHAPTER 02 시제

CHAPTER 05 부정사

CHAPTER 06 동명사

목차

CHAPTER 09 가정법

CHAPTER 10 관계사

CHAPTER 13 비교

CHAPTER 14 전치사

EST CHAPTER 01 2010

문장의 이해

정답 및 해설 p.2

★ POINT 01 ★★★★

구와 절

- 구: 두 개 이상의 단어가 모여 하나의 품사처럼 문장의 일부로 쓰이는 것. 문장에서의 역할에 따라 명사구, 형용사구, 부사구로 나뉜다.

  I like **playing baseball with my friends.** (명사구: 주어 · 목적어 · 보어 역할)
  She doesn't have enough time **to prepare breakfast.** (형용사구: 명사 · 대명사 수식)
  Feeling better, he went out and met his girlfriend. (부사구: 동사 · 형용사 · 부사 · 문장 수식)

- 절: 〈주부+술부〉로 이루어져 하나의 품사처럼 문장의 일부로 쓰이는 것. 두 절이 어법상 대등한 관계로 연결되어 있으면 등위절이라고 하고, 두 절 중 하나가 다른 절에 딸려 있으면 주가 되는 절을 주절, 딸린 절을 종속절이라고 한다. 종속절에는 명사절, 형용사절, 부사절이 있다.

  John is an engineer (등위절) and **Sarah is a musician.** (등위절)
  I heard from Bob (주절) **that Max quit his job.** (종속절 — 명사절)
  They have a dog (주절) **that has unusual eyes.** (종속절 — 형용사절)
  I feel comfortable (주절) **when I'm with you.** (종속절 — 부사절)

A 다음 밑줄 친 부분이 구인지, 절인지 쓰시오.

1 Their service is very easy to use. 교육청 기출 응용
2 I want to buy the T-shirt that she is wearing.
3 I hope we can make their trip memorable. 수능 기출
4 I'm sorry, but I can't tell you about it.
5 I made an effort to get to know my neighbors.
6 Sam broke the window, so his father got angry.
7 I wasn't able to complete my part of our project. 수능 기출

B 다음 밑줄 친 구가 명사구, 형용사구, 부사구 중 어느 것인지 쓰시오.

1 I like the picture on the wall.
2 I learned how to ride a bicycle yesterday.
3 We need to buy some flowers for her birthday party.
4 We offer a fun camp for children aged 7 to 12. 교육청 기출 응용
5 Kelly was happy to travel with Diane.

C 다음 밑줄 친 절이 명사절, 형용사절, 부사절 중 어느 것인지 쓰시오.

1 I immediately knew that something was wrong. 교육청 기출 응용
2 Tell him that you can't finish it by 6 p.m.
3 Let's eat dinner before we watch the movie.
4 This is the park where I go jogging every morning.
5 Turn down the radio, if you don't mind.

POINT 02 ★★★★

★ 문장의 종류

정답 및 해설 p.2

- **평서문: 어떤 사실을 서술하는 문장으로, 긍정문과 부정문이 있다.**

  Keeping your promise is important.
  I won't be at the party tonight.

- **의문문: 의문을 나타내는 문장으로, Yes/No로 답할 수 있는 일반의문문, 의문사가 있는 의문문, 부가의문문 등이 있다.**

  Can you help me? — Yes, I can.
  Where do you live? — I live in Houston.
  You don't know Mary, do you? — No, I don't.

- **명령문: 명령 · 요구 · 금지 등을 나타내는 문장으로, 긍정명령문, 부정명령문, 청유문 등이 있다.**

  Be polite to the elderly.
  Don't worry about him.
  Let's go get something to eat.

- **감탄문: 기쁨 · 슬픔 · 놀라움 등의 감정을 나타내는 문장으로, 〈What+a[an]+형용사+명사(+주어+동사)!〉 또는 〈How+형용사/부사(+주어+동사)!〉의 형태로 쓴다.**

  What a smart boy he is!
  How interesting the movie was!

A 다음 우리말과 같은 뜻이 되도록 어법상 틀린 부분을 고쳐 쓰시오.

1 몇 시에 영화가 시작하니?
What time the movie starts?

2 그는 어제 파티에 갔었지, 그렇지?
He went to the party yesterday, did he?

3 너는 과학 보고서를 다 썼니?
Did finish you the science report? 수능 기출 응용

4 너의 귀중한 시간을 그것에 낭비하지 마라.
Not waste your precious time on that. 수능 기출 응용

5 조용히 해라, 그렇지 않으면 너는 아기를 깨울 것이다.
Do quiet, or you'll wake the baby.

6 이 배우는 꽤 잘생겼지, 안 그래?
This actor is quite handsome, is he?

B 다음 문장을 감탄문으로 바꿀 때 빈칸에 알맞은 말을 쓰시오.

1 The lecture was very inspiring. → How ________ ________ ________ ________!
2 She is a very pretty girl. → What ________ ________ ________ ________ ________!
3 Those flowers are very lovely. → How ________ ________ ________ ________!

POINT 03 ★★★★

1형식 문장 (S+V)

정답 및 해설 p.2

- 〈주어+동사〉의 형태로, 이 형식의 동사는 보어나 목적어를 갖지 않지만, 뒤에 부사구와 같은 수식어구가 붙기도 한다. 단, **be, stay, stand, lie, live** 등과 같은 동사의 경우에는 부사(구)가 반드시 있어야 한다.

  The movie **ended** (at 7 p.m).
  (The movie = S, ended = V)

  My uncle **stayed** in New York.
  (My uncle = S, stayed = V, in New York = 수식어구)

- 〈There+be동사+주어 ~〉도 1형식 문장으로 취급한다.

  There **is** a house on the hill.
  (is = V, a house = S)

A 다음 문장에서 주어를 찾아 S, 동사를 찾아 V로 표시하시오.

1 We stayed at Sally's house.
2 She waited for an hour.
3 We walked around the park.
4 They are in the meeting room.
5 The lion recovered after a few days. 교육청 기출 응용
6 Linda lives in a one-room apartment.
7 There is a small park on the corner.

B 다음 우리말과 같은 뜻이 되도록 주어진 단어를 배열하여 문장을 완성하시오.

1 그의 방은 내 방 바로 위에 있다. (is, his room, just above mine)
_______________ 수능 기출

2 그녀의 개는 지난달에 죽었다. (died, her dog, last month)
____

3 도로에 차가 많다. (there, on the road, are, many cars)
____

4 그들은 3일 동안 이곳에 있을 것이다. (here, will be, they, for three days)
_______________ 수능 기출 응용

5 David와 나는 몇 시간 동안 이야기했다. (for hours, talked, David and I)
____

6 필라테스 수업은 저녁 7시에 시작한다. (in the evening, the pilates lesson, at seven, starts)
____

★ POINT 04 ★★★★

2형식 문장 (S+V+C)

정답 및 해설 p.2

- 〈주어+동사+주격 보어〉의 형태이다. 이때 주격 보어는 주어의 성질 · 상태 · 신분 등을 설명하는 말로 주로 명사(구)나 형용사(구)가 쓰인다.

Michael **became** a firefighter.
S V C

This orange **tastes** sour.
S V C

cf. 2형식 문장에 주로 쓰이는 동사는 다음과 같다.
- 상태(~이다, ~한 상태로 있다): be, keep, stay, remain 등
- 상태의 변화(~이 되다): become, get, grow, turn 등
- 감각(~하다는 느낌이 들다): appear, seem, look, feel, smell, sound, taste 등

★ EXAM TIP 감각동사 뒤에는 부사가 아닌 형용사가 주격 보어로 온다는 데 주의한다.

It **feels** *cold* in this room.

A 다음 문장에서 보어를 찾아 밑줄을 그으시오.

1 The lake is very deep.
2 Cathy is a photographer.
3 Her death remains a mystery.
4 The students looked disappointed. 교육청 기출 응용
5 The flowers in my garden smell sweet.

B 다음 괄호 안에서 알맞은 것을 고르시오.

1 Your job sounds (interesting / interestingly).
2 The whole game seems (unfair / unfairly).
3 I grew (anxious / anxiously) as it got dark. 교육청 기출 응용
4 The boy appears (smart / smartly).
5 This soybean milk turned (sour / sourly).
6 His dream finally came (true / truly).

C 다음 우리말과 같은 뜻이 되도록 주어진 단어를 배열하여 문장을 완성하시오.

1 그는 상태가 나빠지고 있다. (worse, is getting, he) 수능 기출 응용

____

2 그들은 모두 진지해 보인다. (serious, all of them, look) 수능 기출 응용

____

3 그 고양이의 털은 매우 부드럽게 느껴진다 (very soft, the cat's, fur, feels)

____

4 Cindy는 우리 동호회의 회원이 되었다. (became, Cindy, a member of our club)

____

POINT 05 ★★★★

정답 및 해설 p.2

3형식 문장 (S+V+O)

- 〈주어+동사+목적어〉의 형태로, 목적어로는 (대)명사나 명사상당어구(명사구, **to**부정사, 동명사 등)가 쓰인다.

Jackson **made** a lot of money.
S V O

cf. 3형식 동사 중에는 목적어 다음에 전치사구가 반드시 있어야 하는 동사도 있다.
- 동작의 방향 · 목표를 나타내야 하는 동사
  I **put** my bag *on the table*.
- 〈타동사+목적어+전치사〉 구문
  He **robbed** me *of my ring*.

★ EXAM TIP **enter, discuss, marry, reach, resemble은 자동사로 생각하기 쉽지만 타동사이므로 동사 뒤에 전치사를 쓰지 않는다.**

I **discussed** ~~about~~ my problem with my parents.

A 다음 문장에서 목적어를 찾아 밑줄을 그으시오.

1 I prepared dinner for you.
2 He wants to eat a hamburger.
3 I've forgotten his phone number. 수능 기출 응용
4 Please put this book on the bookshelf.
5 He inspired thousands of people through his lectures. 교육청 기출 응용

B 다음 우리말과 같은 뜻이 되도록 주어진 단어를 배열하여 문장을 완성하시오.

1 나는 Billy를 내 친구들에게 소개했다. (Billy, I, my friends, to, introduced)
____

2 그는 침대 위에 자기 코트를 뉘었다. (on the bed, laid, his coat, he)
____

3 그 박물관은 많은 전시회를 연다. (hosts, many, exhibits, the museum) 교육청 기출 응용
____

4 Nate는 우리 아버지를 생각나게 한다. (reminds, my father, me, Nate, of)
____

5 우리는 매운 음식을 먹는 것을 좋아한다. (like, we, spicy food, to eat)
____

6 Tonya는 많은 면에서 그녀의 어머니를 닮았다. (in many ways, Tonya, her mother, resembles)
____

7 그는 자기 방에서 소설을 읽고 있었다. (he, in his room, a novel, was reading)
____

8 그녀는 이 여행에 너무 많은 돈을 썼다. (too much money, spent, on this trip, she) 수능 기출 응용
____

POINT 06 ★★★★

4형식 문장 (S+V+O_1+O_2)

정답 및 해설 p.2

- 〈주어+동사+간접목적어(~에게)+직접목적어(~을/를)〉의 형태로, 간접목적어로는 주로 사람, 직접목적어로는 주로 사물이 쓰인다.

My boyfriend **gave** me a book.
(My boyfriend = S, gave = V, me = O_1, a book = O_2)

cf. 4형식 문장은 〈주어+동사+직접목적어+전치사+간접목적어〉의 3형식 문장으로 전환할 수 있다.
이때 대부분의 동사는 전치사 to를 쓰는데, buy, make, get, find 등의 동사는 for를 쓴다.
I **bought** him a bag. → I bought a bag *for* him. LINK p.47 4형식 문장의 수동태

A 다음 중 3형식 문장은 4형식으로, 4형식 문장은 3형식으로 바꾸어 쓰시오.

1 He sent a letter to me from Greece.
→ ______________________

2 Mike made a small bed for his daughter.
→ ______________________

3 I will get you a notebook.
→ ______________________

4 Her mother gave her a bundle of lilies and roses. 수능 기출 응용
→ ______________________

B 다음 밑줄 친 부분을 어법에 맞게 고쳐 쓰시오.

1 She made <u>a lovely lunch me</u>. 평가원 기출 응용

2 I taught English <u>for my children</u>.

3 He bought a pair of sneakers <u>to his brother</u>.

C 다음 우리말과 같은 뜻이 되도록 괄호 안의 말을 이용하여 문장을 완성하시오.

1 저에게 돈을 좀 주시겠어요? (give)
Could you ________ some money ________ ________? 수능 기출 응용

2 나는 그녀에게 웨딩드레스를 만들어 주었다. (make)
I ________ a wedding dress ________ ________.

3 저희가 당신에게 50달러짜리 쿠폰을 보내드리겠습니다. (send)
We ________ ________ ________ a $50 coupon. 교육청 기출 응용

4 제게 소금 좀 건네주시겠어요? (pass)
Could you ________ ________ the salt, please?

5 그녀는 그에게 책 몇 권을 빌려 주었는데, 그는 돌려주지 않았다. (lend)
She ________ several books ________ ________, but he didn't return them.

POINT 07 ★★★★

5형식 문장 (S+V+O+C) Ⅰ

정답 및 해설 p.2

- 〈주어+동사+목적어+목적격 보어〉의 형태이다. 이때 목적격 보어는 목적어의 성질 · 상태 · 신분 등을 설명하는 말로 주로 명사(구)나 형용사(구)가 쓰인다.

We **will name** this dog Beethoven.
S V O C

Her long silence **made** me anxious.
S V O C

cf. 목적격 보어로 명사(구)나 형용사(구)를 취하는 동사로는 make, keep, leave, call, name, elect, appoint, find, consider 등이 있다.

A 다음 우리말과 같은 뜻이 되도록 주어진 단어를 배열하여 문장을 완성하시오.

1 나는 그 사진을 볼 때마다 기분이 좋아지는 것을 느낀다. (feel, my spirit, lifted, I)
Every time I see the picture, ______________________. 교육청 기출 응용

2 그것들은 내 인생을 생지옥으로 만들었다. (my life, have made, a living hell)
They ______________________. 평가원 기출

3 회사의 모든 사람들이 그를 천사라고 부른다. (an angel, him, calls)
Everyone in the company ______________________.

4 그 사람들은 Martin 씨를 시장으로 선출했다. (Mr. Martin, elected, their mayor)
The people ______________________.

5 우리는 Kate를 잠시 혼자 두는 게 나을 것 같다. (alone, Kate, leave)
We'd better ______________________ for a while.

6 그들은 그를 회사의 사장으로 임명했다. (him, appointed, president of the company)
They ______________________.

B 다음 우리말과 같은 뜻이 되도록 괄호 안의 말을 이용하여 문장을 완성하시오.

1 어떤 약은 사람들을 졸리게 한다. (make, sleepy)
Some medicines ________ ________ ________.

2 Jake는 그 시험이 쉽다고 생각했다. (find, easy)
Jake ________ ________ ________ ________.

3 그의 코 고는 소리가 밤새 나를 깨어 있게 했다. (keep, awake)
His snoring ________ ________ ________ all night.

4 그 문 좀 열어 두시겠어요? (leave, open)
Will you please ________ ________ ________ ________?

5 그들은 자기들의 아기를 Violet이라고 이름 지었다. (name, Violet)
They ________ ________ ________ ________.

★ POINT **08** ★★★★

5형식 문장 (S+V+O+C) II

정답 및 해설 p.2

- 목적격 보어로 부정사가 쓰이기도 하는데, 동사에 따라 **to**부정사 또는 원형부정사를 취한다.
  - to부정사를 취하는 동사: want, like, tell, ask, persuade, advise, order, allow, force 등

    I **want** you to come home early.
    S V O C

  - 원형부정사를 취하는 동사: 사역동사(let, make, have), 지각동사(feel, hear, listen to, see, watch, smell 등)

    His parents **let** him decide where to go for vacation.
    S V O C

  cf. 지각동사의 경우, 동작이 진행 중임을 강조할 때 목적격 보어로 현재분사를 쓰기도 한다.

    I **saw** you dancing the other night.
    S V O C

A 다음 괄호 안에서 알맞은 것을 고르시오.

1 The video encourages students (save / to save) energy. 교육청 기출 응용

2 I won't let it (happen / happening) again.

3 He heard his sister (complain / to complain) about her teacher. 교육청 기출 응용

4 He ordered me (leave / to leave) the room.

B 다음 우리말과 같은 뜻이 되도록 주어진 단어를 배열하여 문장을 완성하시오.

1 나는 그에게 다운로드 링크를 보내 달라고 부탁했다. (to send me the download link, asked, him)
I ______________________________.

2 그녀는 내가 그녀의 펜을 사용하도록 허락했다. (to use her pen, allowed, me)
She ______________________________.

3 너는 내가 도와주길 원하니? (me, want, to give you a hand)
Do you ______________________________? 수능 기출

4 어머니는 나에게 다른 사람들을 존중하라고 하셨다. (told, to respect others, me)
My mother ______________________________.

C 다음 우리말과 같은 뜻이 되도록 괄호 안의 말을 이용하여 문장을 완성하시오.

1 우리는 그녀가 뛰어난 디자이너가 되리라 기대한다. (expect, be)
We ____________________ a great designer.

2 그 부자는 경비병들에게 그를 사자 우리에 넣으라고 명령했다. (order, guards, put) 교육청 기출
The rich man ____________________ him in the lion's cage.

3 그녀의 부모님은 그녀가 저녁 식사 후에 설거지를 하도록 시키셨다. (have, do)
Her parents ____________________ the dishes after dinner.

REVIEW TEST 01 ★

정답 및 해설 p.3

[1-5] 다음 우리말과 일치하도록 빈칸에 알맞은 말을 고르시오.

1

Jack은 어머니를 위해 스카프를 샀다.
Jack bought a scarf ________ his mother.

① to ② of ③ in
④ for ⑤ with

2

나는 그에게 조심해서 운전해 달라고 부탁했다.
I asked him ________ carefully.

① drive ② driving
③ to drive ④ drove
⑤ being driven

3

당신의 아들에게 좀 더 참을성을 가져라.
________ more patient with your son.

① Be ② Is
③ Do ④ Does
⑤ Let

4

Sam은 그녀가 창가 테이블에 앉아 있는 것을 보았다.
Sam saw her ________ at a table by the window.

① sat ② to sit
③ sitting ④ be sat
⑤ have sat

5

Anna는 얼마나 귀여운 소녀인가!
________ a cute girl Anna is!

① How ② What
③ May ④ Which
⑤ Let

[6-8] 다음 〈보기〉와 문장의 형식이 같은 것을 고르시오.

6

보기 | She found the place easily.

① This soup smells good.
② There is snow on the ground.
③ I found the story interesting.
④ He won't let me use his cell phone.
⑤ My sister bought a dress yesterday.

7

보기 | Jim lent me his camera.

① Our budget is very small.
② I don't want to know the truth.
③ Will you lend it to your friend?
④ The police asked him a few questions.
⑤ My grandmother gives lots of money to me.

8

보기 | My pet died last night.

① It doesn't matter at all.
② He didn't want to spend his money.
③ My mom told me to come home early.
④ Everything in the refrigerator went bad.
⑤ Miss Jones saw you cheating on the test.

[9-10] 다음 빈칸에 알맞은 말을 고르시오.

9

Julia went to church, ___________?

① was she ② wasn't she
③ does she ④ did she
⑤ didn't she

10

A: Can you do me a favor?
B: ________________

① Yes, I can. ② No, you can't.
③ Yes, I could. ④ Yes, I am.
⑤ No, you aren't.

[11-14] 다음 우리말과 일치하도록 문장을 완성하시오.

11

이 감자 샐러드는 맛이 신선하다.
This potato salad tastes ___________.

12

이 치즈 케이크 정말 맛있다!
___________ delicious this cheesecake is!

13

저쪽에 버스 정류장이 있다.
________ ________ a bus stop over there.

14

그녀는 그에게 자기 전화번호를 주지 않았다.
She didn't give her number ________ him.

[15-16] 다음 문장의 빈칸에 들어갈 수 없는 말을 고르시오.

15

He ________ me to join his dinner party.

① wants ② allowed
③ told ④ expects
⑤ made

16

My brother ________ very angry.

① was ② became
③ seems ④ stopped
⑤ grew

[17-19] 다음 문장 중 어법상 틀린 것을 고르시오.

17

① She remained silent for a while.
② Are there any empty seats here?
③ I gave him the doctor's address.
④ Mark lives in a large apartment.
⑤ We discussed about the plan yesterday.

18

① I sent a message to Bill.
② What an amazing movie it is!
③ Her new plan sounds wonderful.
④ Not ask such a silly question.
⑤ I hope to win the grand prize.

19

① How intelligent she is!
② Don't show these papers to anyone.
③ They became very close friends. 교육청 기출 응용
④ The dog made my family happier.
⑤ That man robbed me from my wallet!

[20-22] 다음 문장 중 어법상 옳은 것을 고르시오.

20

① What beautiful this river is!
② Kids learns mostly by example. 교육청 기출
③ Shopping makes me feel better.
④ The Christmas tree looked magically.
⑤ I saw something to move slowly.

21

① Asks him how he feels.
② The officer told them stop.
③ Were you hear about the party?
④ Can you give me a hand with the box?
⑤ We ask you donate things you don't need.
교육청 기출 응용

22

① I gave a book for my sister.
② Jake walks school every day.
③ Do you mean what by that?
④ They made him to class president.
⑤ Your actions speak louder than your words.
교육청 기출

23 다음 대화의 (A), (B), (C)에서 각각 알맞은 것을 고르시오.

A: (A) (When / Where) did you stay at our hotel?
B: Last weekend for the medical seminar.
A: Let me (B) (check / to check). Hold on a minute, please. You (C) (stayed / stayed in) room 606, right? 평가원 기출 응용

24 다음 대화의 밑줄 친 부분 중 어법상 틀린 것은?

A: My son ① seems okay, but he doesn't talk with me like he used to and ② doesn't often hang out with his friends.
B: Well, that's a sign of growing up. He reminds ③ me my daughter.
A: ④ Is there anything I can do for him? I'm afraid he might be ⑤ getting worse.
수능 기출 응용

25 다음 글의 빈칸 (A), (B)에 적절한 것끼리 짝지어진 것은?

Some golfers like ____(A)____ on ice near the Arctic. This allows them ____(B)____ beautiful views of the cliffs and peaks of ice mountains. 평가원 기출

	(A)	(B)
①	play	to enjoy
②	playing	enjoying
③	play	enjoying
④	to play	enjoy
⑤	to play	to enjoy

EST CHAPTER 2010

CHAPTER 02

시제

1 현재시제 · 과거시제
2 미래시제
3 미래를 나타내는 현재형 · 진행형
4 진행형
5 현재완료 I (계속 · 경험)
6 현재완료 II (완료 · 결과)
7 과거 vs. 현재완료
8 과거완료 · 미래완료 · 완료진행형

REVIEW TEST 02

POINT 01 ★★★★

현재시제 · 과거시제

정답 및 해설 p.3

- **현재시제: 현재의 사실이나 상태, 변하지 않는 진실, 반복되는 일이나 습관을 나타낼 때 사용하며, 동사의 현재형을 쓴다.**

  I **live** in a tiny apartment in New York.
  The sun **rises** in the east and **sets** in the west.
  Amy **goes** to work at 8 o'clock every morning.

- **과거시제: 이미 끝난 과거의 일이나 상태를 나타낼 때 사용하며, 과거의 특정한 때를 나타내는 표현들(~ ago, last ~, yesterday 등)과 함께 자주 쓰인다.**

  Last year, I **traveled** to Spain with my brother.
  Charles **was** a fantastic basketball player at college.

A 다음 괄호 안에서 알맞은 것을 고르시오.

1 I (hear / heard) the news of his death last year.
2 The sun (is / was) food for many living things on Earth. 수능 기출 응용
3 Abraham Lincoln (is / was) elected president in 1860.

B 다음 괄호 안의 동사를 알맞은 형태로 바꾸어 빈칸에 쓰시오.

1 Chris ________ this car two years ago. (buy)
2 My grandmother ________ of cancer when I was sixteen. (die)
3 Kate currently ________ the world record for the marathon. (hold)
4 Mount Everest ________ one of the highest mountains on Earth. (be)
5 In ancient Egypt, pitching stones ________ the favorite game of children. (be) 수능 기출 응용

C 다음 우리말과 같은 뜻이 되도록 〈보기〉의 말을 이용하여 문장을 완성하시오.

보기 get come have participate

1 우리는 프랑스 유학 중에 결혼했다.
We ________ married while studying in France.

2 한국은 1948년에 처음으로 올림픽에 참가했다.
South Korea first ________ in the Olympic games in 1948.

3 이 패션 잡지는 매주 발간된다.
This fashion magazine ________ out every week.

4 거북은 자동 체온 조절 기능을 가지고 있지 않다. 교육청 기출 응용
A turtle ________ automatic body temperature control.

POINT 02 ★★★★

미래시제

정답 및 해설 p.4

- **〈will+동사원형〉: 미래에 대한 예측이나 의지를 나타낸다.**
  Sarah **will join** us for dinner tomorrow.
  I'll help you finish the science project.
- **〈be going to+동사원형〉: 미래에 대한 예측(= will+동사원형) 및 이미 정해진 미래의 계획을 나타낸다. 즉흥적으로 결심한 일을 나타낼 때는 〈will+동사원형〉을 쓴다.**
  It **is going to snow** for the next two days. (= It **will snow** for the next two days.)
  I'm going to major in physics in college.

A

다음 대화의 괄호 안에서 알맞은 것을 고르시오.

1 A: It's freezing in this room!
B: I (will / am going to) turn on the heater.

2 A: Why are you all dressed up today?
B: I (will / am going to) see an important client.

3 A: I think there's someone at the door.
B: I (will / am going to) go downstairs and answer it.

4 A: You left the car's lights on!
B: Did I? I (will / am going to) turn them off.

5 A: Why don't you hang out with us tonight?
B: I can't. I (will / am going to) meet my boss.

B

다음 괄호 안의 동사를 will 또는 be going to를 이용해 알맞은 형태로 바꾸어 대화를 완성하시오.

1 A: Do you have any plans for tomorrow?
B: I ____________________ a baseball game. (see)

2 A: Why are you taking pictures of your computer? 수능 기출
B: I ____________________ it on a website. (sell)

3 A: You're late again.
B: I promise you this ____________________ the last time. (be) 수능 기출

4 A: Why can't you come to my party tomorrow?
B: I ____________________ my grandparents. (visit)

5 A: When are you expecting your baby?
B: I ____________________ twins next month. (give birth to)

★ POINT 03 ★★★★

미래를 나타내는 현재형 · 진행형

정답 및 해설 p.4

- **현재형: 대중교통 시간표, 공적인 일정 등과 같이 변경될 가능성이 거의 없는 미래의 일을 나타낼 때 현재시제를 사용하기도 한다.**

  The last train for Tokyo **leaves** at 8 in the evening.

★ EXAM TIP 때나 조건을 나타내는 부사절에서는 현재형을 사용하여 미래의 일을 표현한다.

When my parents **come** back, I'll introduce you to them.
If it **is** sunny this weekend, I'll go camping. LINK p.101, p.103 부사절을 이끄는 종속접속사

- **진행형: 가까운 미래에 하기로 계획된 일을 나타낼 때는 현재진행형이나 미래진행형을 사용하기도 한다.**

  Jack **is moving** to a new apartment on Friday.
  I **will be traveling** to New Zealand in September.

A 다음 괄호 안에서 알맞은 것을 고르시오.

1 If we (don't / will not) hurry, we'll miss the bus.
2 When I (get / will get) the money, I'll take you out to dinner.
3 I don't know if I (am able to / will be able to) finish the essay by tomorrow.

B 다음 문장에서 밑줄 친 부분이 어법상 옳으면 동그라미 하고, 틀리면 바르게 고치시오.

1 I'm leaving early tomorrow morning for Africa. 수능 기출 응용
2 I wonder if Betty looks after my kids tonight.
3 You'll get better soon if you will get some rest. 수능 기출 응용
4 The flight arrives at its destination at 9 a.m. tomorrow.
5 When Alex will return next week, I'm having a party for him.
6 The president will be giving a speech tonight.

C 다음 우리말과 같은 뜻이 되도록 괄호 안의 말을 이용하여 문장을 완성하시오.

1 너는 그 회의가 언제 열릴지 아니? (be held)
Do you know when ____________________?
2 내가 거기에 도착하자마자 전화할게. (get)
I'll call you as soon as ____________________.
3 내일 비가 오면, 나는 영화를 보러 가지 않을 것이다. (rain)
If ____________________, I won't go to the movies.

POINT 04 ★★★★

진행형

정답 및 해설 p.4

- **진행형: 진행 중인 일을 나타내며 '~하고 있다'라는 뜻이다.**

  Peter **is reading** a book on a bench. (현재진행형)

  I **was sleeping** on the sofa when Alice called. (과거진행형)

  When you arrive, I **will be watching** TV. (미래진행형)

  cf. 현재진행형과 미래진행형은 예정된 미래의 일을 나타낼 때도 쓸 수 있다. LINK p.24 미래를 나타내는 진행형

★ EXAM TIP **know, remember, like, love, hate, have(가지다), own, see, hear, feel, smell, sound, taste와 같이 생각, 감정, 소유, 감각 등을 나타내는 동사는 진행형으로 쓸 수 없다.**

~~I'm having a black cat.~~ → I **have** a black cat.

A

다음 괄호 안의 동사를 진행형으로 알맞게 바꾸어 문장을 완성하시오.

1 He ____________ a mystery novel now. (read)

2 I ____________ you in front of the mall at 8 p.m. tonight. (wait for)

3 Mary ____________ her mother on the phone when I came in. (talk to)

4 I ____________ hard to get good grades in biology these days. (study)

5 Three days from now I ____________ my vacation in the sun. (enjoy)

6 Anna ____________ music, so she didn't hear the fire alarm. (listen to)

B

다음 우리말과 같은 뜻이 되도록 밑줄 친 부분을 고쳐 쓰시오.

1 어떤 사람들은 관광이 환경에 나쁘다고 생각한다.
Some people <u>are feeling</u> that tourism is bad for the environment.

2 Cindy는 집을 지키는 똑똑한 개를 가지고 있다.
Cindy <u>is having</u> a smart dog to guard her house.

3 다음 주 이 시간에 Iris는 산에서 하이킹을 하고 있을 것이다.
This time next week, Iris <u>will hike</u> in the mountains.

4 오락으로서의 나무 타기의 인기가 급격히 높아지고 있다.
Recreational tree climbing <u>grows</u> rapidly in popularity. 수능 기출 응용

5 나는 아버지가 들어오셨을 때 과제를 하고 있었다.
I <u>am doing</u> the assignment when my father came in. 수능 기출 응용

C

다음 우리말과 같은 뜻이 되도록 괄호 안의 말을 이용하여 문장을 완성하시오.

1 내가 자고 있는 동안 Jacob이 전화했다. (sleep)
Jacob called me ____________.

2 나는 식당에서 피자를 먹고 있는 중이다. (have)
____________ at a cafeteria.

3 그는 내일 이 시간에 일하고 있을 것이다. (work)
____________ at this time tomorrow.

★ POINT
05
★★★★

현재완료 I (계속 · 경험)

정답 및 해설 p.4

- **과거에 일어난 일이 현재까지 영향을 주는 경우에 현재완료형을 사용한다.**
- **계속: 과거에서 현재까지 계속된 동작이나 상태를 나타내며, for 또는 since와 함께 자주 쓰인다.**

  I **have lived** in this city *since* childhood.
  I **have known** Paul *for* ten years.
- **경험: 과거에서 현재까지 경험한 일을 나타낸다.**

  I**'ve visited** this place once before.
  Cathy **has** never **traveled** by plane.

A **다음 우리말과 같은 뜻이 되도록 밑줄 친 부분을 고쳐 쓰시오.**

1 Sue는 전에 그 복사기를 사용해 본 적이 없다.
Sue is never using the copying machine before.

2 Tom과 나는 지금까지 사진 동아리에 2년 동안 속해 있었다.
Tom and I are in the photography club for two years.

3 그녀는 2015년 이후로 지금까지 딸에게서 소식을 듣지 못했다.
She didn't hear from her daughter since 2015.

B **다음 우리말과 같은 뜻이 되도록 괄호 안의 말을 이용하여 문장을 완성하시오.**

1 Sarah는 다리가 부러진 적이 없다. (never, break)
Sarah ________ ________ ________ her leg.

2 나는 어렸을 때부터 고양이를 좋아해 왔다. (like)
I ________ ________ cats since I was young. 수능 기출 응용

3 그녀의 책 중에 무엇이라도 읽어 본 적이 있니? (read)
________ ________ ________ any of her books?

4 Chris는 사업차 파리에 두 번 가 본 적이 있다. (be)
Chris ________ ________ to Paris twice on business.

5 여기 일본에 계신 지 얼마나 되셨나요? (stay)
How long ________ ________ ________ here in Japan?

C **다음 각각의 두 문장을 since 또는 for를 이용하여 한 문장으로 쓰시오.**

1 Robert started to work at this restaurant in 2014. He still works here.
→ Robert ______________________________.

2 The owner started to run the business ten years ago. She still runs it.
→ The owner ______________________________.

POINT 06 ★★★★

현재완료 II (완료 · 결과)

정답 및 해설 p.4

- **완료: 과거에 시작되어 현재에 완료된 일을 나타낸다.**

  Nate **has** *just* **finished** his homework.

  We **have** not **arrived** at the theater *yet*.

  cf. 완료를 나타내는 현재완료는 just, yet, already 등의 부사와 함께 자주 쓰인다.

- **결과: 과거의 일이 현재에 영향을 미침을 나타낸다.**

  Emily **has gone** to Italy with her husband. (→ Emily is in Italy now.)

  I've lost the key to my apartment. (→ I don't have the key now.)

A

다음 우리말과 같은 뜻이 되도록 괄호 안의 말을 이용하여 문장을 완성하시오.

1 그녀는 시애틀로 이사했는데, 그곳을 매우 좋아한다. (move)

She ________ ________ to Seattle, and she loves it.

2 정부가 새로운 노동 관련 법안을 통과시켰다. (pass)

The government ________ ________ a new labor law.

3 Charles가 학교를 떠나서, 나는 그를 더 이상 만나지 않는다. (leave)

Charles ________ ________ school, so I don't see him anymore.

4 우리는 파크스 몰에 막 도착했다. (arrive)

We ________ ________ ________ at the Parks Mall. 평가원 기출 응용

B

다음 문장을 우리말로 해석하고, 밑줄 친 부분이 현재완료의 어떤 용법으로 사용되었는지 쓰시오.

1 We <u>have just accepted</u> his offer.

2 I think I<u>'ve left</u> my bag on the bus.

3 Max <u>hasn't decided</u> where to stay yet.

4 The fire <u>has gone</u> out, so the room is very cold.

5 Car sharing movements <u>have appeared</u> all over the world. 교육청 기출

C

다음 두 문장이 같은 뜻이 되도록 빈칸에 알맞은 말을 쓰시오.

1 My brother went to Canada, and he is still there.

→ My brother ____________________.

2 Bob left his wallet at home, so he doesn't have it now.

→ Bob ____________________.

3 I forgot Amy's cell phone number, so I don't know it now.

→ I ____________________.

★ POINT 07 ★★★★

과거 vs. 현재완료

정답 및 해설 p.4

- **과거시제는 현재와는 상관없는 과거의 사실만을 이야기할 때 사용한다. 반면 현재완료는 과거의 일을 언급하지만 결국 현재의 상황을 말하고자 할 때 사용한다.**

  My car **broke** down. (현재 차의 상태가 어떤지는 알 수 없음)
  My car **has broken** down. (현재에도 차가 고장 나서 사용할 수 없음)

★ EXAM TIP **특정 과거 시점을 나타내는 ~ ago, last ~, yesterday, when, just now는 현재완료와 함께 쓰지 않는다.**

I**'ve seen** the movie **yesterday**. (x)
I **saw** the movie **yesterday**. (o)

A 다음 괄호 안의 말을 이용하여 과거시제 또는 현재완료로 문장을 완성하시오.

1 Samuel __________ his job five years ago. (quit) 평가원 기출 응용
2 I'm full. I __________________ dinner. (just, finish)
3 Sam ______________ his friend yesterday. (run into)
4 Mr. Johnson __________ a heart attack last month. (have)
5 When ____________________ your first car? (you, buy)
6 Nancy _______________ math at a high school since she was 25. (teach)

B 다음 우리말과 같은 뜻이 되도록 괄호 안의 말을 이용하여 문장을 완성하시오.

1 그는 언제 머리를 잘랐니? (get a haircut)
When __________________________?

2 나는 10살 때 처음으로 일본을 방문했다. (visit)
I first __________ Japan when I was ten.

3 남동생은 3일째 아픈 상태이다. (be)
My brother _______________ ill for three days.

4 그의 마지막 경기에서, 그의 실수 때문에 팀이 졌다. (cause) 교육청 기출 응용
In his last game, his mistake __________ his team to lose.

5 Jessica는 열쇠를 잃어버렸다. 그래서 지금 열쇠가 없다. (lose)
Jessica _______________ her key, so she doesn't have it now.

6 어머니가 돌아가신 지 두 달이 지났다. (pass)
Two months _______________ since my mother died. 평가원 기출 응용

7 나는 여태껏 그렇게 이상한 이야기를 들어 본 적이 없다. (never, hear)
I ____________________ such a strange story before.

8 Kate는 집에 없다. 그녀는 친구를 만나러 나갔다. (go out)
Kate is not at home. She ____________________ to meet a friend.

POINT 08 ★★★★

과거완료 · 미래완료 · 완료진행형

정답 및 해설 p.4

- **과거완료 · 미래완료: 과거완료는 과거의 특정 시점 이전에 일어난 일을 나타낼 때, 미래완료는 미래의 특정 시점까지 완료될 일을 나타낼 때 사용한다. 두 시제 모두 현재완료와 마찬가지로 계속, 경험, 완료, 결과의 의미를 나타낼 수 있다.**

  The baseball game **had started** when we arrived. (과거완료: had p.p.)

  Adam **will have finished** the puzzle by 8 o'clock. (미래완료: will have p.p.)

- **완료진행형: 완료형의 계속적 용법과 쓰임이 유사하나 특정 시점에서 일이 진행 중임을 강조할 때 완료진행형을 사용한다.**

  It **has been snowing** for two days. (현재완료진행형: have[has] been v-ing)

  I **had been sleeping** for two hours when the phone rang. (과거완료진행형: had been v-ing)

  We**'ll have been living** in Bangkok for a year next Friday. (미래완료진행형: will have been v-ing)

A 다음 괄호 안에서 알맞은 것을 고르시오.

1 I (have been / had been) blind, but later regained my sight. 평가원 기출 응용

2 I (have never seen / had never seen) an alligator before I came here.

3 I (had studied / will have studied) French for two years when I graduate.

4 Tony (had lived / has been living) in Seattle before he moved to Denver.

5 We (are waiting / will have been waiting) for an hour when his plane arrives.

6 Stop looking at your phone! You (have been using / had been using) it all day long.

B 다음 괄호 안의 말을 이용하여 과거완료 또는 미래완료로 문장을 완성하시오.

1 When I arrived, the musical ____________________. (already, start)

2 Harry ____________________ his homework when I come back home. (finish)

3 Since I ____________________ in public before, I was very nervous. (never, speak)

C 다음 문장을 완료진행형을 이용하여 바꾸어 쓰시오.

1 My computer shut down an hour after I began using it.

→ I ____________________________________ for an hour when it shut down.

2 I started teaching English two years ago. Next year will be my third year.

→ I ____________________________________ for three years next year.

3 The students started working on the project two months ago. They are still working on it. 교육청 기출 응용

→ The students ____________________________________.

REVIEW TEST 02 ★

정답 및 해설 p.4

[1-5] 다음 우리말과 일치하도록 빈칸에 알맞은 말을 고르시오.

1

나는 어제부터 아무것도 먹지 못해 배가 고프다.
I'm hungry because I __________ anything since yesterday.

① didn't eat ② don't eat
③ am not eating ④ haven't eaten
⑤ hadn't eaten

2

내가 전화했을 때 무엇을 하고 있었니?
What __________ when I called?

① are you doing ② did you do
③ were you doing ④ have you done
⑤ are you going to do

3

그들은 한 시간 후에 저녁을 먹을 예정이다.
They __________ dinner in an hour.

① had ② have
③ have eaten ④ had eaten
⑤ are going to have

4

Daniel은 두 시간째 계속 자고 있다.
Daniel __________ for the past two hours.

① sleeps ② slept
③ is sleeping ④ will sleep
⑤ has been sleeping

5

그가 돌아올 때쯤 나는 새 집으로 이사했을 것이다.
I __________ into a new house by the time he comes back.

① moved ② have moved
③ had moved ④ will have moved
⑤ have been moving

[6-8] 다음 빈칸에 들어갈 말이 순서대로 바르게 짝지어진 것을 고르시오.

6

The plane __________ already __________ off when I arrived at the airport.

① is - taking ② has - taken
③ had - taken ④ has - been taking
⑤ will have - taken

7

When the phone __________, Jim __________ spaghetti.

① rang - is cooking ② rang - was cooking
③ rings - was cooking ④ rang - has cooked
⑤ is ringing - cooked

8

A: Have you __________ any movies lately?
B: Yes, I __________ a comedy last night.

① saw - saw ② saw - was seeing
③ seen - saw ④ seen - have seen
⑤ seen - had seen

[9-10] 다음 두 문장의 뜻이 같도록 빈칸에 알맞은 말을 고르시오.

9

Wendy started to study biology three years ago, and she is still studying it.
= Wendy ________ biology for three years.

① studied ② is studying
③ has studied ④ had studied
⑤ will have been studying

10

Roy joined the travel club last summer, but he quit this summer.
= Roy ________ in the travel club for a year.

① is ② was ③ has been
④ will be ⑤ will have been

[11-12] 다음 중 밑줄 친 부분의 쓰임이 나머지와 다른 것을 고르시오.

11

① I've seen her somewhere before.
② I've never been abroad in my life.
③ Have you ever had a part-time job?
④ Ben has watched that movie three times.
⑤ Ivy has gone to London to live with her parents.

12

① I've just heard the terrible news.
② It has rained heavily for two days.
③ I have loved Jay since I first met him.
④ They have known each other for 15 years.
⑤ Cindy has had a bad cold since last Sunday.

[13-15] 다음 밑줄 친 부분을 바르게 고친 것을 고르시오.

13

His family has gone to Japan five years ago.

① goes ② went
③ is going ④ has been going
⑤ will have gone

14

If it will snow tomorrow, we will build a snowman.

① snows ② snowed
③ is going to snow ④ has snowed
⑤ will have snowed

15

Sandra has used her computer for two years before it broke down.

① uses ② is using
③ had used ④ has been using
⑤ will have used

[16-19] 다음 중 밑줄 친 부분이 어법상 틀린 것을 고르시오.

16

① I missed my yoga class yesterday.
② I was feeling scared at night as a child.
③ I'm going to see a doctor tomorrow.
④ We offer quailty training to all employees.
⑤ Amy had never seen lions in the wild before she came here.

17

① We are having a good time here.
② I've lost trust in their customer service.
③ Do you know when he will be available?
④ We expanded our business since 2015.
⑤ They will have opened 10 more stores by next year.

18

① I have read the book three times.
② They have started dating last month.
③ Our sales have been on the rise recently.
④ He has gone to India and can't be reached.
⑤ I will let you know as soon as I have the details.

19

① It's been snowing all day.
② The boss will be coming back next week.
③ My family is going on a holiday soon.
④ The audience was laughing at him. 교육청 기출 응용
⑤ Jim has already left when I got there.

[20-21] 다음 밑줄 친 부분 중 어법에 맞지 않는 것을 골라 바르게 고치시오.

20

I'm not sure when it ① started to snow. I know it ② had already started when I ③ drove to Mike's house around 8 a.m. And it ④ has been snowing heavily when I came back home.

21

① I'm going to move to Washington D.C. next month. My wife ② has moved there last spring. My two daughters also ③ live there. We ④ will make Philadelphia our primary residence. 평가원 기출 응용

[22-23] 다음 글의 밑줄 친 부분 중 어법상 틀린 것을 고르시오.

22

I recently ① began attending a famous high school in Oxford on scholarship. It ② takes two hours or more each way to commute. In the beginning, I ③ was willing to accept the challenge. However, as the long days continue, I'm not sure this school is right for me. Also my relationship with my family ④ got worse since I started. I ⑤ come home too tired to talk with them. 평가원 기출 응용

23

① I've enjoyed your class for the past two years. When I told you about my difficulties in your class, you ② have given me words of encouragement. I ③ will never forget it. Now I'm sad that Bayside High ④ is losing one of its greatest teachers. I appreciate all the effort ⑤ you've put into teaching. 평가원 기출 응용

24 **다음 글의 빈칸 (A), (B)에 적절한 것끼리 짝지어진 것은?**

Jane and Kevin ____(A)____ their second wedding ceremony tomorrow. They have gone through a difficult time. Kevin had a car accident, and his legs were paralyzed. Jane lovingly took care of him, and a miracle happened: He was able to walk again. So, they ____(B)____ their love with this ceremony. 수능 기출 응용

	(A)	(B)
①	have	confirm
②	are having	are going to confirm
③	have had	confirmed
④	are having	have confirmed
⑤	have had	have confirmed

EST 2010

CHAPTER 03

조동사

★ POINT 01 ★★★★

can, be able to, could (능력 · 가능)

정답 및 해설 p.5

- **can은 능력 · 가능(~할 수 있다)을 나타내며, be able to로 바꾸어 쓸 수 있다.**

  I **can** speak Spanish. = **I'm able to** speak Spanish. (현재의 능력)

  cf. 일상 영어에서는 be able to보다 can을 자주 사용한다.

- **과거의 능력을 나타낼 때는 could, 미래의 능력을 나타낼 때는 will be able to를 사용한다.**

  He **could** swim when he was seven years old. (과거의 능력)

  cf. I **was able to** finish the book in two days. (과거 특정 상황에서 실제로 해낸 일)

  I **will be able to** complete the project. (미래의 능력)

★ EXAM TIP **조동사 두 개를 연달아 쓰지 않으므로, 조동사 뒤에는 반드시 can 대신 be able to를 써야 한다.**

A 다음 빈칸에 can 또는 be able to 중 적절한 것을 골라 쓰시오. (둘 다 가능한 경우, can을 쓰시오.)

1 Ted will ____________ win this match.

2 I ____________ speak three different languages.

3 He ____________ make a desk by himself.

4 I thought that I would ____________ find another job. 교육청 기출

5 Wendy ____________ swim in the ocean.

6 Jane hopes to ____________ travel around Europe.

B 다음 괄호 안에서 알맞은 것을 고르시오.

1 She (is able to / was able to) pass her driving test the first time.

2 Kate may (can / be able to) lift the box easily.

3 Robert (can / could) play the piano when he was young.

4 He wants to (can / be able to) get there by 2 o'clock.

5 I won't (can / be able to) finish by the deadline. 수능 기출 응용

6 I (was able to / will be able to) complete it yesterday. 수능 기출 응용

C 다음 밑줄 친 부분을 어법에 맞게 고쳐 쓰시오.

1 I won't <u>can make</u> it in time.

2 I <u>can write</u> poems when I was eight.

3 Paul might <u>was able to see</u> her someday.

4 My sister <u>is able</u> to enter a good college next year.

5 He used to <u>can eat</u> spicy food when he was younger.

6 I <u>am able</u> to see famous paintings at the gallery tomorrow.

★ POINT 02 ★★★★

can, could (가능성 · 허가 · 요청)

정답 및 해설 p.5

- **can은 가능성(종종 ~할 수 있다), 허가(~해도 된다) 및 요청(~해 주시겠습니까)을 나타낸다. 허가를 구하거나 요청할 때 could를 쓰면 더 정중한 표현이 된다.**

Anyone **can** get cancer. (가능성)
You **can** stop working and go home now. (허가)
Can[Could] I come in and wait? (허가)
Can[Could] you give me a call tonight? (요청)

A

다음 문장을 밑줄 친 부분에 유의하여 우리말로 해석하시오.

1 It can be very cold in March.
2 You can come visit us anytime!
3 Even experts can make mistakes.
4 Could I borrow your lecture notes?
5 You can use my laptop now.
6 You can't use your cell phone in the office.
7 Can you put some more powder on my face?
8 Can I use this coupon with my membership card? 수능 기출 응용

B

다음 짝지어진 세 문장 중 밑줄 친 부분의 쓰임이 다른 것을 고르시오.

1 (1) Can I open the window?
(2) Can you find the ring for me? 수능 기출 응용
(3) You can park anywhere in the parking lot.
2 (1) The schedule can be changed without notice.
(2) You can be a good writer without any experience. 교육청 기출
(3) You can start anytime you are ready.
3 (1) Can you please pass the salt?
(2) Can the rumor be true?
(3) Can you tell me your address?

C

다음 우리말과 같은 뜻이 되도록 괄호 안의 말을 이용하여 문장을 완성하시오.

1 저희 어머니를 위한 선물을 추천해 주시겠어요? (recommend)
__________________ a gift for my mother?
2 원하면 쉬어도 된다. (rest)
You __________________ if you want.
3 자외선에 대한 직접 노출은 피부에 부정적인 영향을 일으킬 수 있다. (cause) 교육청 기출
Direct exposure to ultraviolet light __________________ negative effects on the skin.

POINT 03 ★★★★

may, might (추측 · 허가)

정답 및 해설 p.5

- **may는 불확실한 추측(아마 ~할 것이다)을 나타낸다. might는 may보다 추측에 대한 확신이 떨어질 때 사용한다.**

He **may** come tomorrow or the next day.
There **might** be life on other planets.

- **may는 허가(~해도 된다)를 나타낼 수 있다.**

You **may** eat whatever you like.
May I see your ticket and passport?

A 다음 〈보기〉에서 알맞은 말을 골라 써넣어 대화를 완성하시오.

보기 She might be sick. I may not be able to finish it today. May I ask your price range? No, you may not. It may rain.

1 A: How about going to the beach this afternoon?
B: We'd better not. ______________________

2 A: ______________________
B: Don't worry. You don't have to.

3 A: Do you know why Anne is absent?
B: I'm not sure. ______________________

4 A: Mom, may I have some dessert?
B: ______________________ You haven't finished your vegetables.

5 A: ______________________
B: Well, I don't want to spend more than $50. 교육청 기출

B 다음 우리말과 같은 뜻이 되도록 괄호 안의 말을 이용하여 문장을 완성하시오.

1 Wilson 선생님께 연필깎이가 있을지도 모른다. (may, have) 교육청 기출
Mrs. Wilson ______________________ a pencil sharpener.

2 주목해 주시겠어요? (may, have)
______________________ your attention, please? 수능 기출

3 우리 계획은 잘 풀리지 않을지도 모른다. (might, work out)
Our plan ______________________ well.

4 원한다면 지금 떠나도 좋다. (may, leave)
You ______________________ now, if you want to.

5 누군가의 쓰레기가 다른 이에게는 보물일지 모른다. (may, be)
One person's trash ______________________ another's treasure. 수능 기출

POINT 04 ★★★★

must, have to (의무 · 추측)

정답 및 해설 p.5

- **must는 의무(~해야 한다)를 나타낸다. 이때 must는 have to로 바꾸어 쓸 수 있으며, 과거, 미래의 의무를 나타낼 때는 각각 had to, will have to를 사용한다.**

  You **must** pay a fine. = You **have to** pay a fine.

- **must의 부정형인 must not은 '~하면 안 된다'라는 금지의 의미이고, don't have to(= don't need to = need not)는 '~할 필요가 없다'라는 뜻이다.**

  Can I park here? — No, you **must not**.

  Must I finish the report today? — No, you **don't have to**.

  cf. 조동사 need는 '~할 필요가 있다'라는 뜻으로 주로 부정문과 의문문에서 쓰인다.

  You **need** not apologize to him.

- **must는 강한 추측(~임에 틀림없다)을 나타내며, 이때 must의 부정은 cannot(~할 리가 없다)이다.**

  Laura **must** be in her twenties.

  She **cannot** be at home now.

A 다음 두 문장이 같은 뜻이 되도록 빈칸에 알맞은 말을 쓰시오.

1 I must do my homework now.

→ I ______________________ my homework now.

2 You don't need to go to the dentist today.

→ You ______________________ to the dentist today.

3 Students have to sign up for our program in advance. 교육청 기출

→ Students ______________________ up for our program in advance.

B 다음 빈칸에 must 또는 have to 중 적절한 것을 골라 쓰시오. (둘 다 가능한 경우 must를 쓸 것)

1 You __________ not lie to me.

2 You don't __________ lock the door.

3 We __________ wear a swimming cap here. 수능 기출 응용

4 This boy __________ be your brother Kevin. 교육청 기출

5 Paul will __________ go to the airport tomorrow.

C 다음 괄호 안에서 알맞은 것을 고르시오.

1 Sarah may (must / have to) work on Saturdays.

2 It (can't / must not) be Fred. He is in Brazil now.

3 Kelly doesn't look well. She (must / need) be sick.

4 It's only 2 o'clock. We (must not / don't need to) hurry.

5 I (have to / had to) perform a dangerous task yesterday. 수능 기출 응용

6 We (must not / don't have to) drive a car without a license.

7 You (had to / will have to) wait until the product is in stock again.

POINT 05 ★★★★

should, ought to (충고 · 제안)

정답 및 해설 p.6

- **should와 ought to는 '~해야 한다, ~하는 것이 좋다'라는 충고 · 제안의 의미로 사회적 관습이나 양심에 근거하여 마땅히 해야 하는 일을 나타낼 때 사용한다.**

You **should** be quiet in a library.

You **ought to** respect your parents.

cf. should의 부정형은 should not[shouldn't]이고, ought to의 부정형은 ought not to이다.

We **should not[ought not to]** waste our resources.

A 다음 괄호 안에서 알맞은 것을 고르시오.

1 You (should / ought to) not break your promise.

2 This is your last chance. You (have to / ought not to) miss it.

3 It looks like a storm is coming. You (should not / don't have to) go outside.

4 We don't have much time. You (might / ought to) make up your mind now.

5 You (could / should) be careful with your money in a big city like L.A.

6 We're true friends, so we (can't / ought to) help each other in times of need.

B 다음 〈보기〉에서 알맞은 말을 골라 괄호 안의 조동사를 이용하여 문장을 완성하시오.

보기				
	bring	focus	keep	try
	wear	run around	see a doctor	

1 운전자들은 제한 속도를 지켜야 한다. (ought to)
Drivers ____________________ to the speed limit.

2 박물관에서는 뛰어다니면 안 된다. (should)
You ____________________ in the museum.

3 야외 활동을 위해 운동화를 가져와야 한다. (ought to)
You ____________________ sneakers for outdoor activities. 수능 기출 응용

4 우리는 단기적인 손실에 집중해서는 안 된다. (should)
We ____________________ on short-term losses. 교육청 기출

5 채소를 썰 때는 장갑을 껴야 한다. (should)
You ____________________ gloves while cutting vegetables. 수능 기출

6 Nancy는 두통에 대해 의사의 진찰을 받아야 한다. (ought to)
Nancy ____________________ about her headache.

7 너는 단기간에 살을 많이 빼려 해서는 안 된다. (should)
You ____________________ to lose a lot of weight in a short period of time.

POINT 06 ★★★★

had better, would rather (충고 · 선택)

정답 및 해설 p.6

- **〈had better+동사원형〉은 '~하는 게 좋을 것이다'라는 뜻으로, 충고대로 따르지 않으면 불이익을 당할 수 있다는 의미를 내포한다. 부정형은 had better not이다.**

  You**'d better** return it now, or you'll pay a late fee.
  You **had better not** tell Daniel.

- **〈would rather+동사원형〉은 선택의 상황에서 쓰는 표현으로 '(그보다는) ~하고 싶다'라는 의미이다. 부정형은 would rather not이다.**

  I'd rather take the subway. The traffic is too heavy.
  I'd rather not attend the meeting.

  cf. would rather는 than과 함께 쓰이는 경우가 많다.
  I **would rather** stay home *than* go to her party.

A **다음 밑줄 친 부분을 어법에 맞게 고쳐 쓰시오.**

1 You'd better skip not breakfast.
2 I'd rather going to the concert with her.
3 I'd better got started right away. 평가원 기출

B **다음 괄호 안의 말과 had better 또는 would rather를 이용하여 문장을 완성하시오.**

1 You ____________, or you'll miss the train. (hurry up)
2 I ____________ home than go out with him. (stay)
3 It's freezing outside. You ____________ a coat. (wear)
4 I ____________ in the library than study at home. (study)
5 It's already 4 o'clock. We ____________ cooking. (start)
6 You ____________ a doctor, or your condition will only get worse. (see)

C **다음 우리말과 같은 뜻이 되도록 괄호 안의 말을 이용하여 문장을 완성하시오.**

1 창가에는 아무것도 걸지 않는 게 좋을 거야. (hang) 교육청 기출
We ____________ anything next to the window.

2 나는 오늘 밤 오페라를 보러 가고 싶지 않아. (go)
I ____________ to the opera tonight. 수능 기출 응용

3 너는 건강을 위해 균형 잡힌 식단을 유지하는 게 좋아. (keep)
You ____________ a balanced diet for your health.

4 나는 차라리 그 쇼를 TV로 보고 싶어. (watch)
I ____________ the show on TV.

5 나는 집에 있기보다는 여행을 가고 싶다. (go on a trip)
I ____________ than stay at home.

★ POINT 07 ★★★★

used to, would (습관)

정답 및 해설 p.6

- **used to는 '~하곤 했다, ~이었다'라는 뜻으로 과거에 반복되던 행동, 습관이나 지속된 상태를 나타내며, '현재는 그렇지 않다'라는 의미를 내포한다.**

  When I lived in Canada, I **used to** go snowboarding.

- **would는 '~하곤 했다'라는 의미로 과거의 습관을 나타낸다.**

  I **would** take a nap after school.

★ EXAM TIP 과거에 지속되던 상태를 나타낼 때는 **would**를 사용할 수 없다.

There **used to[~~would~~]** be a bookstore here.

A

다음 주어진 문장을 참고해서 used to를 이용하여 문장을 완성하시오.

1 Nate was an actor when he was young, but now he is a movie director.
→ Nate ______________________ when he was young.

2 I went out with Greg, but now I don't go out with him anymore.
→ I ______________________ with Greg.

3 There was a fire station on the corner, but now there is a hospital.
→ There ______________________ on the corner.

4 I went camping every weekend, but now I don't go camping anymore.
→ I ______________________ every weekend.

B

다음 빈칸에 used to 또는 would 중 적절한 것을 골라 쓰시오. (둘 다 가능한 경우 would를 쓸 것)

1 I __________ be a shy person.

2 Amy __________ work at an art gallery.

3 My uncle __________ own a small gift shop.

4 There __________ be a pine tree in the garden.

5 Matt __________ sometimes complain about the city of Chicago. 평가원 기출 응용

6 My brother and I __________ play games for hours on weekends.

C

다음 문장을 밑줄 친 부분에 유의하여 우리말로 해석하시오.

1 Helen <u>would</u> often cry until she was exhausted. 평가원 기출 응용

2 Patrick <u>used to</u> visit Thailand on business.

3 I <u>used to</u> live in this house when I was a little boy. 교육청 기출 응용

4 He <u>would</u> go to the bus station just to watch the buses. 교육청 기출

5 Laura <u>used to</u> have a complex about her height.

POINT 08 조동사+have p.p.

정답 및 해설 p.6

- **〈조동사+have p.p.〉는 과거 사실에 대한 추측이나 유감을 나타낸다.**

  She **may[might] have been** Tom's wife. (과거 사실에 대한 불확실한 추측: ~했을지도 모른다)
  Ted **must have been** busy. (과거 사실에 대한 확실한 추측: ~했음에 틀림없다)
  My sister **can't have accepted** his proposal. (과거 사실에 대한 부정적인 추측: ~했을 리가 없다)
  I **should have driven** carefully. (과거 사실에 대한 후회·유감: ~했어야 했다)

A 다음 우리말과 같은 뜻이 되도록 어색한 부분을 자연스럽게 고치시오.

1 그는 감기에 걸렸던 것이 틀림없다.
He may have had a cold.

2 Maria가 네게 거짓말을 했을 리 없다.
Maria must not have told you a lie.

3 나는 Paul에게 사과를 했어야 했다.
I must have apologized to Paul.

B 다음 두 문장이 같은 뜻이 되도록 적절한 조동사를 이용하여 문장을 완성하시오.

1 I'm sure she trained very hard. 교육청 기출
→ She ________________________.

2 I had to call you earlier, but I didn't.
→ I ________________________.

3 I'm not certain, but I think I saw the movie.
→ I ________________________.

C 다음 우리말과 같은 뜻이 되도록 괄호 안의 말을 이용하여 문장을 완성하시오.

1 나는 그녀와 헤어지지 말았어야 했다. (break up)
I ________________ with her.

2 그녀가 그 결혼식을 잊었을 리 없다. (forget)
She ________________ about the wedding.

3 내 여동생은 그 공포 영화를 봤을지도 모른다. (see)
My sister ________________ the horror movie.

4 그들은 정책을 바꾸었음에 틀림없다. (change)
They ________________ their policy. 수능 기출 응용

5 Tom은 파리에 있었을 때 Susan을 만났을지도 모른다. (meet)
Tom ________________ Susan when he was in Paris.

6 너는 그것보다는 좀 더 잠을 잤어야 했다. (sleep)
You ________________ more than that. 수능 기출

REVIEW TEST 03 ★

정답 및 해설 p.6

[1-5] 다음 우리말과 일치하도록 빈칸에 알맞은 말을 고르시오.

1

Cathy는 예전에 그 병원의 간호사였다.
Cathy ________ be a nurse at the hospital.

① might ② would
③ used to ④ was able to
⑤ would rather

2

그는 아들이 자랑스러울 게 틀림없다.
He ________ be proud of his son.

① can ② must
③ may ④ doesn't need to
⑤ had better

3

나가지 않는 게 좋을 거야. 밖이 추워.
You ________ go out. It's cold outside.

① could not ② may not
③ don't have to ④ had better not
⑤ would not

4

나는 그녀의 휴대전화 번호를 알려 달라고 했어야 했다.
I ________ for her cell phone number.

① had better ask ② would rather ask
③ must have asked ④ may have asked
⑤ should have asked

5

너는 내 정원에 들어가도 된다.
You ________ go into my garden.

① may ② must ③ ought to
④ will ⑤ would rather

[6-8] 다음 두 문장의 뜻이 같도록 빈칸에 알맞은 말을 고르시오.

6

He must be taken to the hospital immediately.
= He ________ be taken to the hospital immediately.

① can't ② has to ③ would rather
④ may ⑤ used to

7

When I lived in Vancouver, I went skiing in the winter, but now I don't anymore.
= When I lived in Vancouver, I ________ go skiing in the winter.

① may ② should ③ must
④ would ⑤ can

8

Ms. Brown is certainly not German.
= Ms. Brown ________ be German.

① can't ② won't ③ must not
④ don't have to ⑤ should not

[9-12] 다음 우리말과 일치하도록 괄호 안의 말을 이용하여 문장을 완성하시오.

9

너는 그에게 진실을 말하지 않는 것이 좋겠다. (tell)
You ____________________ him the truth.

10

그가 나에게 거짓말을 했을지도 모른다. (lie)
He ____________________ to me.

11

나는 차라리 녹차를 마시겠다. (have)
I ____________________ green tea.

12

너는 입장료를 낼 필요가 없다. (pay)
You ________________________________
the admission fee.

[13-15] 다음 문장의 빈칸에 알맞은 것을 고르시오.

13

You __________ waste your money. You ought to save money for the future.

① may not ② need not
③ shouldn't ④ would not
⑤ don't have to

14

Peter __________ be a genius. He has an IQ of 165.

① should ② had better
③ can't ④ must
⑤ used to

15

Anna __________ be tired. She got enough rest last night.

① may ② will
③ can't ④ must
⑤ could

[16-21] 다음 중 밑줄 친 부분이 어법상 <u>틀린</u> 것을 고르시오.

16

① I <u>may have met</u> her before.
② His wallet <u>must be</u> very old.
③ Applicants <u>must be able to</u> speak French.
④ <u>I'd rather to play</u> tennis than go shopping.
⑤ There <u>used to be</u> a department store here.

17

① <u>May I see</u> your plane ticket?
② You <u>had better not go</u> out today.
③ We <u>don't have to stay</u> here now.
④ You <u>ought to not avoid</u> this problem.
⑤ He <u>must have forgotten</u> about the appointment.

18

① Leo <u>used to live</u> in Hawaii.
② I <u>cannot apply</u> for the position.
③ I <u>should haven't said</u> that to her.
④ You <u>have to have</u> a heart operation.
⑤ I <u>will be able to leave</u> for Italy next year.

19

① I have to write a history report.

② I tried to wear contact lenses, but I couldn't.

③ You had rather go see a doctor right away.

④ You won't be able to change it. 교육청 기출 응용

⑤ We used to dry peppers on a mat in the yard. 교육청 기출 응용

20

① You don't need to bring your ID.

② You ought to keep your promises.

③ I used to eat at that restaurant every week.

④ May you please send me a map of the city?

⑤ Inconvenience can lead to an invention. 교육청 기출 응용

21

① I would rather leave now.

② I had to call in sick this morning.

③ You shouldn't have gone to bed so late.

④ Jack cannot have done anything wrong.

⑤ You will must apply for a visa by Friday.

22 다음 중 대화가 어색한 것은?

① A: Can I take photos in the museum?
B: No, you can't.

② A: Do you want me to bring some snacks?
B: You don't have to. We have some cupcakes. 교육청 기출

③ A: How may I help you? 교육청 기출 응용
B: I'm here to purchase tickets for the city tour.

④ A: I couldn't enter the contest because of the age limit.
B: You can be very disappointed.

⑤ A: Can I ask you a couple of questions?
B: Okay, but I have to leave soon. 수능 기출 응용

23 다음 글의 밑줄 친 부분 중 어법상 바르지 못한 것은?

Starting today, you ① will can watch concerts more comfortably since you ② will not have to carry your coats or bags. You ③ can check your belongings at the room located on the first floor. There ④ will be no charge for this service. 수능 기출 응용

24 다음 글의 (A), (B), (C)에서 각각 알맞은 것을 고르시오.

To donate blood, you (A) (should / may) weigh more than 50 kilograms. And you (B) (can't / don't have to) donate blood if you've donated in the past two months. Now, if you (C) (are able to / ought to) donate blood, please fill out this form. 평가원 기출 응용

25 다음 글의 빈칸 (A), (B)에 적절한 것끼리 짝지어진 것은?

You probably know that exercise is a good way to lose weight. But you ____(A)____ work out at the gym to burn calories. Little movements add up, which ____(B)____ help you lose weight. These can be anything, such as pacing back and forth while talking on the phone. 평가원 기출 응용

	(A)	(B)
①	should	can
②	must	may
③	may not	must
④	must not	used to
⑤	don't have to	can

EST

2010

CHAPTER 04

★★★★

수동태

POINT 01 ★★★★

수동태의 기본 개념

정답 및 해설 p.7

- **행위를 하는 주체에 초점을 둘 때는 능동태를, 행위에 영향을 받는 대상에 초점을 둘 때는 수동태를 사용한다. 수동태의 기본 형태는 〈be p.p.(+by+행위자)〉이다.**

  Julie Smith wrote this novel. (능동태)

  This novel **was written** by Julie Smith. (수동태)

  cf. 의지와 관계없는 상태를 나타내는 동사(have 등)나 상호 관계를 나타내는 동사(resemble, fit 등)는 수동태로 쓰지 않는다.

  She has a very unusual name. ~~A very unusual name **is had** by her.~~

- **행위자를 모를 때 또는 행위자가 중요하지 않거나 일반인일 때는 〈by+행위자〉를 생략한다.**

  The wine **was made** in France.

  Halloween **is celebrated** in America.

A 다음 괄호 안에서 알맞은 것을 고르시오.

1 I (made / was made by) sandwiches for the picnic.

2 The boy (punished / was punished) for lying.

3 Daily breakfast (includes / is included) in the room rate.

4 Peter's mother (impressed / was impressed by) his kind offer. 수능 기출 응용

5 Jessica closely (resembles / is resembled by) her mother in appearance.

B 다음 문장을 수동태로 바꾸어 쓰시오.

1 A snake bit Cleopatra. 평가원 기출 응용

→ ______________________________

2 The flame blinded me. 교육청 기출

→ ______________________________

3 A famous artist drew these beautiful pictures.

→ ______________________________

4 Thousands of people visit this museum each day.

→ ______________________________

C 다음 우리말과 같은 뜻이 되도록 괄호 안의 말을 이용하여 문장을 완성하시오.

1 그 건물들은 테러리스트들에 의해 파괴되었다. (destroy)

The buildings ____________ terrorists.

2 코카콜라는 1886년에 John Pemberton에 의해 개발되었다. (invent)

Coca-Cola ____________ John Pemberton in 1886.

3 그는 최고의 연사 중 하나로 선정되었다. (select) 교육청 기출 응용

He ____________ as one of the top speakers.

★ POINT 02 ★★★★

4형식 문장의 수동태

정답 및 해설 p.7

- **4형식 문장은 목적어(간접목적어, 직접목적어)가 두 개이기 때문에 각각을 주어로 하는 두 개의 수동태 문장을 쓸 수 있다. 하지만 buy, make, get과 같은 동사의 경우 간접목적어를 주어로 수동태를 쓰지 않는다.**

She gave the waitress a tip. LINK p.15 4형식 문장

(the waitress: 간접목적어, a tip: 직접목적어)

→ The waitress **was given** a tip by her.

→ A tip **was given to** the waitress by her.

cf. 직접목적어를 주어로 수동태 문장을 쓸 때, 대부분의 동사는 간접목적어 앞에 전치사 to를 쓰는데 buy와 make는 for를 쓴다.

A 다음 괄호 안에서 알맞은 것을 고르시오.

1 My girlfriend (got / was got) me a tie for my birthday.

2 A first draft of our plan (was sent to / was sent for) you. 수능 기출 응용

3 A letter (was written / was written to) me by Sam.

4 This recipe (was given to / was given for) me by my mother.

5 The cake (was made to / was made for) me by my boyfriend.

B 다음 문장을 수동태로 바꾸어 쓰시오.

1 A friend taught me Korean.

→ I ______________________________.

→ Korean ______________________________.

2 He offered me a new position. 평가원 기출 응용

→ I ______________________________.

→ A new position ______________________________.

3 I sent her a thank-you note.

→ She ______________________________.

→ A thank-you note ______________________________.

4 They told me the story of the company.

→ I ______________________________.

→ The story of the company ______________________________.

5 Robert made her a cup of coffee.

→ A cup of coffee ______________________________.

6 I bought my mother a bunch of flowers.

→ A bunch of flowers ______________________________.

POINT 03 5형식 문장의 수동태 I

정답 및 해설 p.7

- **5형식 문장을 수동태로 바꿀 경우, 능동태의 목적어가 수동태의 주어가 되고 목적격 보어는 보통 〈be p.p.〉 다음에 그대로 쓴다.**

The court found her guilty.
→ *She* **was found** guilty by the court.
The doctor told him to take more vitamin C. LINK p.68 목적격 보어로 쓰이는 to부정사
→ *He* **was told** to take more vitamin C by the doctor.

A 다음 문장을 수동태로 바꾸어 쓰시오. (행위자는 밝힐 필요 없음)

1 We consider the project a failure.
→ ______________________

2 People called him a genius.
→ ______________________

3 My father told me to stop playing the piano. 수능 기출 응용
→ ______________________

4 He asked me to paint a picture on the wall. 수능 기출 응용
→ ______________________

5 They call the 18th century the golden age of botanical painting. 수능 기출
→ ______________________

B 다음 우리말과 같은 뜻이 되도록 괄호 안의 말을 이용하여 능동태 문장을 완성한 후, 수동태로 바꾸어 쓰시오.

1 그 난로는 그 방을 따뜻하게 유지한다. (keep, warm)
The stove ______________________.
→ The room ______________________.

2 그는 나에게 운동을 좀 하라고 충고했다. (advise, get some exercise)
He ______________________.
→ I ______________________.

3 그 영화는 그 여배우를 유명하게 만들었다. (make, famous)
The movie ______________________.
→ The actress ______________________.

4 경찰은 그들에게 그 건물에 들어가지 말라고 경고했다. (warn, enter)
The police ______________________.
→ They ______________________.

POINT 04 ★★★★

5형식 문장의 수동태 II

정답 및 해설 p.7

- **지각동사(see, hear, feel 등)의 목적격 보어로 쓰인 원형부정사는 수동태 문장으로 쓸 때 to부정사로 바뀐다.** LINK p.69 목적격 보어로 쓰이는 원형부정사

  I heard him talk about you.
  → He was **heard** to talk about you.
  cf. He was heard talking about you. 형태로 전환하는 것도 가능하다.

- **사역동사 중 make만 수동태로 쓰이며, 이때 목적격 보어로 쓰인 원형부정사는 수동태 문장으로 쓸 때 to부정사로 바뀐다.**

  This movie made me feel better.
  → I **was made** to feel better by this movie.

A

다음 문장에서 어법상 틀린 부분을 고쳐 쓰시오.

1 The dogs were heard bark on the road.
2 We are made believing that true love always works out.
3 She saw Susan to swim across the river.

B

다음 문장을 수동태로 바꾸어 쓰시오.

1 The clerk made me pay for the damage.
→ ______________________________

2 My boss made me work overtime.
→ ______________________________

3 Someone heard Pam cry in her dorm room.
→ ______________________________

4 His mother made him apologize to me.
→ ______________________________

5 A witness saw the suspect argue with the victim.
→ ______________________________

C

다음 우리말과 같은 뜻이 되도록 괄호 안의 말을 이용하여 문장을 완성하시오.

1 나는 방과 후에 더 늦게까지 남겨졌다. (make, stay)
I ______________ later after school.

2 누군가 Tony가 험한 말을 하는 것을 들었다. (hear, say)
Tony ______________ something rude.

3 공원에서 한 젊은 커플이 거니는 광경이 보였다. (see, take a walk)
A young couple ______________ in the park.

POINT 05

수동태의 여러 가지 형태

정답 및 해설 p.8

- **진행형 수동태: 〈be+being p.p.〉**
  A tall building **is being constructed** by the company.
- **완료형 수동태: 〈have+been p.p.〉**
  The flight to Mexico **has been canceled**.
- **조동사가 있는 수동태: 〈조동사+be p.p.〉**
  This disease **can be cured** by medicine.

A **다음 문장을 수동태로 바꾸어 쓰시오.**

1 Tourists are destroying the Alps. 평가원 기출 응용

→ ______________________________

2 We must do something to help those people.

→ ______________________________

3 They are repairing my laptop now.

→ ______________________________

4 An adult should accompany students. 교육청 기출 응용

→ ______________________________

5 We can use plastics in place of natural materials. 평가원 기출 응용

→ ______________________________

6 People have used this oil for cooking for centuries.

→ ______________________________

B **다음 우리말과 같은 뜻이 되도록 괄호 안의 말을 이용하여 문장을 완성하시오.**

1 그 소포는 내일 배달될 것이다. (will, deliver)
The package ________________ tomorrow.

2 그 홀에서는 모터쇼가 열리고 있는 중이었다. (hold)
A motor show ________________ in the hall.

3 이 케이크는 냉장고에 보관되어야 한다. (must, keep)
This cake ________________ in the refrigerator.

4 상위 10위는 공개 온라인 투표를 통해 선정될 것이다. (will, pick) 교육청 기출
The top 10 entries ________________ through public online voting.

5 환불은 행사 2주 전까지만 주어질 수 있다. (can, give) 교육청 기출
Refunds ________________ up to two weeks before the event.

6 그의 문체는 젊었을 때부터 아버지의 영향을 받아 왔다. (influence)
His writing style ________________ by his father since he was young.

POINT 06 ★★★★

주의해야 하는 수동태 I

정답 및 해설 p.8

- **동사구를 포함하는 수동태: 동사가 부사나 전치사와 결합해 하나의 동사처럼 쓰이는 동사구를 수동태로 쓸 때는 동사만 〈be p.p.〉로 바꾸고, 나머지 부분은 그대로 쓴다.**

  He looked after the sick people for a week.
  → The sick people **were looked after** by him for a week.

- **명령문의 수동태: 〈Let+목적어+be p.p.〉의 형태로 쓴다. 명령문의 수동태는 문어적이며 잘 쓰이지 않는다.**

  Tell the truth. → **Let** the truth **be told**.
  Don't forget the past. → Don't **let** the past **be forgotten**.

A **다음 문장을 수동태로 바꾸어 쓰시오.**

1 Don't break your promise.
→ ______________________

2 He put off his visit until Tuesday.
→ ______________________

3 Jennifer made fun of my clothes.
→ ______________________

4 A speeding car ran over two deer.
→ ______________________

5 Their grandmother takes care of the children.
→ ______________________

6 Many of the employees look up to the director.
→ ______________________

B **다음 우리말과 같은 뜻이 되도록 밑줄 친 부분을 고쳐 쓰시오.**

1 너의 재능을 썩히지 마라.
Don't let your talent waste.

2 그녀는 친구들에게 험담을 들었다.
She spoken ill of by her friends.

3 그 일이 즉시 마쳐지게 하라.
Let the job finished immediately.

4 그의 어리석은 계획은 우리의 비웃음을 샀다.
His stupid plan was laughed by us.

5 가난하다고 해서 그들이 멸시당해서는 안 된다.
They should not look down on for being poor.

POINT 07 ★★★★

주의해야 하는 수동태 II

정답 및 해설 p.8

- **목적어가 that절인 문장의 수동태: 〈It+be동사+p.p.+that ~〉의 형태로 쓴다. 또는 that절의 주어를 수동태 문장의 주어로 할 수 있는데, 이때 that절의 동사는 to부정사로 바뀐다.**

People believe that he is honest.
→ **It is believed that** he is honest.
→ **He is believed to be** honest.

cf. that절의 시제가 주절보다 앞서면, that절의 동사는 〈to have p.p.〉의 형태가 된다.
People say that she lived for more than 100 years.
→ **It is said that** she lived for more than 100 years.
→ **She is said to have lived** for more than 100 years.

A 다음 문장을 수동태로 바꾸어 쓰시오.

1 People say that this country is the land of opportunity.
→ It ______________________________.

2 They believe that a broken mirror is a sign of bad luck.
→ It ______________________________.

3 He reported that the criminal was tall and thin.
→ It ______________________________.

B 다음 두 문장이 같은 뜻이 되도록 문장을 완성하시오.

1 All life is thought to be precious. 수능 기출 응용
→ It ______________________________.

2 It is said that hats are popular among men this season.
→ Hats ______________________________. 수능 기출 응용

3 James Dean is considered to be one of the greatest actors of all time.
→ It ______________________________.

C 다음 우리말과 같은 뜻이 되도록 괄호 안의 말을 이용하여 문장을 완성하시오.

1 그가 나이보다 어려 보인다고들 말한다. (look younger)
It ______________ than his age.

2 그는 남아프리카 출신이라고 믿어진다. (be from)
He ______________ South Africa.

3 그 예술가는 그 걸작이 완성되었을 때 70세였다고 전해진다. (be) 수능 기출 응용
The artist ______________ 70 years of age when the masterpiece was completed.

4 우리의 인생 경험은 지능에 중대한 영향을 미친다고 생각된다. (have) 교육청 기출 응용
Our life experience ______________ a profound effect upon intelligence.

POINT 08

by 이외의 전치사를 쓰는 수동태

정답 및 해설 p.8

- **수동태의 행위자를 나타낼 때 보통 by를 쓰는데, by 이외의 전치사를 쓰는 경우도 있다.**
  He **was worried about** the results of the exam.
- **많이 사용되는 표현**
  - be surprised at: ~에 놀라다
  - be pleased with: ~로 기뻐하다
  - be disappointed in[with]: ~에 실망하다
  - be interested in: ~에 흥미가 있다
  - be filled with: ~로 가득 차 있다
  - be worried about: ~에 대해 걱정하다
  - be satisfied with: ~에 만족하다
  - be scared of: ~을 두려워하다
  - be covered with: ~로 덮여 있다
  - be composed of: ~로 구성되다

A 다음 문장의 빈칸에 알맞은 전치사를 쓰시오.

1 I was disappointed ________ the book.

2 The second jar was covered ________ cloth. 평가원 기출 응용

3 The music class is composed ________ 10 students.

4 The high school grounds were filled ________ well-dressed people. 수능 기출

B 다음 문장에서 어법상 틀린 부분을 고쳐 쓰시오.

1 My dog is scared in everything.

2 I'm very satisfied of my current job.

3 I have been interested with this field. 평가원 기출 응용

4 We were surprised of how good the food was!

C 다음 우리말과 같은 뜻이 되도록 괄호 안의 말을 이용하여 문장을 완성하시오.

1 나는 새 노트북 컴퓨터에 만족한다. (satisfy)
I ________________ my new laptop.

2 그는 자기 몸무게를 걱정했었다. (worry)
He ________________ his weight.

3 나는 남동생이 성공을 해서 기쁘다. (please)
I ________________ my brother's success.

4 Julie는 멕시코 문화에 관심이 있다. (interest)
Julie ________________ Mexican culture.

5 이 책은 다섯 개의 챕터로 구성되어 있다. (compose)
This book ________________ five chapters.

REVIEW TEST 04 ★

정답 및 해설 p.8

[1-5] 다음 우리말과 일치하도록 빈칸에 알맞은 말을 고르시오.

1

그 물품은 내일 당신의 사무실로 배달될 것이다.
The goods will __________ to your office tomorrow.

① deliver ② be delivering
③ be delivered ④ be to deliver
⑤ being delivered

2

야구가 가장 인기 있는 스포츠 중 하나라고들 말한다.
Baseball __________ one of the most popular sports.

① is said that ② is said being
③ is said to be ④ says to be
⑤ says being

3

나는 나의 낮은 시험 점수가 걱정이다.
I'm worried ________ my low exam scores.

① at ② in ③ of
④ from ⑤ about

4

Danny가 나에게 TV를 켜게 했다.
I was made __________ the TV by Danny.

① turn on ② to turn on
③ turning on ④ to be turned on
⑤ being turned on

5

손님들을 위해 점심이 준비되고 있는 중이다.
Lunch __________ for the guests.

① is preparing ② is prepared
③ is being prepared ④ has been prepared
⑤ will be prepared

[6-8] 다음 문장을 바꿔 쓸 때 빈칸에 알맞은 말을 고르시오.

6

I heard him sing a cheerful song.
→ He was heard __________ a cheerful song.

① sing ② sung ③ to be sung
④ to sing ⑤ being sung

7

Show your talents to everybody.
→ Let your talents __________ to everybody.

① show ② showing ③ be shown
④ to show ⑤ to be shown

8

Microsoft has released a new version of Windows.
→ A new version of Windows __________.

① is released ② was released
③ has being released ④ has been released
⑤ had been released

[9-10] 다음 문장의 빈칸에 알맞은 말을 고르시오.

9

Some photos were shown __________ the witness.

① to ② of ③ at
④ about ⑤ for

10

The operation should __________ as soon as possible.

① do ② be done
③ to do ④ be doing
⑤ to be done

[11-13] 다음 두 문장의 빈칸에 공통으로 알맞은 것을 고르시오.

11

• The girl's eyes were filled __________ tears.
• We're very pleased __________ our new products.

① with ② of ③ by
④ about ⑤ from

12

• I was disappointed __________ his lack of enthusiasm.
• She is interested __________ fashion and cooking.

① of ② in ③ at
④ about ⑤ with

13

• A doll was given __________ her by him.
• Large turtles are said __________ live for hundreds of years.

① by ② that ③ for
④ at ⑤ to

[14-16] 다음 문장을 수동태로 바꿀 때 빈칸에 알맞은 말을 쓰시오.

14

They made us a blueberry cake.
→ A blueberry cake ____________________.

15

The doctor told me to get more rest.
→ I was told ____________________.

16

People believe that the children are still alive.
→ It ______________ the children are still alive.

[17-19] 다음 중 밑줄 친 부분이 어법상 틀린 것을 고르시오.

17

① Ross will be fired soon.
② They were made to work in the head office.
③ He was seen to play basketball yesterday.
④ All my appointments are taken care of by my secretary.
⑤ Christmas gifts were bought to her children by her.

18

① This box is covered with dust.
② She was made do household chores.
③ The conference room is being cleaned now.
④ The police car was heard to come.
⑤ You will be notified of the results by e-mail.
수능 기출 응용

19

① Visas are not required for tourists.
② Some dogs are used by the police. 교육청 기출
③ The green wall was painted by my father.
④ Alcoholic drinks are made from the plant.
⑤ Central America has hit hard by the hurricane.
교육청 기출 응용

[20-21] 다음 문장 중 어법상 옳은 것을 고르시오.

20

① The fire was immediately put out.
② Your application is currently being review.
③ Don't let your children exposed to the chemicals.
④ All shoes will be repaired and given for children. 교육청 기출
⑤ Soon after I got out of school, I was offered to a job. 교육청 기출

21

① The room was filled of light.
② The witness was made testify in court.
③ An interesting study recently published by the association. 교육청 기출 응용
④ He is considered to be the best player on the team.
⑤ Before you donate blood, you will be asking about your medical history. 수능 기출 응용

22 다음 밑줄 친 부분 중 어법에 맞지 않는 것을 골라 바르게 고치시오.

In the past, old money ① cut into small pieces and ② buried in landfills. But now, old money ③ is used to make new things. It ④ may be used to make writing paper.
평가원 기출 응용

[23-24] 다음 글의 밑줄 친 부분 중 어법상 틀린 것을 고르시오.

23

My bike ① was hit by a car yesterday and it ② broke. However, I ③ didn't get hurt because I was in a convenience store when it ④ happened. The driver of the car ⑤ was seen hit my bike by a lady. 수능 기출 응용

24

The Goddess Sedna was believed ① having separated the land animals from the sea animals. ② It was thought that bringing these animals together ③ would bring bad luck. There were other beliefs concerning animals. When a dead seal ④ was brought into the house, everyone had to stop working. Then, the spirit of the dead seal ⑤ had to be given a drink of water. 평가원 기출 응용

25 다음 글의 빈칸 (A), (B)에서 각각 알맞은 것을 고르시오.

Coffee (A) (buys / is bought) by consumers in one of two forms: whole or ground. Unopened cans of coffee may be kept in the cupboard and (B) (used / is used) within a year. However, opened cans of coffee (C) (should be kept / should keep) in a cool, dry environment. 수능 기출 응용

EST CHAPTER 2010

05

부정사

POINT 01 ★★★★

to부정사의 명사적 용법 I - 주어 · 목적어 · 보어

정답 및 해설 p.9

• **to부정사는 문장에서 명사처럼 주어, 목적어, 보어 역할을 한다.**

To become a famous fashion designer is difficult. (주어)
(= *It* is difficult **to become** a famous fashion designer.)

cf. to부정사가 주어의 역할을 하는 경우, 대개 to부정사는 문장의 뒤쪽으로 가고 빈 자리에 가주어 it을 쓴다.

I hope **to work** with you again. (목적어) LINK p.75 to부정사만을 목적어로 취하는 동사

Her job is **to translate** English into French. (보어)

A 다음 괄호 안에서 알맞은 것을 고르시오.

1 (Learn / To learn) from your mistakes is important.

2 Do you want (buy / to buy) Kate's birthday gift now? 수능 기출 응용

3 Her plan (is become / is to become) a software engineer.

B 다음 우리말과 같은 뜻이 되도록 〈보기〉에서 알맞은 말을 골라 빈칸에 적절한 형태로 써넣으시오.

보기 go help travel win

1 그녀의 꿈은 복권에 당첨되는 것이었다.
Her dream was ______________ the lottery.

2 빈곤한 나라를 돕는 것은 매우 중요하다.
It is very important ______________ poor countries. 교육청 기출

3 우리는 보스턴에서 필라델피아까지 여행할 계획이다.
We are planning ______________ from Boston to Philadelphia. 수능 기출 응용

4 하루 안에 그곳에 갔다가 돌아오는 것은 불가능하다.
It is impossible ______________ there and back in a day.

C 다음 우리말과 같은 뜻이 되도록 주어진 단어를 배열하여 문장을 완성하시오.

1 나는 새 차를 사기로 결정했다. (a new car, buy, to, decided, I)

____

2 우리의 목표는 고객들을 만족시키는 것이다. (is, the customers, our aim, please, to)

____

3 짠 음식을 피하는 것이 건강에 좋다. (avoid, to, is good, it, salty foods, for your health)

____

4 그 회사는 아시아 시장에 진출하길 원한다. (to, the company, the Asian market, enter, wants)

____

POINT 02 ★★★★

to부정사의 명사적 용법 II – 의문사+to부정사

정답 및 해설 p.9

- 〈의문사+to부정사〉는 문장 안에서 주어, 목적어, 보어 역할을 할 수 있는데, 주로 동사 뒤에서 목적어로 쓰인다.

Where to meet him has not yet been decided. (주어)
I don't know **how to drive.** (목적어)
My question is **when to start** the project. (보어)

cf. 〈의문사+to부정사〉는 보통 〈의문사+주어+should[can]+동사원형〉으로 바꾸어 쓸 수 있다.
Could you advise me on **what to do**?
→ Could you advise me on *what I should*[*can*] *do*?

A 다음 두 문장이 같은 뜻이 되도록 빈칸에 알맞은 말을 쓰시오.

1 Tell me where I should stay.
→ Tell me ________ ________ ________.

2 He did not know where he should turn for help. 교육청 기출
→ He did not know ________ ________ ________ ________ ________.

3 Chris told us when we should get off the bus.
→ Chris told us ________ ________ ________ ________ the bus.

4 I feel bad for Ann, but I don't know how I can help her.
→ I feel bad for Ann, but I don't know ________ ________ ________ ________.

B 다음 우리말과 같은 뜻이 되도록 괄호 안의 말을 이용하여 문장을 완성하시오.

1 그는 내게 바퀴를 갈아 끼우는 방법을 알려주었다. (change)
He taught me ____________________ a wheel.

2 표를 어디서 살 수 있는지 알려주시겠어요? (buy)
Can you tell me ____________________ the ticket?

3 나는 언제 직장을 그만둘지 결정할 수가 없다. (quit)
I can't decide ____________________ my job.

4 Lauren은 다음에 무엇을 해야 할지 결정할 수 없었다. (do)
Lauren could not decide ____________________ next.

5 그 책은 건강을 유지하기 위해 무엇을 먹어야 하는지 알려준다. (eat)
The book tells you ____________________ to stay healthy.

6 너는 이 식당에서 거기에 가는 방법을 아니? (get)
Do you know ____________________ from this restaurant? 수능 기출 응용

7 마케팅 매니저로 누구를 고용할지 결정했나요? (hire)
Have you decided ____________________ for the marketing manager position?

★ POINT 03 ★★★★

to부정사의 형용사적 용법 I - 명사 수식

정답 및 해설 p.9

- **to부정사는 명사 뒤에서 형용사처럼 명사를 수식할 수 있다. 수식받는 명사가 부정사구 안에 있는 전치사의 목적어가 되는 경우 전치사를 빠뜨리지 않도록 주의해야 한다.**

We don't have enough time **to finish** it.

She finally had someone **to talk to**. (← talk to someone)

A

다음 괄호 안에서 알맞은 것을 고르시오.

1 I bought a new house (to live / to live in).

2 I have some photos (show / to show) him.

3 Adam has (to tell something / something to tell) you.

4 There was no (to go time / time to go) sightseeing in London.

B

다음 밑줄 친 부분을 어법에 맞게 고쳐 쓰시오.

1 I'd like to have a friend to play.

2 I have to prove evidence her innocence.

3 They didn't have anything eat for two days.

4 The reception will be a great opportunity get to know each other.

C

다음 우리말과 같은 뜻이 되도록 주어진 단어를 배열하여 문장을 완성하시오.

1 그녀는 선택할 수 있는 선물들의 목록을 받았다. (a list of gifts, from, to, choose, received)
She ______________________________. 교육청 기출 응용

2 우리는 접대할 손님이 12명 있다. (to, have, twelve customers, serve)
We ______________________________. 평가원 기출

3 마침내 그가 연설을 할 차례였다. (his turn, to, was, give a speech)
Finally, it ______________________________. 교육청 기출

4 제게 앉을 의자를 주시겠어요? (on, a chair, to, me, give, sit)
Would you ______________________________?

5 그녀는 아이들을 돌봐 줄 사람이 필요하다. (needs, to, someone, her kids, look after)
She ______________________________.

6 Cindy는 그와 결혼을 하겠다는 결심을 했다. (him, made, marry, the decision, to)
Cindy ______________________________.

7 여러분의 글쓰기 능력을 향상시킬 이 기회를 놓치지 마세요. (to, miss, your writing, improve, this opportunity)
Don't ______________________________. 수능 기출 응용

★ POINT 04 ★★★★

to부정사의 형용사적 용법 II - be+to부정사

정답 및 해설 p.9

- **〈be+to부정사〉는 예정, 의무, 운명, 의도, 가능 등 여러 가지 의미를 나타내며, 주로 격식체에서 쓰인다.**

We **are to visit** New York next week. (예정: ~할 예정이다)
You **are to come** back here by 7 o'clock. (의무: ~해야 한다)
He **was never to return** home again. (운명: ~할 운명이다)
If you **are to succeed**, you'll have to work hard. (의도: ~하고자 하다)
No one **was to be** seen on the street. (가능: ~할 수 있다)

cf. 가능을 나타내는 〈be+to부정사〉는 주로 수동태로 쓰인다.

A 다음 우리말과 같은 뜻이 되도록 〈be+to부정사〉 구문을 이용하여 문장을 완성하시오.

1 그 영화는 10분 후에 시작할 예정이다. (start)
The movie ____________________ in ten minutes.

2 하늘에는 구름 한 점도 보이지 않았다. (see)
Not a cloud ____________________ in the sky.

3 Ted는 세계적인 극작가가 될 운명이었다. (become)
Ted ____________________ a world-famous playwright.

4 학생들은 수업에 정시에 도착해야 한다. (arrive)
Students ____________________ to class on time.

5 졸업식은 다음 주 월요일에 열릴 예정이다. (hold)
The graduation ceremony ____________________ next Monday.

B 다음 두 문장이 같은 뜻이 되도록 〈be+to부정사〉 구문을 이용하여 문장을 완성하시오.

1 We are going to have a pop quiz tomorrow.
→ We ____.

2 The camera can't be found anywhere.
→ The camera ____.

3 Tim and Jane would eventually fall in love.
→ Tim and Jane ____.

4 You must not miss the deadline again.
→ You ____.

5 If you intend to get there by noon, you should leave now.
→ If you ____, you should leave now.

6 Participants must keep the place clean.
→ Participants ____.

★ POINT 05 ★★★★

to부정사의 부사적 용법 I – 목적 · 결과

정답 및 해설 p.10

- **to부정사는 부사처럼 쓰여 목적이나 결과를 나타낼 수 있다.**

I'll do my best **to help** you. (목적)

cf. 격식체에서는 목적의 의미를 강조하기 위해 to부정사 앞에 in order나 so as를 붙이기도 한다.

He went to the store *in order*[*so as*] **to buy** some vegetables.

Sally grew up **to be** a famous ballerina. (결과)

A 다음 두 문장이 같은 뜻이 되도록 to부정사를 이용하여 빈칸을 채우시오.

1 I'm going to China. I will study Chinese there.

→ I'm going to China ____________________.

2 Leo tried to persuade her, but failed.

→ Leo tried to persuade her, only ____________________.

3 The poet left the country, and he never returned.

→ The poet left the country, never ____________________.

B 다음 우리말과 같은 뜻이 되도록 괄호 안의 말을 이용하여 문장을 완성하시오.

1 그들은 옷을 만들기 위해 플라스틱을 사용한다. (make)

They use plastics ____________________ clothes. 평가원 기출 응용

2 나는 그를 화나게 하지 않으려고 조용히 있었다. (upset)

I remained silent ____________________ him.

3 일어나 보니 엄마가 내 옆에 앉아 계셨다. (find)

I awoke ____________________ my mother sitting beside me.

4 나는 이 보고서를 작성하기 위해 그 모든 프로그램이 필요하다. (write up)

I need all the programs ____________________ this report. 수능 기출 응용

5 나는 주차장에 갔다가 차를 도둑맞은 것을 알았다. (find)

I went to the parking lot, only _______________ that my car had been stolen.

C 다음 문장을 밑줄 친 부분에 유의하여 우리말로 해석하시오.

1 I took a taxi <u>not to waste</u> time.

2 I'll do anything <u>to achieve</u> my dream.

3 I came home <u>to find</u> my pillow torn apart. 교육청 기출 응용

4 Samuel grew up <u>to be</u> a warm and generous man.

5 Tim traveled to Seattle <u>to visit his brother</u>.

POINT 06 ★★★★

to부정사의 부사적 용법 II – 원인 · 판단의 근거 · 조건

정답 및 해설 p.10

- **to부정사는 부사처럼 쓰여 감정의 원인이나 판단의 근거 또는 조건을 나타낼 수 있다.**

I was surprised **to get** an A in math. (원인)
Betty was foolish **to trust** him. (판단의 근거)
To hear him sing, you would take him for a professional singer. (조건)
(= If you heard him sing, ~.)

A **다음 문장을 밑줄 친 부분에 유의하여 우리말로 해석하시오.**

1 I'm sorry to hear the bad news. 수능 기출 응용
2 Simon was relieved to find out his kids were safe.
3 The people were brave to speak out against the government.
4 To hear her talk, you would think she was an expert.
5 Jessica will be happy to get your e-mail.

B **다음 우리말과 같은 뜻이 되도록 괄호 안의 말을 이용하여 문장을 완성하시오.**

1 나는 그가 수학 경시 대회에서 우승했다는 말을 들어 너무 기쁘다. (hear)
I'm so ____________________ that he won the math competition.

2 우리는 그 중요한 시합에 져서 실망했다. (lose)
We were ____________________ the important match.

3 나에게 자전거를 빌려주다니 Alex는 친절하다. (lend)
Alex is ____________________ me his bicycle.

4 나는 이 영화를 보게 되어 정말 흥분된다. (watch)
I'm really ____________________ this movie. 교육청 기출 응용

5 그 제안을 정중히 거절하다니 Brad는 현명했다. (refuse)
Brad was ____________________ the proposal politely.

C **다음 두 문장이 같은 뜻이 되도록 문장을 완성하시오.**

1 The boss saw his best worker go. He was sorry.
→ The boss ____. 교육청 기출 응용

2 Angela drove me home in her car. She was very nice.
→ Angela ____.

3 I heard that Hans had moved to Mexico. I was surprised.
→ I ____.

4 If you heard her speak Japanese, you would take her for a Japanese.
→ To ____.

5 I found the gallery closed. I was disappointed.
→ I ____.

★ POINT 07 ★★★★

to부정사의 부사적 용법 III - 형용사 · 부사 수식

정답 및 해설 p.10

- **to부정사는 형용사나 부사를 수식하여 정도를 나타내기도 한다. 특히 〈too ~ to-v(너무 ~해서 …할 수 없는)〉와 〈enough to-v(~할 수 있을 만큼 충분히 …한)〉 구문으로 잘 쓰인다.**

This coat is *good* **to wear** in winter.
You're **too** *young* **to watch** it. (= You're so *young* that you can't watch it.)
She was *smart* **enough to solve** the riddle.
(= She was so *smart* that she could solve the riddle.)

A 다음 두 문장이 같은 뜻이 되도록 빈칸에 알맞은 말을 쓰시오.

1 He is so tall that he can reach the top shelf.
→ He is ________ ________ ________ ________ the top shelf.

2 I was so tired that I couldn't clean the room.
→ I was ________ ________ ________ ________ the room.

3 She was kind enough to lend me her favorite book.
→ She was ________ ________ that ________ ________ me her favorite book.

4 He was too poor to buy a ticket for a flight to his hometown. 교육청 기출 응용
→ He was ________ ________ that ________ ________ ________ a ticket for a flight to his hometown.

B 다음 우리말과 같은 뜻이 되도록 주어진 단어를 배열하여 문장을 완성하시오.

1 Daniel은 너무 바빠서 점심을 먹을 수가 없었다. (too, lunch, to, eat, busy)
Daniel was ________________________________.

2 이 앱은 사용하기가 아주 어렵다. (use, very, to, difficult)
This app is ________________________________.

3 우리는 아래의 동물들을 볼 만큼 낮게 날았다. (enough, see, low, to, the animals below)
We flew ________________________________.

4 그는 너무 어려서 그 소설을 이해할 수 없었다. (understand, young, to, the novel, too)
He was ________________________________.

C 다음 문장을 밑줄 친 부분에 유의하여 우리말로 해석하시오.

1 I'm not brave enough to try it. 평가원 기출 응용

2 Steven was hard to get along with.

3 It's too late to call his father now. 수능 기출 응용

4 This city is dangerous to walk alone in at night.

5 The chair looks easy to move around in. 교육청 기출 응용

POINT 08 ★★★★

독립부정사

정답 및 해설 p.10

- **독립부정사는 숙어처럼 굳어진 표현으로, 독립적으로 쓰여 문장 전체를 수식한다.**

  To tell (you) the truth, his speech was boring. (사실대로 말하면)

- **기타 독립부정사**

  – to be honest[frank]: 솔직히 말해서, 사실은
  – strange to say: 이상한 이야기이지만
  – to be sure: 확실히
  – to begin with: 우선, 먼저
  – so to speak: 말하자면
  – to make matters worse: 설상가상으로

A 다음 우리말과 같은 뜻이 되도록 〈보기〉의 단어를 이용하여 문장을 완성하시오.

보기 begin honest speak strange sure tell worse

1 설상가상으로 폭우가 쏟아지기 시작했다.
_______________, it began to rain heavily.

2 사실대로 말하면 나는 그가 하는 말에 신경 쓰지 않는다.
_______________, I don't care what he says.

3 솔직히 말해 나는 무대 위에 서는 게 무서워.
_______________, I'm afraid of being on stage. 교육청 기출

4 그 호텔은 형편없었어! 우선, 직원이 무례했어.
The hotel was terrible! _______________, the staff were rude.

5 Tommy는 말하자면 반의 코미디언이다.
Tommy is a classroom comedian, _______________.

6 이상한 말 같지만, 나는 사실 텔레비전을 즐겨 보지 않는다.
_______________, I don't really enjoy television.

7 그 차는 확실히 비싸긴 하지만, 그만한 가치가 있다.
The car is expensive, _______________, but it's worth the cost.

B 다음 문장을 밑줄 친 부분에 유의하여 우리말로 해석하시오.

1 He is my role model, <u>so to speak</u>.
2 <u>Strange to say</u>, I've never taken the subway.
3 <u>To begin with</u>, I'd like some chicken soup.
4 Will is reliable, <u>to be sure</u>, but he can be rude.
5 <u>To make matters worse</u>, our star player broke his leg.
6 <u>To tell the truth</u>, I don't want to take the job.
7 <u>To be frank</u>, the steak was so tough that I couldn't even cut it.

POINT 09 ★★★★

to부정사의 의미상 주어

정답 및 해설 p.10

- **to부정사의 의미상 주어가 문장의 주어 또는 목적어와 일치하거나 막연한 일반인을 가리키는 경우에는 생략한다.**

  She decided **to stay** at home.

  I want *him* **to call** me back.

- **to부정사의 의미상 주어를 따로 밝혀 주어야 할 경우에는 보통 to 앞에 〈for+목적격〉을 쓴다. 단, 사람에 대한 평가를 나타내는 형용사(kind, nice, rude, wise, clever, silly, foolish 등) 뒤에서는 〈of+목적격〉으로 의미상 주어를 나타낸다.**

  It is not easy **for me to read** this book.

  It was very kind **of him to help** me.

A 다음 괄호 안에서 알맞은 것을 고르시오.

1 The slope was too steep (for / of) us to ski down. 수능 기출 응용

2 It is unusual (for / of) her to get up so early.

3 It was wise (for / of) you to change your mind. 평가원 기출 응용

4 It is very clever (for / of) her to solve the mystery.

5 We can't wait (for / of) world leaders to take action. 평가원 기출

6 It is impossible (for / of) a man of many trades to be skilled in all of them. 교육청 기출

7 It was foolish (for / of) him to spend all his money on drinks.

B 다음 우리말과 같은 뜻이 되도록 괄호 안의 말을 이용하여 문장을 완성하시오.

1 네가 그녀를 도운 것은 잘한 일이었다. (help)
It was nice ____________________ her.

2 그의 지원을 기대하다니 그녀는 바보 같았다. (expect)
It was silly ____________________ his support.

3 우리는 네가 그 프로젝트에 참여하길 바란다. (participate in)
We want ____________________ the project.

4 직장을 그만두다니 그는 어리석었다. (quit)
It was foolish ____________________ his job.

5 내가 새 노트북을 살 때가 된 것 같다. (buy)
I think it's time ____________________ a new laptop.

6 그녀에게 사람들 앞에서 발표를 하기란 어려웠다. (do)
It was difficult ____________________ a presentation in front of people.

★ POINT **10** ★★★★

to부정사의 부정 · 시제 · 태

정답 및 해설 p.10

- **to부정사의 부정은 to 바로 앞에 not 또는 never를 써서 나타낸다.**
  I try **not to eat** too much spicy food.
- **to부정사가 나타내는 때가 술어동사의 시제와 같거나 그보다 미래일 때는 〈to-v〉를 쓰고, to부정사가 나타내는 때가 술어동사의 시제보다 앞설 때는 〈to have p.p.〉를 쓴다.**
  I expect him **to be** a great pianist. (= I expect that he will be a great pianist.)
  Lauren seems **to have been** ill. (= It seems that Lauren was ill.)
- **to부정사의 수동태는 〈to be p.p.〉를 쓴다.**
  She waited **to be called** upon.

A 다음 괄호 안에서 알맞은 것을 고르시오.

1 She agreed (not to / to not) publish the book.
2 I hope (to invite / to be invited) to Peter's birthday party.
3 My mother told me (never to / to never) start smoking.
4 Tony appears (to be / to have been) handsome when he was young.
5 I want (to accept / to be accepted) as one of the members.
6 We expect him (to finish / to be finished) the work by tomorrow.

B 다음 우리말과 같은 뜻이 되도록 괄호 안의 말을 이용하여 문장을 완성하시오.

1 나는 똑똑한 학생으로 여겨지기를 바란다. (consider)
I wish ____________________ a smart student.

2 나는 그 팀에 뽑혀서 너무 기뻤다. (choose)
I was very pleased ____________________ for the team.

3 여기서 교통사고가 있었던 것 같다. (be)
There seems ____________________ a traffic accident here.

4 그녀는 그 코트가 그녀의 사무실로 보내지길 원한다. (send)
She wants the coat ____________________ to her office. 평가원 기출

5 다른 사람들이 일하는 중에는 방해하지 않도록 하세요. (not, bother)
Please try ____________________ anybody while they're working. 수능 기출

6 알 수 없는 출처에서 온 이메일 첨부 파일은 절대로 열지 않는 것이 현명하다. (never, open)
It is wise ____________________ e-mail attachments from an unknown source.
교육청 기출 응용

7 당신의 글이 더 효과적이길 바란다면, 상투어를 사용하지 않기 위해 노력하세요. (use)
If you want your writing to be more effective, try ____________________ clichés.
교육청 기출 응용

★ POINT 11 ★★★★

목적격 보어로 쓰이는 to부정사

정답 및 해설 p.11

- **〈동사+목적어+to-v〉 형태의 구문에서 to부정사는 목적어의 상태나 동작을 보충 설명하는 목적격 보어의 역할을 한다. 이러한 형태로 잘 쓰이는 동사에는 tell, ask, want, get, advise, allow, order 등이 있다.**

She *told* me **to get** out of her car.

He *got* his children **to help** with the household chores.

cf. 〈동사+목적어+to-v〉 구문이 수동형으로 쓰이면, 동사 바로 다음에 to-v가 오게 된다.

They *were asked* **to follow** the rules.

A 다음 밑줄 친 부분을 어법에 맞게 고쳐 쓰시오.

1 I allowed my kids have a dog.

2 My father gets for me to clean the bathroom.

3 The officer warned him stop immediately.

B 다음 우리말과 같은 뜻이 되도록 괄호 안의 말을 이용하여 문장을 완성하시오.

1 갈등은 우리로 하여금 행동하게 한다. (force, act)

Conflict ______________________. 교육청 기출

2 제가 거기 몇 시에 가길 바라세요? (want, be)

What time do you ______________________ there? 교육청 기출

3 나는 그녀에게 에어컨을 켜 달라고 부탁했다. (ask, turn on)

I ______________________ the air conditioner.

4 우리 형은 내가 자기 노트북 컴퓨터를 쓰도록 허락하지 않는다. (allow, use)

My brother ______________________ his laptop computer.

5 엄마는 항상 나에게 정크푸드를 멀리하라고 말씀하신다. (tell, stay away)

My mom always ______________________ from junk food.

6 그는 나에게 그 나라를 최대한 빨리 떠나라고 조언했다. (advise, leave)

He ______________________ the country as soon as possible.

C 다음 문장을 밑줄 친 부분에 유의하여 우리말로 해석하시오.

1 The judge ordered him to be released.

2 They got her to jump into the river. 평가원 기출 응용

3 My doctor tells me to avoid sugar and salt.

4 The teacher warned him not to be late again.

5 We encourage you to take advantage of this program. 수능 기출

6 She doesn't allow her child to eat cookies before a meal.

POINT 12 ★★★★

목적격 보어로 쓰이는 원형부정사

정답 및 해설 p.11

- ★ EXAM TIP 지각동사(see, hear, feel, smell 등)와 사역동사(have, make, let)는 목적격 보어로 원형부정사를 쓴다.

  I *heard* him **complain[complaining]** about the lecture.

  cf. 지각동사의 경우 목적격 보어로 원형부정사 대신 현재분사를 써서 동작이 진행 중임을 강조하기도 한다.

  He *made* me **sit** next to John.

- **준사역동사 help는 목적격 보어로 원형부정사와 to부정사 둘 다를 취할 수 있다.**

  They *helped* us **(to) plant** trees.

A 다음 괄호 안에서 알맞은 것을 고르시오.

1 Can't you see the clouds (coming / to come)? 수능 기출
2 I will have my son (wash / to wash) his clothes.
3 I asked my sister (bring / to bring) a magazine.
4 The cartoon made me (laugh / to laugh). 교육청 기출 응용
5 My boss allowed me (have / to have) another chance.
6 Anna heard him (leave / to leave) the office.
7 She felt something (touch / to touch) her foot.
8 He wouldn't let me (know / to know) the results.

B 다음 〈보기〉에서 알맞은 말을 골라 빈칸에 적절한 형태로 써넣으시오.

보기	bark	apply for	lower	beat	look

1 Jill felt her heart __________ fast.
2 This suit makes me __________ thin.
3 What made you __________ this position? 평가원 기출 응용
4 He heard a dog __________ loudly outside.
5 This helps you __________ the level of your anxiety and stress. 교육청 기출

C 다음 우리말과 같은 뜻이 되도록 괄호 안의 말을 이용하여 문장을 완성하시오.

1 나의 트레이너는 나에게 매일 운동을 하도록 시킨다. (make, work out)
My trainer ____________________ every day.

2 그 경찰관은 그녀가 불법으로 주차하는 것을 보았다. (see, park)
The police officer ____________________ illegally.

3 우리 어머니는 내가 늦게까지 깨어 있게 두지 않으셨다. (let, stay up)
My mother didn't ____________________ late.

REVIEW TEST 05 ★

정답 및 해설 p.11

[1-5] 다음 우리말과 일치하도록 빈칸에 알맞은 말을 고르시오.

1

Cindy는 아들에게 집을 청소하게 했다.
Cindy made her son __________ the house.

① clean ② cleaning
③ to clean ④ cleaned
⑤ to have cleaned

2

당신이 Green 씨를 만나는 것은 불가능하다.
It is impossible for you __________ Mr. Green.

① meet ② meeting ③ to meet
④ met ⑤ having met

3

그는 자신감이 없는 것 같다.
He seems __________ confidence.

① lack ② to lack
③ lacked ④ to lacking
⑤ to have lacked

4

그런 말을 하다니 그녀는 무례하다.
It's rude __________ her to say things like that.

① to ② for ③ of
④ on ⑤ with

5

우리는 휴가를 어디로 갈지 결정했다.
We decided on __________ go on a vacation.

① what to ② when to ③ how to
④ where to ⑤ whom to

[6-8] 다음 두 문장의 뜻이 같도록 빈칸에 알맞은 말을 고르시오.

6

Jim is so strong that he can move the bookshelf.
= Jim is __________ to move the bookshelf.

① strong ② strong enough
③ enough strong ④ not strong
⑤ too strong

7

This suitcase is so heavy that I can't carry it.
= This suitcase is __________ for me to carry.

① so heavy ② heavy enough
③ too heavy ④ heavy too
⑤ enough heavy

8

It seems that Ted was poor before.
= Ted seems to __________ before.

① be poor ② was poor
③ being poor ④ have been poor
⑤ having been poor

[9-12] 다음 우리말과 일치하도록 괄호 안의 말을 이용하여 문장을 완성하시오.

9

나는 다음 의장으로 당선되기를 희망한다. (elect)
I hope __________ __________ __________ as the next chairman.

10

그는 귀여운 소녀가 거리에서 노래하는 것을 들었다. (sing)
He heard a cute girl __________ on the street.

11

나는 너무 행복해서 뭐라고 말해야 할지 모르겠다. (say)
I'm so happy that I don't know __________ __________ __________.

12

제 차를 고쳐 줄 사람을 보내 주시겠어요? (fix)
Could you send someone __________ __________ my car?

[13-15] 다음 문장의 빈칸에 알맞은 것을 고르시오.

13

She didn't let me __________ her phone number.

① know ② knew
③ to know ④ knowing
⑤ to have known

14

It is very dangerous __________ you to go there alone.

① to ② for ③ of
④ on ⑤ with

15

Emily was __________ her parents again.

① never seen ② never seeing
③ never saw ④ never to see
⑤ to never have seen

[16-17] 다음 중 밑줄 친 부분의 쓰임이 다른 것을 고르시오.

16

① I took a taxi to get there on time.
② He needs self-confidence to win the game.
③ I'd be happy to drop by your house.
④ She made a promise to go shopping with me.
⑤ I'm pleased to announce the winner of the contest.

17

① Jane grew up to be a pop musician.
② It is easy to learn how to ride a bicycle.
③ My sister hopes to work with you again.
④ My wish is to go back to my hometown.
⑤ He promised to come to my graduation.

[18-20] 다음 중 밑줄 친 부분이 어법상 틀린 것을 고르시오.

18

① I told him not to forgive her.
② You are to come to class every day.
③ Strange to say, he is not my brother.
④ Danny found a new apartment to live.
⑤ It was not easy to understand what she said.

19

① You are to get up immediately.

② My boss made me quit my job.

③ I was glad to get an e-mail from him.

④ He appears to be happy at his new school.

⑤ Laughter started spread through the room. 교육청 기출 응용

20

① I plan to be here until July. 평가원 기출 응용

② His answer seemed to be a lie.

③ Peter asked his mother to come. 수능 기출 응용

④ I am too busy to attend the meeting.

⑤ At what age should a child learn use a computer? 평가원 기출 응용

[21-22] 다음 문장 중에서 어법상 옳은 것을 고르시오.

21

① Paul wanted buy some souvenirs.

② The job needs be done right away.

③ I'm honored to having been the president.

④ It's nice for you to remember my birthday.

⑤ It is not easy to distinguish between male and female fruit flies. 교육청 기출 응용

22

① We were thrilled learn that you won.

② I was a fool of make such a mistake. 교육청 기출

③ My father allowed me take a trip with Lucy.

④ Officials hired a team to beautifying the city. 교육청 기출

⑤ I need someone to pick up the buyers at the airport. 교육청 기출

23 다음 글의 밑줄 친 부분 중 쓰임이 다른 것은?

When you move to a new town, the toughest thing to do is ① to get to know your new neighbors. One way ② to do this is ③ to invent a reason to talk to them. I like ④ to call it the "cup-of-sugar" technique. 수능 기출 응용

24 다음 글의 밑줄 친 부분 중 어법상 틀린 것은?

It's important ① to have an hour of family time each day. If this isn't possible, you should try ② to get together at least once a week. Having dinner with your family can be a good way ③ to spend time together. It's a time ④ learn conversation skills and respect.

25 다음 글의 빈칸 (A), (B)에 적절한 것끼리 짝지어진 것은?

In the distance, she sees her son ___(A)___ towards the house. She loves these moments. She looks around the house and smiles. How much she wanted ___(B)___ in a house near the beach! 평가원 기출 응용

	(A)	(B)
①	coming	living
②	coming	to live
③	to come	live
④	come	living
⑤	to come	to live

EST CHAPTER 2010

06

동명사

POINT 01 ★★★★

동명사의 역할

정답 및 해설 p.12

- **동명사는 〈동사원형+ing〉 형태로 문장에서 주어, 보어, 목적어 역할을 한다.**

Losing weight is not easy. (주어)
= To lose

My favorite winter activity is **snowboarding**. (보어)
= to snowboard

I *like* **listening** to rock music. (동사의 목적어)
= to listen

I'm afraid *of* **swimming** in the ocean. (전치사의 목적어)

cf. 전치사의 목적어 자리에는 to부정사를 쓸 수 없다.

★ EXAM TIP 동명사구가 주어로 쓰이면 단수 취급하여 뒤에 단수형 동사가 와야 한다.

Watching movies is a good way to learn English.

A 다음 괄호 안에서 알맞은 것을 고르시오.

1 (Sit / Sitting) on the grass is not permitted. 수능 기출 응용

2 My lifetime goal is (write / writing) a mystery novel.

3 I'm interested in (invest / investing) my money in your company.

B 다음 두 문장이 같은 뜻이 되도록 빈칸을 채우시오.

1 To find a well-paying job is difficult.
→ ______________ is difficult.

2 The cat started to lick his hand. 교육청 기출 응용
→ The cat started ______________.

3 Her job is to assist the disabled.
→ Her job is ______________.

C 다음 우리말과 같은 뜻이 되도록 주어진 단어를 배열하여 문장을 완성하시오.

1 지각하는 것은 좋은 버릇이 아니다. (not, is, late, a good habit, being)
______________ 교육청 기출

2 나는 기말 보고서 쓰는 것을 끝마쳤다. (writing, final report, I, finished, my)
______________ 수능 기출 응용

3 너무 많은 초콜릿을 먹는 것은 너를 뚱뚱해지게 한다. (eating, chocolate, too much, you, makes, fat)
____

4 내가 가장 좋아하는 취미는 비디오 게임을 하는 것이다. (playing, my favorite pastime, video games, is)
____

5 그는 수학 시험에서 부정행위를 한 것이 부끄러웠다. (was, he, ashamed of, the math test, on, cheating)
____

정답 및 해설 p.12

★ POINT 02 ★★★★

동명사 vs. to부정사 I

- **동명사만을 목적어로 취하는 동사: enjoy, avoid, mind, quit, stop, finish, keep, deny, give up, put off 등**
  I *avoid* **eating** junk food and sweets.
- **to부정사만을 목적어로 취하는 동사: want, hope, expect, decide, plan, choose, promise, refuse 등**
  He *decided* **to study** abroad in Australia.

A 다음 괄호 안의 동사를 빈칸에 알맞은 형태로 바꾸어 쓰시오.

1 I kept ______________ you last night. (call) 수능 기출 응용
2 They plan ______________ a new library. (build)
3 Do you mind ______________ me find my bag? (help)
4 He didn't expect ______________ Kate at the party. (see)
5 We've just finished ______________ information. (gather) 수능 기출 응용
6 They refused ______________ me a refund. (give)
7 Stop ______________ TV and go to bed. (watch)

B 다음 〈보기〉에서 알맞은 말을 골라 빈칸에 적절한 형태로 써넣으시오.

보기	teach	watch	play	provide	support

1 Dave promised ______________ my plan.
2 I enjoyed ______________ the show last week. 교육청 기출 응용
3 We hope ______________ you with the best service possible. 교육청 기출
4 It's difficult to quit ______________ mobile games.
5 I gave up ______________ my sister how to drive.

C 다음 우리말과 같은 뜻이 되도록 괄호 안의 말을 이용하여 문장을 완성하시오.

1 Linda는 머리를 금발로 염색하기로 결정했다. (decide, dye)
Linda ____________________ her hair blonde.

2 그녀는 범행을 저지른 것을 부인했다. (deny, commit)
She ____________________ the crime.

3 그는 마지막 순간까지 숙제하는 것을 미뤘다. (put off, do)
He ____________________ his homework until the last minute.

POINT 03

동명사 vs. to부정사 II

정답 및 해설 p.12

- **동명사와 to부정사를 모두 목적어로 취하는 동사: like, love, prefer, hate, start, begin, continue 등**

  I *hate* **doing[to do]** household chores.

- **동명사와 to부정사를 모두 목적어로 취하지만 의미가 달라지는 동사: remember, forget, regret, try 등**

  I *forgot* **turning** off the lights. (과거에 한 일)

  I *forgot* **to turn** off the lights. (앞으로 할 일)

★ EXAM TIP

remember v-ing: ~했던 것을 기억하다	**forget v-ing: ~했던 것을 잊다**
remember to-v: ~할 것을 기억하다	**forget to-v: ~할 것을 잊다**
regret v-ing: ~했던 것을 후회하다	**try v-ing: (시험 삼아) ~해 보다**
regret to-v: ~하게 되어 유감이다	**try to-v: ~하려고 노력하다**

A

다음 괄호 안의 동사를 빈칸에 알맞은 형태로 바꾸어 쓰시오.

1 I regret ______________ her my secret. (tell)

2 Nancy prefers ______________ in the back row. (sit)

3 My boss always tries ______________ polite to his employees. (be)

4 Don't forget ______________ pictures when people come in. (take) 교육청 기출 응용

5 When you see her, remember ______________ hello for me. (say)

6 He moved to the U.S. and continued ______________ films. (make) 수능 기출 응용

7 He began ______________ about the weather. (complain) 평가원 기출 응용

B

다음 우리말과 같은 뜻이 되도록 괄호 안의 말을 이용하여 문장을 완성하시오.

1 그는 패스트푸드 먹는 것을 포기했다. (eat)

He ____________________ fast food.

2 수업 시간에 활발하게 참여하도록 노력해라. (participate)

____________________ actively in class. 평가원 기출 응용

3 Tim은 현관문을 잠갔던 것을 기억한다. (lock)

Tim ____________________ the front door.

4 초대에 응할 수 없다고 말하게 되어 유감입니다. (say)

I ____________________ that I can't accept your invitation.

5 Matt는 우산을 가져오는 것을 깜박했다. (bring)

Matt ____________________ his umbrella.

6 그녀는 영화 보러 가는 것을 좋아한다. (go)

She ____________________ to the movies.

POINT 04 ★★★★

동명사의 의미상 주어

정답 및 해설 p.12

- **동명사의 의미상 주어가 문장의 주어 또는 목적어와 일치하거나 일반인을 가리키는 경우에는 생략한다.**

  Thank *you* for **inviting** me. (목적어가 동명사의 의미상 주어)

- **동명사의 의미상 주어는 동명사 바로 앞에 소유격이나 목적격으로 나타낸다.**

  I don't like **his[him] coming** to our meeting.

  Andy('s) resigning surprised everyone.

A **다음 두 문장이 같은 뜻이 되도록 빈칸을 채우시오.**

1 She complained that he was rude to her.
→ She complained of ____________________ rude to her.

2 I was afraid that he might talk to me.
→ I was afraid of ____________________ to me. 평가원 기출 응용

3 We are worried that she is in bad condition.
→ We are worried about ____________________ in a bad condition.

4 I was sure that we would arrive there before 5 o'clock.
→ I was sure of ____________________ there before 5 o'clock.

5 She insisted that her daughter major in economics.
→ She insisted on ____________________ in economics.

B **다음 우리말과 같은 뜻이 되도록 주어진 단어를 배열하여 문장을 완성하시오.**

1 나는 그가 내게 거짓말하는 것이 지겹다. (lying, him, me, to)
I'm tired of ____________________________.

2 제가 당신의 이메일 주소를 여쭤봐도 될까요? (asking, e-mail address, my, your)
Do you mind ____________________________?

3 Jessica는 피고가 유죄임을 의심하지 않는다. (guilty, being, the accused)
Jessica has no doubt of ____________________________.

4 너희 부모님은 네가 음악에 재능이 있는 것을 자랑스러워하신다. (for, you, music, a talent, having)
Your parents are proud of ____________________________.

5 그는 내가 디자이너로서 성공할 거라고 확신한다. (as, succeeding, a designer, me)
He is confident of ____________________________.

6 그 유명인은 사람들이 자기 사진을 찍는 것을 싫어한다. (taking, people, picture, his)
The celebrity hates ____________________________.

POINT 05 ★★★★

동명사의 부정 · 시제 · 태

정답 및 해설 p.12

- **동명사의 부정은 동명사 앞에 not이나 never와 같은 부정어를 써서 나타낸다.**

  I'm thinking of **not going** to the party.

- **동명사가 나타내는 때가 술어동사의 시제와 같거나 그보다 미래일 때는 〈v-ing〉를 쓰고, 동명사가 나타내는 때가 술어동사의 시제보다 앞설 때는 〈having p.p.〉를 쓴다.**

  He is proud of **being** handsome. (= He is proud that he *is* handsome.)

  He is proud of **having worked** for you. (= He is proud that he *worked* for you.)

  cf. 동사에 따라서는 단순형의 동명사 〈v-ing〉 그대로 술어동사의 시제보다 앞선 때를 나타내는 경우가 있다.

- **동명사의 수동태는 〈being p.p.〉를 쓴다. 동명사가 술어동사보다 앞서 일어난 일을 나타낼 때는 〈having been p.p.〉를 쓴다.**

  She was disappointed at not **having been invited**.

A 다음 괄호 안에서 알맞은 것을 고르시오.

1 Most people are afraid of (rejecting / being rejected) by others.

2 She insisted on (buying / having bought) dinner for us tonight.

3 Ray complained of (having treated / having been treated) badly.

4 Tom is fond of (drinking / having drunk) coffee every morning.

5 We think he doesn't have a chance of (electing / being elected).

6 He regrets (having not finished / not having finished) high school.

B 다음 우리말과 같은 뜻이 되도록 괄호 안의 말을 이용하여 문장을 완성하시오.

1 너에게 진실을 말하지 않았던 것이 아쉽다. (tell)
I am sorry for ______________________ you the truth.

2 그는 그 자동차 사고에 연루된 것을 부인한다. (be)
He denies ______________________ involved in the car crash.

3 나는 전에 본 적이 있는 얼굴을 잘 알아본다. (recognize)
I'm good at ______________________ faces I've seen before.

4 그녀는 내가 자기를 기다리지 않아 화가 났다. (wait for)
She got angry with me for ______________________ her.

5 나는 사람들에게 비난받는 것이 두렵다. (criticize)
I'm afraid of ______________________by people.

6 우리는 환경 문제를 야기한 것에 대해 기술을 탓하는 경향이 있다. (bring) 수능 기출 응용
We tend to blame technology for ______________________ on the environmental problems.

7 Sally는 그 책을 받은 걸 기억할 수 없었다. (give)
Sally couldn't remember ______________________ the book.

★ POINT 06 ★★★★

동명사를 사용한 관용 구문

정답 및 해설 p.12

• **자주 쓰이는 동명사를 사용한 관용 구문은 다음과 같다.**

go v-ing: ~하러 가다
feel like v-ing: ~하고 싶다
It is no use v-ing: ~해도 소용없다
be used to v-ing: ~에 익숙하다
cannot help v-ing: ~하지 않을 수 없다
be busy v-ing: ~하느라 바쁘다
be worth v-ing: ~할 가치가 있다
look forward to v-ing: ~할 것을 고대하다[기대하다]
have trouble[difficulty] v-ing: ~하는 데 어려움을 겪다
spend ... v-ing: ~하느라 …를 소비하다

A **다음 우리말과 같은 뜻이 되도록 어법상 틀린 부분을 고쳐 쓰시오.**

1 그는 여름에 낚시하러 가는 것을 좋아한다.
He likes to go fish in the summer.

2 Charles는 바닥에 앉는 것에 익숙하지 않았다.
Charles was not used to sit on the floor.

3 우리는 푸짐한 식사를 한 후 낮잠을 자고 싶어지는 경향이 있다.
We tend to feel like to take a nap after a heavy meal. 교육청 기출 응용

4 그곳에서 당신을 만나기를 기대합니다.
We look forward to see you there. 교육청 기출

5 그는 세계를 여행하며 젊은 시절을 보냈다.
He spent his youth to travel around the world. 평가원 기출 응용

B **다음 우리말과 같은 뜻이 되도록 괄호 안의 말을 이용하여 문장을 완성하시오.**

1 이 유명한 소설은 읽을 가치가 있다. (read)
This famous novel __________ __________ __________.

2 지금 나에게 사과해 봐야 소용없다. (apologize)
It is __________ __________ __________ to me now.

3 나는 전공을 선택하느라 어려움을 겪고 있다. (choose)
I'm __________ __________ __________ my major. 교육청 기출

4 Emily는 그를 직접 만나 보기를 고대한다. (see)
Emily __________ __________ __________ __________ him in person.

5 그녀는 자신의 고장 난 시계를 고치는 데 세 시간을 보냈다. (repair)
She __________ __________ __________ __________ her broken watch.

6 나는 발표를 준비하느라 바쁘다. (get ready)
I __________ __________ __________ __________ for the presentation. 수능 기출

7 미안하지만 나는 너의 의도를 의심하지 않을 수 없다. (doubt)
I'm sorry, but I __________ __________ __________ your intentions.

REVIEW TEST 06 ★

정답 및 해설 p.12

[1-6] 다음 우리말과 일치하도록 빈칸에 알맞은 말을 고르시오.

1

요즘 우리 아버지는 고기 드시는 걸 피하신다.
These days, my father avoids ________ meat.

① eat ② eating
③ to eat ④ having eaten
⑤ be eating

2

나는 Amy에게 소포를 보내는 걸 잊었다.
I forgot ________ a package to Amy.

① send ② sending ③ sent
④ to send ⑤ having sent

3

좋은 소식을 듣기를 고대하고 있겠다.
I will be looking forward to ________ some good news.

① hear ② hearing ③ to hear
④ be heard ⑤ having heard

4

그녀는 비싼 신발 한 켤레를 훔쳤다고 의심받고 있다.
She is suspected of ________ an expensive pair of shoes.

① steal ② stolen ③ being stolen
④ to steal ⑤ having stolen

5

그는 그 상을 받는 데 성공했다.
He succeeded in ________ the prize.

① win ② won
③ winning ④ being won
⑤ to win

6

나는 화장을 하는 것에 익숙하지 않다.
I'm not used ________ make-up.

① wear ② wearing
③ to wear ④ to wearing
⑤ to have worn

[7-8] 다음 문장의 빈칸에 들어갈 수 없는 말을 고르시오.

7

John ________ collecting comic books.

① enjoys ② began
③ quit ④ planned
⑤ loves

8

I ________ to find work abroad.

① expect ② hope
③ want ④ tried
⑤ gave up

[9-12] 다음 우리말과 일치하도록 괄호 안의 말을 이용하여 문장을 완성하시오.

9

그 도둑은 경찰에게 잡힐까 봐 두려웠다. (catch)
The thief was afraid of __________ __________ by the police.

10

나는 네가 가난한 것이 부끄럽지 않다. (be)
I'm not ashamed of __________ __________ poor.

11

당신께 더 빨리 전화 드리지 못해 죄송합니다. (call)
I apologize for __________ __________ you sooner.

12

나는 어머니에게 거짓말했던 것을 후회한다. (lie)
I regret __________ __________ to my mother.

[13-14] 다음 문장의 빈칸에 알맞은 것을 고르시오.

13

I couldn't help __________ when I saw him.

① smile ② smiled
③ smiling ④ to smile
⑤ of smiling

14

Kelly was proud of __________ into Harvard University.

① admitting ② to admit
③ be admitted ④ being admitted
⑤ to have admitted

[15-17] 다음 두 문장이 같은 뜻이 되도록 동명사를 이용하여 빈칸을 채우시오.

15

I'm sorry that she is so sick.
→ I'm sorry about __________________.

16

It is not right to gossip about people.
→ __________________ is not right.

17

He denied that he had met the suspect that night.
→ He denied __________________ the suspect that night.

[18-20] 다음 중 밑줄 친 부분이 어법상 틀린 것을 고르시오.

18

① I don't like being left alone.
② I tried selling my computer.
③ He refused answering my question.
④ I'm busy writing a review for the book.
⑤ Writing a long essay is not easy.

19

① I feel like to go to a concert.
② Remember to lock the back door.
③ Linda's job is taking care of young children.
④ I'm sick of cleaning the house every day.
⑤ My friends and I are going fishing on Saturday. 수능 기출 응용

20

① Jake was accused of having betrayed his uncle.
② Do you mind wearing a swimming cap?
③ I truly enjoyed having worked with all of you.
④ I just finished to decorate the room. 교육청 기출 응용
⑤ Taking photos is allowed inside the exhibition hall. 수능 기출

[21-22] 다음 문장 중 어법상 옳은 것을 고르시오.

21

① I couldn't help cry watching the movie.
② We decided not taking on the project.
③ Don't forget to bring your towel.
④ Negative feelings are part of be human.
⑤ Keep a safe distance from the car ahead is important. 교육청 기출

22

① She spent most of her time studying.
② I really want winning the competition.
③ An architect's job is construct houses.
④ I plan doing something for my parents.
⑤ He's responsible for to manage a small team.

23 다음 글의 빈칸 (A), (B)에 적절한 것끼리 짝지어진 것은?

There are children who don't want to learn ___(A)___. Do you know why? It's partly because they think their parents will stop ___(B)___ bedtime stories to them if they can read. 평가원 기출 응용

	(A)	(B)
①	read	to read
②	reading	to read
③	read	reading
④	to read	reading
⑤	to read	having read

24 다음 글의 밑줄 친 부분 중 어법상 바르지 못한 것은?

Research shows that people who exercise in the evening have more trouble ① sleeping. However, ② exercising in the morning can increase your energy for the day. Other research also shows that ③ start the day with morning exercise is the key to ④ losing weight. 평가원 기출 응용

25 다음 글의 (A), (B), (C)에서 각각 알맞은 것을 고르시오.

The doctor said that it was not worth (A) (to treat / treating) the puppy since there wasn't much chance of it (B) (to survive / surviving). However, I didn't want to give up the puppy, so I decided (C) (doing / to do) everything in my power to save it.

수능 기출 응용

EST CHAPTER 2010

07

분사

정답 및 해설 p.13

★ POINT 01 ★★★★

분사의 쓰임

- **한정 용법: 형용사처럼 쓰여 앞이나 뒤에서 명사를 수식한다.**

  She tried to open the **locked** *door*.

  I saw *a dog* **sitting** on a chair.

  cf. 분사에 목적어, 수식어구가 붙어 길어지면 명사의 뒤에서 수식한다.

- **서술 용법: 주어나 목적어에 대해 설명하는 주격 보어, 목적격 보어의 역할을 한다.**

  He looks **tired** and **stressed** today.

  I found *her* **sleeping** in her bed.

A 다음 괄호 안에서 알맞은 것을 고르시오.

1 (Win / Winning) videos will air on the TV show. 교육청 기출

2 The man (wears / wearing) a blue tie is my boyfriend.

3 This is a photo (took / taken) on my trip to Spain.

4 Max was reading a book (wrote / written) in French.

5 A picture of (an eating bear / a bear eating) fish hung on the wall.

B 다음 두 문장이 같은 뜻이 되도록 분사를 이용하여 문장을 완성하시오.

1 Do you know the woman? She is called Anne.
→ Do you know the woman ____________________?

2 He was singing. He was surrounded by a lot of people.
→ He was singing ____________________.

3 There are a lot of nannies. They are working in American homes.
→ There are a lot of nannies ____________________. 평가원 기출

4 I saw two men. They were wandering around the cars.
→ I saw two men ____________________. 평가원 기출 응용

C 다음 우리말과 같은 뜻이 되도록 주어진 단어를 배열하여 문장을 완성하시오.

1 우리 선생님은 내 발표에 만족하신 것 같았다. (with, satisfied, my presentation)
My teacher looked ____________________.

2 방문자들은 주차권에 도장을 받아야 합니다. (their, stamped, parking tickets, have) 수능 기출
Visitors must ____________________.

3 Erin은 자고 있는 그녀의 아기를 팔에 안고 있다. (her, baby, sleeping)
Erin is holding ____________________ in her arms.

POINT 02 ★★★★

현재분사 vs. 과거분사

정답 및 해설 p.13

- **현재분사(v-ing): '~하고 있는, ~하는'이라는 진행 또는 능동의 의미를 나타낸다.**

  She saw him **lying** on the ground. (진행)

  I read an **exciting** novel. (능동)

  cf. 동명사와 현재분사는 형태가 같지만 동명사는 명사의 역할(~하는 것, ~하기)을, 현재분사는 형용사의 역할(~하고 있는)을 한다.

  His hobby is **reading** comic books. (동명사)

  Joe is **reading** comic books in his room. (현재분사)

- **과거분사(p.p.): '~한, ~당한'이라는 완료 또는 수동의 의미를 나타낸다.**

  Tom walked on **fallen** leaves. (완료)

  I had my cell phone **repaired**. (수동)

A 다음 괄호 안에서 알맞은 것을 고르시오.

1 I saw the man (stealing / stolen) a bicycle.
2 She couldn't open the (locking / locked) door.
3 He bought a (using / used) car and slept in it. 평가원 기출 응용
4 Michael kept the windows (closing / closed).
5 There were six people (hurting / hurt) in the car crash.
6 Don't forget to tell him about the (barking / barked) dog. 수능 기출 응용
7 The building has remained (deserting / deserted).
8 There are a lot of people (selling / sold) fake items on the Internet.

B 다음 우리말과 같은 뜻이 되도록 괄호 안의 말을 이용하여 문장을 완성하시오.

1 우리는 타고 있는 초를 껐다. (burn)
We blew out the __________ candles.

2 그들은 집에서 그 곤충들을 제거되게 했다. (remove)
They had the insects __________ from their homes. 교육청 기출 응용

3 나는 그 소년이 시험에서 부정행위를 하는 것을 적발했다. (cheat)
I caught the boy __________ on the test.

4 나는 그 방에서 울고 있는 어린 여자아이를 안다. (cry)
I know the little girl __________ in the room.

5 그 사고로 그는 다리가 부러졌다. (break)
The accident left his leg __________.

6 한번은 할아버지께서 덤불을 바라보고 계시는 것을 지켜보았다. (look)
I once watched my grandfather __________ at a bush. 교육청 기출 응용

★ POINT 03 ★★★★

감정을 유발하는 v-ing vs. 감정을 느끼는 p.p.

정답 및 해설 p.13

- **사람의 감정을 나타내는 동사는 분사형으로 자주 쓰인다. 이때 능동의 뜻(~한 감정을 느끼게 하는)일 경우에는 현재분사를, 수동의 뜻(~한 감정을 느끼게 되는)일 경우에는 과거분사를 쓴다.**

  J.K. Rowling is an **amazing** writer. (능동: 놀라운)

  He was **amazed** at my cooking skills. (수동: 놀란)

A 다음 괄호 안에서 알맞은 것을 고르시오.

1 His speech was (boring / bored) as usual.

2 I'm very (exciting / excited) to work here. 수능 기출 응용

3 The results were not particularly (surprising / surprised).

4 They were (shocking / shocked) by the plane crash.

5 This is an (exciting / excited) and dynamic place to work. 수능 기출

6 She felt so (embarrassing / embarrassed) to have made a big mistake.

B 다음 괄호 안의 말을 알맞게 바꾸어 문장을 완성하시오.

1 Don't give me a __________ answer. (confuse)

2 Read this book if you are __________ in Greek myths. (interest)

3 You can enjoy __________ activities such as kite flying for free. (excite) 수능 기출 응용

4 He was __________ to death during the conference. (bore)

5 My grades were very __________ this semester. (satisfy)

6 Many students will be __________ at the decision. (disappoint) 교육청 기출 응용

C 다음 우리말과 같은 뜻이 되도록 〈보기〉의 말을 이용하여 문장을 완성하시오.

보기 amaze confuse disgust interest please

1 서로 다른 관심사를 가진 친구들이 있는 것은 삶을 흥미롭게 해 준다.
Having friends with different interests keeps life __________. 교육청 기출 응용

2 네가 승진했다는 소식을 들으니 우리는 정말 기쁘다.
We're very __________ to hear that you got promoted.

3 이유는 모르겠지만 그는 매우 혼란스러워 보인다.
I don't know why, but he seems very __________.

4 나는 그런 혐오스러운 이야기를 듣고 싶지 않다.
I don't want to hear such a __________ story.

5 그는 그 마을이 너무 많이 변한 것에 놀랐다.
He was __________ at how much the village had changed.

★ POINT 04 ★★★★

분사구문의 형태

정답 및 해설 p.14

- 분사구문이란 〈접속사+주어+동사〉 형태의 부사절을 현재분사 〈v-ing〉가 이끄는 부사구로 나타낸 것이다.
- 부사절을 분사구문으로 바꾸는 방법

  ① 접속사를 생략한다. ② 부사절의 주어가 주절의 주어와 같으면 생략한다.
  ③ 부사절과 주절의 시제가 같으면 부사절의 동사를 〈v-ing〉로 바꾼다.

  ~~When he~~ arrived in Seattle, he headed straight to the hotel.
  → **Arriving** in Seattle, he headed straight to the hotel.
  ~~As I~~ wasn't able to concentrate, I went to bed.
  → **Not being** able to concentrate, I went to bed.

  cf. 분사구문의 부정은 부정어(not, never)를 분사 앞에 써서 나타낸다.

A 다음 밑줄 친 부분을 분사구문으로 바꾸어 쓰시오.

1 As I was busy, I couldn't call you.
→ ______________________, I couldn't call you.

2 While I was playing badminton yesterday, I dropped my phone by mistake.
→ ______________________, I dropped my phone by mistake. 수능 기출 응용

3 If you go straight ahead, you'll see a bank on the right.
→ ______________________, you'll see a bank on the right.

4 After we joined the drama club together, we became closer friends.
→ ______________________, we became closer friends.

5 When you travel by car, you may suffer from these symptoms. 수능 기출 응용
→ ______________________, you may suffer from these symptoms.

6 Since it wanted to make a good impression, the company sent its best employee.
→ ______________________, the company sent its best employee. 교육청 기출 응용

B 다음 우리말과 같은 뜻이 되도록 괄호 안의 말을 이용하여 분사구문을 완성하시오.

1 이것을 보고, 모두들 놀랐다. (see)
________ ________, everyone was surprised. 교육청 기출

2 돈이 없어서 나는 내 머리를 직접 자르기로 결심했다. (not, have)
________ ________ ________, I decided to cut my hair myself.

3 친구들과 농구를 하다가 그는 팔을 다쳤다. (play)
________ ________ with his friends, he hurt his arm.

4 학교에 지각해서 나는 선생님께 꾸중을 들었다. (be)
________ ________ for school, I was scolded by my teacher.

5 왼쪽으로 돌면, 우체국이 보일 거예요. (turn)
________ ________, you'll find the post office.

POINT 05 ★★★★

분사구문의 의미

정답 및 해설 p.14

- **분사구문은 문맥에 따라 주로 때(동시동작, 연속동작), 이유의 의미로 쓰인다.**

  He stood at the door, **looking** at her with a smile. (동시동작: ~하면서)
  (← He stood at the door while he was looking ~.)
  Turning off the alarm, she went back to sleep. (연속동작: ~하고)
  (← She turned off the alarm and she went ~.)
  Having a headache, I got off work early. (이유: ~하므로)
  (← As I had a headache, I got ~.)

  cf. 드물게 조건(만약 ~하면), 양보(비록 ~이지만)의 의미로 쓰일 때도 있다.
  Listening to music, you'll never hear the birds. (← If you listen to music, ~.)
  Being short, she runs faster than me. (← Though she is short, ~.)

A 다음 문장을 밑줄 친 부분에 유의하여 우리말로 해석하시오.

1 I fell asleep watching TV at home.
2 Exercising regularly, he never gets fat.
3 Smiling, Breaden walked down the aisle. 수능 기출 응용
4 Searching the Internet, she found my blog.
5 Fighting with her brother, the girl started to cry.

B 다음 밑줄 친 부분을 분사구문으로 바꾸어 쓰시오.

1 When I am with you, I feel comfortable.
→ ______________________, I feel comfortable.
2 If you always tell the truth, you will be admired.
→ ______________________, you will be admired.
3 As I didn't wear contact lenses, I couldn't see you. 평가원 기출 응용
→ ______________________, I couldn't see you.

C 다음 밑줄 친 분사구문을 절로 바꾸어 쓰시오.

1 Being only twelve, I couldn't watch that movie. 평가원 기출 응용
→ ______________________, I couldn't watch that movie.
2 I quickly shook the presents, testing their weight. 교육청 기출 응용
→ I quickly shook the presents, ______________________.
3 Receiving the phone call, my sister started to yell.
→ ______________________, my sister started to yell.
4 Behaving like that, you will not succeed.
→ ______________________, you will not succeed.

★ POINT 06 ★★★★

분사구문의 시제와 태

정답 및 해설 p.14

- **분사구문이 주절의 동사와 같은 때를 나타내는 경우에는 〈v-ing〉를, 주절의 동사보다 이전에 일어난 일을 나타내는 경우에는 〈having p.p.〉를 쓴다.**

Not knowing what to do, he just stood there.
(← As he didn't know what to do, he just stood there.)

(Having been) Born in a small town, he knew everyone in it.
(← As he had been born in a small town, he knew everyone in it.)

cf. 〈Being[Having been]+과거분사/형용사/명사〉로 시작하는 수동 분사구문에서 Being이나 Having been은 보통 생략된다.

A 다음 밑줄 친 부분을 분사구문으로 바꾸어 쓰시오.

1 After I had watched the comedy show, I felt better.
→ ______________________, I felt better.

2 While I looked for work in Tokyo, I stayed in a small hotel.
→ ______________________, I stayed in a small hotel.

3 Because he had seen the movie before, he didn't want to go again.
→ ______________________, he didn't want to go again.

4 Although she was stuck in an elevator, Lucy remained calm.
→ ______________________, Lucy remained calm.

5 As I slept for three hours last night, I am very sleepy now.
→ ______________________, I am very sleepy now.

6 If it is used sparingly, this shampoo will last a long time.
→ ______________, this shampoo will last a long time.

B 다음 우리말과 같은 뜻이 되도록 괄호 안의 말을 이용하여 분사구문을 완성하시오.

1 그는 난관에 직면하여 그것을 받아들이고 극복했다. (face)
__________ with a challenge, he accepted it and overcame it. 수능 기출 응용

2 그를 기다리면서 나는 뜨거운 커피 한 잔을 마셨다. (wait)
__________ for him, I had a cup of hot coffee.

3 그는 그 업계에서 10년 일했었기 때문에 그 주제에 대해 잘 안다. (work)
__________ in the industry for 10 years, he has a solid understanding of the subject.

4 아침에 지갑을 잃어버렸기 때문에 나는 버스를 탈 돈이 없다. (lose)
__________ my wallet in the morning, I have no money to take a bus.

5 그녀는 어제 여행 준비를 끝마쳤기 때문에 지금 할 일이 없다. (finish)
__________ preparing for the trip yesterday, she has nothing to do now.

POINT 07 ★★★★

독립 분사구문

정답 및 해설 p.14

- **독립 분사구문: 분사구문의 주어가 주절의 주어와 다를 때는 의미상 주어를 분사 앞에 쓴다.**

It being sunny, we went to the beach. (← As it was sunny, ~.)
There being no food at home, I ordered some Chinese food.
(← As there was no food at home, ~.)
cf. 〈There+be〉 구문을 분사구문으로 쓸 때는 There를 생략하지 않고 being 앞에 쓴다.

- **비인칭 독립 분사구문: 분사구문의 주어가 일반인인 경우, 주어를 생략하고 하나의 숙어처럼 쓴다.**

– generally[strictly, frankly] speaking: 일반적으로[엄밀히, 솔직히] 말하자면
– judging from: ~로 판단하건대
– speaking of: ~ 얘기가 나왔으니 말인데
– considering that: ~을 감안한다면
Generally speaking, our economy is improving.

A 다음 밑줄 친 부분을 분사구문으로 바꾸어 쓰시오.

1 As there was nothing to do, I watched TV all day.
→ ____________________, I watched TV all day.

2 Our class was canceled, so we went to the beach.
→ ____________________, we went to the beach.

3 As her thoughts wandered, Hannah vaguely heard her mother's voice. 수능 기출
→ ____________________, Hannah vaguely heard her mother's voice.

4 When the plane started to land, he got ready to go.
→ ____________________, he got ready to go.

5 As it is very hot these days, Mary drinks lots of ice water.
→ ____________________, Mary drinks lots of ice water.

6 As the marketing director complained, we began to work harder.
→ ____________________, we began to work harder.

B 다음 우리말과 같은 뜻이 되도록 비인칭 독립 분사구문을 이용하여 문장을 완성하시오.

1 솔직히 말해서 그녀의 무례한 태도가 싫다.
____________________, I hate her rude attitude.

2 그의 반응으로 판단하건대 그는 그 회의에 대해 몰랐다.
____________________ his reaction, he didn't know about the meeting.

3 John Grisham 얘기가 나와서 말인데, 나 지금 그 사람 책을 읽고 있어.
____________________, I am reading his book now.

4 네가 원어민이 아닌 것을 감안한다면 너의 프랑스어 실력은 훌륭하다.
____________________ you're not a native speaker, your French is excellent.

POINT 08 ★★★★

〈with+(대)명사+분사〉 구문

정답 및 해설 p.14

- **〈with+(대)명사 + 분사〉 구문: '~가 …하고 있는[된 채로]'이라는 뜻으로 일종의 분사구문이다. (대)명사와 분사가 의미상 능동 관계일 때는 현재분사를, 수동 관계일 때는 과거분사를 쓴다.**

  I took a walk **with my dog following** me.

  She was sitting on a bench **with her legs crossed**.

A 다음 두 문장이 같은 뜻이 되도록 빈칸에 알맞은 말을 쓰시오.

1 She lay on the couch, and her eyes were closed.
→ She lay on the couch with her eyes __________.

2 I went out, and the heater was turned on.
→ I went out with the heater __________ on.

3 While his mouth watered, he stretched out his arm. 수능 기출 응용
→ With his mouth __________, he stretched out his arm.

4 Marvin hugged me, and tears were running down his cheeks.
→ Marvin hugged me with tears __________ down his cheeks.

5 I watched TV while my husband read a book beside me.
→ I watched TV with my husband __________ a book beside me.

6 She was playing the violin and her feet were tapping on the floor.
→ She was playing the violin with her feet __________ on the floor.

B 다음 우리말과 같은 뜻이 되도록 괄호 안의 말을 이용하여 문장을 완성하시오.

1 나는 입을 다문 채로 구석에 앉아 있었다. (shut)
I was sitting in the corner with __________ __________ __________.

2 그것의 뚜껑을 제거한 채로 기계를 작동시키지 마십시오. (cover, remove)
Don't operate the machine with __________ __________ __________.

3 그녀는 TV를 켜 놓은 채로 설거지를 하고 있다. (turn on)
She is washing dishes with __________ __________ __________ __________.

4 그녀는 머리를 단정히 빗어 넘긴 채로 검정 원피스를 입고 있었다. (comb)
She wore a black dress, with __________ __________ __________ back neatly.

5 그는 발에서 피가 나는 채로 걷고 또 걸었다. (bleed)
He walked and walked, with __________ __________ __________.

6 그것들의 이름이 겉에 쓰인 채로, 씨앗을 봉투에 넣어 포장해라. (write)
Package your seeds in envelopes __________ __________ __________ __________ on the outside. 교육청 기출

REVIEW TEST 07 ★

정답 및 해설 p.14

[1-5] 다음 우리말과 일치하도록 빈칸에 알맞은 말을 고르시오.

1

난 내 시험 성적이 만족스럽지 않다.
I'm not ________ with my test results.

① satisfy ② satisfying
③ satisfied ④ to satisfy
⑤ having satisfied

2

Kelly는 멀리서 그녀의 이름이 불리는 것을 들었다.
Kelly heard her name ________ from a distance.

① call ② calling ③ called
④ to call ⑤ having called

3

그는 중국에서 살았기 때문에 중국어를 할 줄 안다.
________ in China, he can speak Chinese.

① Live ② Living ③ To live
④ Being lived ⑤ Having lived

4

그것은 거울을 보고 있는 여자의 그림이다.
It is a painting of a woman ________ into a mirror.

① look ② looking
③ looked ④ to look
⑤ having looked

5

Jack은 이탈리아에서 만들어진 서류 가방을 샀다.
Jack bought a briefcase ________ in Italy.

① make ② makes ③ making
④ made ⑤ to make

[6-9] 다음 두 문장의 뜻이 같도록 빈칸에 알맞은 말을 고르시오.

6

When he left the office, he didn't say anything.
= ________ the office, he didn't say anything.

① Leave ② Leaving
③ Left ④ He leaving
⑤ Having left

7

Because my parents are away for the week, I'm alone in the house.
= ________ away for the week, I'm alone in the house.

① Being ② To be
③ My parents being ④ My parents were
⑤ My parents having been

8

Having been in the same class for three years, we are very close to each other.

= __________ we have been in the same class for three years, we are very close to each other.

① While ② If ③ When
④ As ⑤ Though

9

After I had been late for work several times, I decided to get up earlier.
= __________ late for work several times, I decided to get up earlier.

① Be ② Being
③ Had been ④ Have been
⑤ Having been

[10-13] 다음 우리말과 일치하도록 괄호 안의 말을 이용하여 문장을 완성하시오.

10

나는 그에 대한 놀라운 사실을 발견했다. (surprise)
I discovered a __________ fact about him.

11

종일 아무것도 못 먹어서, 나는 피곤하고 배가 고팠다. (eat)
__________ __________ all day, I was tired and hungry.

12

Jay는 라디오를 켜 놓은 채로 샤워를 했다. (turn on)
Jay took a shower with __________ __________ __________ __________.

13

일반적으로 말해서, 여자들은 로맨틱 코미디를 좋아한다. (speak)
__________ __________, women like romantic comedies.

[14-16] 다음 문장의 빈칸에 알맞은 것을 고르시오.

14

Who is that boy __________ at us?

① waved ② waving ③ waves
④ to wave ⑤ being waved

15

__________ from his accent, he is from New York.

① Judge ② Judged ③ Judging
④ Judges ⑤ Having judged

16

She went out for a walk with her dogs __________ her.

① follows ② followed ③ following
④ to follow ⑤ having followed

[17-20] 다음 중 밑줄 친 부분이 어법상 틀린 것을 고르시오.

17

① I'd like to have my hair cutting.
② We were excited by his arrival.
③ The weather being good, I'll go hiking.
④ Frankly speaking, I've never met her.
⑤ I sat down, putting my bag on the seat beside me. 교육청 기출 응용

18

① I saw him crossing the road.

② Having studied late last night, I'm tired.

③ His mother calling his name, the boy ran away.

④ The steak in this restaurant is disappointed.

⑤ The match fell from my trembling fingers. 교육청 기출

19

① I'm interested in English literature. 교육청 기출 응용

② Having done my homework, I went out.

③ Considering that he is young, he will be a great pianist.

④ Carts pulled by horses could transport goods more quickly. 교육청 기출 응용

⑤ He tried to speak again, not know what to say. 교육청 기출

20

① I heard something moving slowly. 교육청 기출 응용

② Having a full stomach makes people feel satisfying. 교육청 기출

③ Post a photo of yourself wearing our product.

④ Pictures painted by Van Gogh often sell for millions of dollars.

⑤ Orphaned during the war, he was raised by his relatives. 수능 기출 응용

[21-22] 다음 글의 빈칸 (A), (B)에 적절한 것끼리 짝지어진 것을 고르시오.

21

> ___(A)___ in Germany, she lost her sight at 18. But she was not ___(B)___ about her situation. 평가원 기출 응용

	(A)	(B)
①	Bearing	frustrating
②	Born	frustrate
③	Born	frustrating
④	Born	frustrated
⑤	Bearing	frustrated

22

> I watched David ___(A)___ soccer yesterday. He scored two goals in the game. His performance has been ___(B)___ this season.

	(A)	(B)
①	played	satisfying
②	playing	satisfying
③	playing	satisfied
④	to play	satisfying
⑤	play	satisfied

23 다음 글의 밑줄 친 부분 중 어법상 바르지 못한 것은?

> You're more likely to be ① disappointed if you set expectations too high. Here is an example. ② Having been watched a new movie, your friend tells you that it is really ③ amazing. You go to see it. But if it's not 100% ④ amazing, you'll be ⑤ disappointed. 평가원 기출 응용

24 다음 글의 (A), (B), (C)에서 각각 알맞은 것을 고르시오.

> I put the bag of food inside my shirt. I tried to look calm, (A) (walking / walked) towards the fence. I was about fifty feet from the fence, when I saw a (B) (barking / barked) dog (C) (running / to run) towards me. 평가원 기출 응용

EST 2010

CHAPTER 08

접속사

1 등위접속사
2 상관접속사
3 명사절을 이끄는 종속접속사 I - that
4 명사절을 이끄는 종속접속사 II - if, whether
5 접속사 역할을 하는 의문사
6 부사절을 이끄는 종속접속사 I (시간)
7 부사절을 이끄는 종속접속사 II (시간)
8 부사절을 이끄는 종속접속사 III (조건)
9 부사절을 이끄는 종속접속사 IV (양보)
10 부사절을 이끄는 종속접속사 V (기타)

REVIEW TEST 08

정답 및 해설 p.15

★ POINT 01 ★★★★

등위접속사

- **등위접속사: 문법적 역할이 대등한 단어, 구, 절을 연결한다.**

It'll be hot **and** humid tomorrow. (첨가)
I like Charles, **but** he likes Linda. (대조)
Do you have any brothers **or** sisters? (선택)
I sat for too long, **so** I'd like to go for a walk. (결과)

cf. 〈명령문+and[or]〉는 '~해라, 그러면[그러지 않으면] …'이라는 뜻이다.
Tell me the truth, **and** I will forgive you. (= If you tell me the truth, I ~)
Hurry up, **or** you will miss the school bus. (= If you don't hurry up, you ~)

A 다음 괄호 안에서 알맞은 것을 고르시오.

1 Max proposed to Anna (and / but) she accepted.
2 He made an attractive offer, (or / but) I refused.
3 I don't have much money, (so / but) I can't buy it.
4 Which do you prefer, pants (or / and) skirts?
5 We didn't get any homework in history (or / so) English. 수능 기출 응용

B 다음 두 문장이 같은 뜻이 되도록 빈칸을 채우시오.

1 If you don't keep quiet, you'll be punished.
→ Keep quiet, ______________________.
2 If you exercise every day, you'll be fitter.
→ Exercise every day, ______________________.
3 If you don't take a taxi, you'll be late for the meeting.
→ Take a taxi, ______________________.

C 다음 우리말과 같은 뜻이 되도록 〈보기〉에서 알맞은 말을 골라 주어진 단어와 함께 문장을 완성하시오.

보기 and but or so

1 집에 가서 잠을 좀 자라. (some, get, sleep)
Go home ______________________. 수능 기출
2 그녀는 한 달에 사흘 또는 나흘 초과근무를 한다. (a month, four, days, three)
She works overtime ______________________.
3 이 책상은 더 비싸지만, 고객 평가가 더 좋아. (better, customer, has, reviews, it)
This desk is more expensive, ______________________. 교육청 기출 응용
4 교외에서는 대중교통이 제한되어 있어서, 사람들이 어디든지 차를 몰고 간다. (drive, people, everywhere)
Public transportation is limited in the suburbs, ______________________.
교육청 기출 응용

POINT 02 ★★★★

상관접속사

정답 및 해설 p.15

- **상관접속사: 짝을 이루어 쓰이는 등위접속사를 지칭한다.**

Both my sister **and** I play the cello. (A와 B 둘 다)
You can have **either** green tea **or** coffee. (A나 B 둘 중 하나)
Neither he **nor** I like horror movies. (A도 B도 아닌)
Not only you **but also** she lives in Italy. (A뿐만 아니라 B도)
(= She **as well as** you lives in Italy.)

cf. both A and B가 주어 자리에 오는 경우 동사는 복수형을 쓰며, either A or B, neither A nor B, not only A but also B(= B as well as A)가 주어 자리에 오는 경우 동사는 B에 일치시킨다. LINK p.180 수의 일치

A 다음 두 문장이 같은 뜻이 되도록 〈보기〉의 말을 이용하여 문장을 완성하시오.

보기 both ~ and　　either ~ or　　neither ~ nor　　not only ~ but also

1 He acted as writer or as director on several films. 수능 기출 응용
→ He acted as ______________________ on several films.

2 He didn't recognize her. He didn't remember her name. 교육청 기출 응용
→ He ______________________.

3 I got an A in math as well as in science.
→ I got an A ______________________.

4 I want to open a checking account. And I want to open a savings account.
→ I want to open ______________________.

B 다음 문장에서 어법상 틀린 부분을 고쳐 쓰시오.

1 Either Tony or you is wrong.
2 Not only he but also I plays the guitar well.
3 Neither you nor she are responsible for this failure.

C 다음 우리말과 같은 뜻이 되도록 문장을 완성하시오.

1 그 요리법에 우유나 물 중 하나를 사용할 수 있다.
You can use ________ milk ________ water for the recipe.

2 문제는 그가 영어를 말하지도 쓰지도 못한다는 것이다.
The problem is that he ________ speaks ________ writes English.

3 그는 잘생겼을 뿐만 아니라 유머 감각도 있다.
He is ________ ________ good-looking ________ ________ humorous.

4 강의도 듣고 필기도 하는 것은 어렵게 생각될지도 모른다.
You may find it difficult to ________ listen to the lecture ________ take notes.

POINT 03 ★★★★

명사절을 이끄는 종속접속사 I - that

정답 및 해설 p.15

- **종속접속사: 종속절을 주절에 연결해 준다.**
- **종속접속사 that은 문장에서 주어, 목적어, 보어 역할을 하는 명사절을 이끈다.**

It is a pity **that** he failed the exam. (주어)
(= **That** he failed the exam is a pity.)

cf. 종속접속사 that이 이끄는 절이 문장에서 주어의 역할을 하는 경우, 그 자리에 가주어 it을 쓰고 that절은 문장 뒤로 보낸다.

I didn't know **(that)** he was Sue's boyfriend. (목적어)

cf. 목적어로 쓰인 명사절을 이끄는 that은 생략되기도 한다.

The fact is **that** she is hiding something. (보어)

A

다음 문장에서 명사절을 이끄는 접속사 that이 들어갈 자리에 ✓표 하시오.

1 He hopes he will be rich.
2 They believe I'm highly gifted. 수능 기출
3 It's a relief your injury is not serious.
4 It is amazing she survived the accident.
5 My concern is he only stays in his room after he comes home. 수능 기출
6 The best thing about driverless cars is people won't need a license to operate them. 교육청 기출 응용

B

다음 우리말과 같은 뜻이 되도록 주어진 단어를 배열하여 문장을 완성하시오.

1 대부분의 사람들은 친구가 중요하다고 생각한다. (friends, that, important, are)
Most people think ______________________. 교육청 기출 응용
2 문제는 지금 내게 돈이 없다는 것이다. (that, I, no, money, have)
The problem is ______________________ now.
3 나는 그녀가 범죄를 저질렀을 것 같지 않다. (the, crime, she, that, committed)
I doubt ______________________.
4 그가 지난달부터 실종 상태라는 것은 충격적이다. (he, that, missing, been, has)
It is shocking ______________________ since last month.
5 진실은 그가 나를 더는 사랑하지 않는다는 것이다. (he, that, love, doesn't, me)
The truth is ______________________ anymore.

C

다음 문장을 밑줄 친 부분에 유의하여 우리말로 해석하시오.

1 It is true <u>that</u> Owen didn't finish college.
2 The trouble is <u>that</u> we don't have enough time to prepare for the test.
3 I have to inform you <u>that</u> our hours of operation will change starting next month. 교육청 기출 응용

POINT 04 ★★★★

명사절을 이끄는 종속접속사 II - if, whether

정답 및 해설 p.15

- **if나 whether가 명사절을 이끄는 경우 '~인지 아닌지'라는 의미를 나타낸다.**

It isn't important **if[whether]** they agree or not.
(= **Whether** they agree or not isn't important.)
I still wonder **if[whether]** I made the right decision.
The question is **whether** the information is accurate.

cf. if는 문장 앞에서 주어 역할을 하는 절이나 보어 역할을 하는 절을 이끌 수 없다.

A **다음 빈칸에 if 또는 whether를 써서 문장을 완성하시오. (둘 다 가능한 경우, if를 쓰시오.)**

1 Peter doubts __________ he can do his duties. 수능 기출 응용
2 __________ he likes me or not doesn't matter to me.
3 All I'm worried about is __________ she is all right.
4 Let's look around to see __________ we can find something. 수능 기출
5 We are asking __________ the route for bus 15 could be changed slightly. 교육청 기출

B **다음 괄호 안에서 알맞은 것을 고르시오.**

1 Some people believe (if / that) social media is a waste of time.
2 I'm not sure (that / whether) she is honest or not.
3 I thought (if / that) she would be able to fix the computer.
4 (If / Whether) you succeed or not is entirely up to you.

C **다음 우리말과 같은 뜻이 되도록 주어진 단어를 배열하여 문장을 완성하시오.**

1 웨이터는 나에게 차를 더 원하느냐고 물었다. (more, wanted, tea, if, I)
The waiter asked me ______________________________.
2 나는 그녀가 뜨개질에 관심이 있는지 궁금하다. (is, interested, if, knitting, in, she)
I wonder ______________________________.
3 네가 나와 함께 가든 안 가든 나는 상관없다. (me, whether, you, with, go)
I don't mind ______________________________ or not.
4 나는 Steven이 시장으로 선출될지가 의문이다. (Steven, mayor, whether, elected, be, will)
I doubt ______________________________.
5 웹사이트의 정보를 믿을 수 있는지 어떻게 알 수 있나요? (whether, trust, the information, can, I)
How can I know ______________________________ on websites? 교육청 기출 응용

★ POINT 05 ★★★★

접속사 역할을 하는 의문사

정답 및 해설 p.16

- 의문사가 접속사 역할을 하여 종속절을 이끄는 경우가 있다. 이 경우 종속절을 간접의문문이라 하기도 한다. 어순은 〈의문사+주어+동사〉이며, 의문사가 주어일 경우에는 〈의문사(주어)+동사〉로 쓴다. LINK p.185 의문문의 화법 전환

I don't know **where** he is. (← I don't know .... + Where is he?)

Tell me **what** happened to you. (← Tell me .... + What happened to you?)

cf. 주절이 do you think[guess, believe, imagine] 등일 경우에는 의문사를 문장 맨 앞에 둔다.

Who do you think she is? (← Do you think ...? + Who is she?)

A 다음 두 문장을 한 문장으로 만드시오.

1 Do you know ...? + Where is the closest library?

→ ______________________________

2 Do you think ...? + Who will be there?

→ ______________________________

3 I'd like to know .... + When will my order be shipped?

→ ______________________________

4 I don't remember .... + When did the concert take place?

→ ______________________________

5 He isn't sure .... + Which camera should he buy?

→ ______________________________

6 Do you believe ...? + What is the best solution?

→ ______________________________

B 다음 우리말과 같은 뜻이 되도록 주어진 단어를 배열하여 문장을 완성하시오.

1 나는 어떤 그래프를 사용할지 결정하지 못했다. (use, which, I'll, graph)
I haven't decided ______________________________. 수능 기출

2 과학은 우리에게 우리가 어디 있는지와 우리가 무엇인지를 알려 준다. (we, what, are, and, are, where, we)
Science tells us ______________________________. 수능 기출

3 언제 태어나셨는지 제게 말씀해 주시겠어요? (you, born, when, were)
Would you tell me ______________________________? 평가원 기출 응용

4 Sarah에게 그 등을 어디서 구했는지 물어보자. (where, got, the lamp, she)
Let's ask Sarah ______________________________. 교육청 기출 응용

5 너는 그가 왜 학교에 결석하고 있는지 아니? (he, absent, why, has been, school, from)
Do you know ______________________________?

POINT 06 ★★★★

부사절을 이끄는 종속접속사 I (시간)

정답 및 해설 p.16

- **시간을 나타내는 종속접속사: when(~할 때), while(~하는 동안에), as(~할 때, ~하면서, ~함에 따라), since(~한 이래로) 등**

When she fell off her horse, she got hurt.
The phone rang **while** I was eating dinner.
As spring comes, flowers begin to bloom.
It has been five years **since** my father retired.

cf. 시간을 나타내는 부사절에서는 현재형을 써서 미래의 일을 나타낸다. LINK p.24 미래를 나타내는 현재형
I'll give you a call **when** I *finish* my class.

cf. 접속사 as와 since는 이유(~하기 때문에)를 나타내기도 한다.
As she was tired, she went to bed right away.
Since you did the dishes, I'll do the laundry.

A 다음 괄호 안에서 알맞은 것을 고르시오.

1 (When / While) I entered the classroom, nobody was there.
2 (When / Since) he started hanging out with Chris, he has changed a lot.
3 Nancy was very nervous (while / since) she was waiting for the test results.

B 다음 문장을 밑줄 친 부분에 유의하여 우리말로 해석하시오.

1 As we got closer, the tower looked bigger.
2 While he was swimming, I prepared pizza for dinner.
3 Diane sings as she puts on her makeup every morning.
4 I have known Nate since he was ten.
5 Carol was waiting for her friend when she noticed a sign above her head. 교육청 기출 응용

C 다음 우리말과 같은 뜻이 되도록 주어진 단어와 적절한 접속사를 이용하여 문장을 완성하시오.

1 내 차례가 가까워짐에 따라, 내 심장은 기대로 점점 빨리 뛰었다. (turn, come)
________ ________ ________ ________ closer, my heart beat faster with anticipation. 교육청 기출

2 당신이 일을 하는 동안 저는 무엇을 해야 하나요? (work)
What am I supposed to do ________ ________ ________ ________? 수능 기출 응용

3 Mary가 나를 떠난 이래로 난 아주 우울하다. (leave)
I've been very depressed ________ ________ ________ ________.

4 그는 어렸을 때 나무에 오르는 것을 좋아했다. (be, young)
________ ________ ________ ________, he liked to climb trees. 평가원 기출 응용

정답 및 해설 p.16

★ POINT 07 ★★★★

부사절을 이끄는 종속접속사 II (시간)

- **시간을 나타내는 종속접속사: until(~할 때까지), by the time(~할 때쯤에는), as soon as(~하자마자), the moment(~하는 순간), every time(~할 때마다) 등**

My family lived in Brazil **until** I was five.
The mall will be closed **by the time** you get there.
As soon as[The moment] he saw me, he stopped crying.
Laura cries **every time** she watches a sad movie.

A 다음 괄호 안에서 알맞은 것을 고르시오.

1 Don't open the box (by the time / until) I tell you to.
2 The train had already left (until / by the time) I got to the station.
3 Please call me (the moment / by the time) you get this message.
4 I will have worked here for fifteen years (as soon as / by the time) I retire.

B 다음 〈보기〉에서 알맞은 말을 골라 빈칸에 쓰시오.

보기	as soon as	by the time	every time	until

1 __________ I see him, he's eating something.
2 I searched the streets __________ my feet ached. 교육청 기출
3 __________ she heard the news, she fainted.
4 It will be after midnight __________ this meeting is finished.

C 다음 우리말과 같은 뜻이 되도록 괄호 안의 말을 이용하여 문장을 완성하시오.

1 Robert는 집에 도착하자마자 동생을 불렀다. (arrive) 교육청 기출 응용
______________________________, he called his brother over.
2 그들의 우정은 Lewis가 1963년에 사망할 때까지 지속되었다. (die)
Their friendship lasted ______________________________. 평가원 기출
3 네가 여기 올 때쯤이면 저녁이 준비되어 있을 것이다. (get)
The dinner will be ready ______________________________.
4 내가 그 파일을 열 때마다 컴퓨터가 멈춰 버린다. (open)
My computer freezes ______________________________.
5 그녀를 본 순간 나는 우리가 함께 할 운명이란 걸 알았다. (see)
______________________________, I knew we were meant to be together.

POINT 08 ★★★★

부사절을 이끄는 종속접속사 III (조건)

정답 및 해설 p.16

- **조건을 나타내는 종속접속사: if(만약 ~한다면), unless(만약 ~하지 않는다면 = if ~ not), as long as(~하는 한, ~하기만 한다면) 등**

If you do this for me, I'll take you out to dinner.

Unless you hurry, you'll miss the train. (= *If* you do*n't* hurry, you'll ~)

cf. 조건을 나타내는 부사절에서는 현재형을 써서 미래의 일을 나타낸다. LINK p.24 미래를 나타내는 현재형

If I *meet* her tomorrow, I will tell her the truth.

A 다음 두 문장이 같은 뜻이 되도록 if 또는 unless를 이용하여 문장을 완성하시오.

1 If it isn't raining hard, I ride my bike to work.
→ ________________, I ride my bike to work.

2 Families don't get strong unless parents invest precious time in them.
→ Families don't get strong ________________. 교육청 기출

3 I can be there unless it's next Monday.
→ I can be there ________________. 수능 기출

4 If he doesn't come, I'll cancel the party.
→ ________________, I'll cancel the party.

B 다음 우리말과 같은 뜻이 되도록 어법상 틀린 부분을 고쳐 쓰시오.

1 그렇게 하라는 지시를 받지 않는다면 컴퓨터를 끄지 마십시오.
→ Don't shut down the computer unless you aren't instructed to do so.

2 네가 이 기회를 잡지 않으면 언젠가 후회하게 될 것이다.
→ If you take this opportunity, you'll regret it someday.

3 9시까지 돌아오는 한 외출해도 된다.
→ You can go out as soon as you're back by nine.

C 다음 우리말과 같은 뜻이 되도록 주어진 단어를 배열하여 문장을 완성하시오.

1 더 많은 정보가 필요하면 얼마든지 제게 문의하세요. (if, further, information, need, you)
________________, feel free to contact me.

2 예약을 하지 않으면 우린 그 뮤지컬을 볼 수 없다. (we, unless, a reservation, make)
________________, we can't see the musical.

3 6시까지 준비하지 않으면 나는 너 없이 갈 거다. (by, you're, unless, ready, six)
________________, I'll leave without you. 평가원 기출 응용

4 끊임없이 시도하는 한 늘 길은 있다. (keep, trying, you, as long as)
There is always a way ________________.

POINT 09 ★★★★

부사절을 이끄는 종속접속사 IV (양보)

정답 및 해설 p.16

- **양보를 나타내는 접속사: although[though](비록 ~이지만), even though(비록 ~이지만), even if(만약 ~할지라도), whether ~ or not(~이든 아니든), while(~인 반면에) 등**

Although[Though] he is good at singing, he is not good at dancing.
She wasn't disappointed **even though** she failed to get a promotion.
Even if I were rich, I wouldn't want to help him.
Whether you like it **or not**, you should go to school.
While Thomas is clever, he is not friendly.

A 다음 우리말과 같은 뜻이 되도록 〈보기〉에서 알맞은 말을 골라 빈칸에 쓰시오.

보기	even if	even though	if	whether	while

1 내일 비가 오면 외출하지 않을 거야.
I won't go out __________ it rains tomorrow.

2 만약 내가 실수를 하더라도 그녀는 나를 이해할 것이다.
__________ I make mistakes, she'll understand me.

3 네가 동의하든 안하든 결과는 같을 것이다.
__________ you agree or not, the result will be the same.

4 눈은 표면을 보는 반면, 귀는 표면 아래를 꿰뚫는다.
__________ the eye sees the surface, the ear penetrates below the surface. 수능 기출 응용

5 비록 공룡은 거대했지만 어떤 공룡도 165피트 이상으로 길지는 않았다.
__________ dinosaurs were large, no dinosaur was over 165 feet long. 평가원 기출 응용

B 다음 우리말과 같은 뜻이 되도록 주어진 단어를 배열하여 문장을 완성하시오.

1 내가 상황을 설명했음에도 불구하고 그녀는 내게 화를 냈다. (my, even though, explained, situation, I)
______________________________, she got angry at me. 평가원 기출 응용

2 그 교사는 참을성이 뛰어났는데도, 그 학생의 행동에 상처받았다. (was, though, the teacher, patient)
______________________________, he was hurt by the student's behavior. 교육청 기출 응용

3 만약 이 프로젝트가 실패한다 해도 그것은 도전할 가치가 있다. (even if, fails, this, project)
______________________________, it's worth the challenge.

4 내가 영어에서 A를 받은 반면 Thomas는 C를 받았다. (an A, I, in English, got, while)
______________________________, Thomas got a C.

5 배가 많이 고팠지만, 나는 한 입도 먹지 않았다. (I, hungry, very, was, although)
______________________________, I didn't eat a bite.

POINT 10 ★★★★

부사절을 이끄는 종속접속사 V (기타)

정답 및 해설 p.16

- **〈so+형용사/부사+that …〉 / 〈such+(a[an])+형용사+명사+(that) ~〉: 너무 ~해서 …하다**

  She is **so** kind **that** everybody likes her. (결과)

  It was **such** a great experience **that** I will never forget it. (결과)

- **〈so (that) ~〉: ~하도록, ~하기 위하여**

  Be quiet **so that** I can study. (목적)

A

다음 문장을 밑줄 친 부분에 유의하여 우리말로 해석하시오.

1 I'll help you with the work so that you can go home early.

2 My planner remembers my schedule so that I don't have to. 교육청 기출 응용

3 The radio is so loud that I can't concentrate on studying.

4 She was so upset that she went home without accepting my apology. 교육청 기출

B

다음 두 문장이 같은 뜻이 되도록 빈칸을 채우시오.

1 Kate is too proud to ask him for help.

→ Kate is ________ proud ________ she won't ask him for help.

2 Let me know your phone number. I might need to contact you.

→ Let me know your phone number ________ ________ I ________ contact you.

3 His personality is so warm that everybody loves him.

→ He has ________ ________ warm personality ________ everybody loves him.

C

다음 우리말과 같은 뜻이 되도록 괄호 안의 말을 이용하여 문장을 완성하시오.

1 그 차는 너무 낡아서 도로에서 고장 날 수도 있다. (old)

________ ________ ________ ________ ________ ________ it could break down on the road.

2 그 아이들이 잠을 잘 수 있도록 불을 꺼라. (can, sleep)

Put out the lights ________ ________ ________ ________ ________ ________.

3 그는 낮에 레코드 회사를 방문할 수 있도록 밤에 일하는 직업을 얻었다. (can, visit)

He got a job working at night ________ ________ ________ ________ ________ record companies during the day. 평가원 기출

4 이것은 너무 좋은 영화여서 다시 보고 싶다. (good, film)

This is ________ ________ ________ ________ ________ I want to see it again.

REVIEW TEST 08 ★

정답 및 해설 p.16

[1-5] 다음 우리말과 일치하도록 빈칸에 알맞은 말을 고르시오.

1

나는 내일 눈이 올지 안 올지 궁금하다.
I wonder _______ it will snow tomorrow or not.

① and ② unless ③ when
④ whether ⑤ either

2

만약 최악의 상황이 벌어지더라도 희망을 버려서는 안 된다.
__________ the worst happens, you shouldn't give up hope.

① While ② As ③ Though
④ Even if ⑤ Unless

3

Nicole도 Susan도 나와 함께 쇼핑하러 가지 않았다.
__________ Nicole nor Susan went shopping with me.

① Both ② Either ③ Neither
④ If ⑤ As well as

4

문제는 우리에게 충분한 시간과 돈이 없다는 것이다.
The trouble is _________ we don't have enough time and money.

① if ② unless ③ whether
④ that ⑤ though

5

남편은 중국 음식을 좋아하는 반면 나는 이탈리아 음식을 좋아한다.
__________ my husband likes Chinese food, I like Italian food.

① That ② While ③ Though
④ Since ⑤ Even if

[6-9] 다음 두 문장의 뜻이 같도록 빈칸에 알맞은 말을 고르시오.

6

This book is not only interesting but also informative.
= This book is informative ___________ interesting.

① when ② as long as ③ if not
④ so that ⑤ as well as

7

Billy can speak French. He can speak German.
= Billy can speak __________ French and German.

① both ② neither ③ either
④ whether ⑤ but

8

The moment he saw the teacher, he ran away.
= __________ he saw the teacher, he ran away.

① While ② Since ③ If
④ That ⑤ As soon as

9

If you are not busy, I'd like to talk to you.
= __________ you are busy, I'd like to talk to you.

① Unless ② Though ③ Even if
④ Whether ⑤ Neither

[10-13] 다음 우리말과 일치하도록 문장을 완성하시오.

10

어두워짐에 따라 날씨가 더 추워졌다.
__________ it became darker, the weather got colder.

11

비록 최선을 다했지만 나는 경주에서 우승하지 못했다.
__________ __________ I did my best, I couldn't win the race.

12

학교에 늦지 않도록 네 형을 깨워라.
Wake up your brother __________ __________ he won't be late for school.

13

그녀가 왜 또 지각했는지 아니?
Do you know __________ __________ __________ __________ again?

[14-16] 다음 두 문장의 빈칸에 공통으로 들어갈 말을 고르시오.

14

• I don't know __________ he is married.
• Call me anytime __________ you want to join our club.

① if ② unless ③ that
④ whether ⑤ though

15

• __________ she was 15, she has lived alone.
• __________ he doesn't work hard, I don't want to help him.

① As ② Because ③ Since
④ While ⑤ As long as

16

• __________ I'm short and not active, my brother is tall and active.
• __________ I was taking a shower, a thief broke into my house.

① As ② While ③ Even though
④ If ⑤ When

[17-20] 다음 문장 중 어법상 틀린 것을 고르시오.

17

① Do you think who is Tom's girlfriend?
② My uncle is not only gentle but also kind.
③ She was so embarrassed that she couldn't say anything.
④ Either she or I am making a presentation tomorrow.
⑤ Even though she isn't interested in me, I like her.

18

① Neither Jack nor Robert agreed with me.
② Not only I but also Patrick like to go skiing.
③ She asked me if my brother is single.
④ Think positively, and everything will be fine.
⑤ Unless you want to get fired, don't make the same mistake again.

19

① I'm happy as long as you're happy.
② My phone rang as I reached the front door.
③ Don't be discouraged even if you fail.
④ She won't go there unless she will have to.
⑤ I asked whether she had ever done that.
교육청 기출

20

① Leave now, or you will be sorry.
② I wondered what did the box contain.
③ You can get a 10% discount if you have a membership. 교육청 기출
④ Even though he lived 2,500 years ago, his ideas are still relevant. 교육청 기출 응용
⑤ The musical has been performed thousands of times since it opened.

[21-22] 다음 글의 빈칸 (A), (B)에 적절한 것끼리 짝지어진 것을 고르시오.

21

A: Now, lift your face up ___(A)___ I can glue your beard on.
B: I hope my beard doesn't fall off ___(B)___ I'm jumping. 수능 기출

	(A)	(B)		(A)	(B)
①	such that	while	②	as	unless
③	because	unless	④	so that	while
⑤	as	if			

22 다음 글의 빈칸 (A), (B)에 적절한 것끼리 짝지어진 것은?

Our lives are ___(A)___ filled with responsibilities that it's almost impossible for us to sit still and just do nothing. However, ___(B)___ you allow yourself to do nothing and to be bored for an hour, the feelings of boredom will be replaced with feelings of peace. 평가원 기출 응용

	(A)	(B)		(A)	(B)
①	unless	if	②	so	though
③	so	if	④	so that	although
⑤	so that	even if			

23 다음 글의 밑줄 친 부분 중 어법상 바르지 못한 것은?

① When we walk into a supermarket, we can find many tropical fruits. ② If we look at the labels, we'll see that the mangoes are from India and the pineapples are from the Philippines. That means ③ if they have been flown in from those countries ④ so that we can eat them fresh! 수능 기출 응용

24 다음 글의 (A), (B)에서 각각 알맞은 것을 고르시오.

(A) (When / Since) you make a complaint, try not to get angry at the person you are speaking to. It would be better (B) (if / unless) you could calmly present sufficient evidence to support your claim. 평가원 기출 응용

EST CHAPTER 2010

09

★★★★

가정법

★ POINT 01 ★★★★

가정법 과거

정답 및 해설 p.17

- **쓰임: 현재 사실과 반대되는 일, 실현 가능성이 거의 없는 일을 상상해서 말할 때 사용하며, '만약 ~하면 …할 텐데'라는 의미이다.**
- **형태: 〈If+주어+과거형 동사 ~, 주어+조동사의 과거형 + 동사원형 …〉**

  If you **had** a million dollars, what **would** you **do**?

  I **would accept** his offer if I **were** you.

  cf. 가정법 과거에서 if절의 동사가 be동사일 경우, 주어의 인칭과 수에 상관없이 were를 쓰는 것이 원칙이다.
- **실현 가능성이 희박한 미래의 일을 가정할 때는 if절에 were to를 써서 나타낸다.**

  If I **were to** be a high school student again, I **would study** harder.

  cf. 어느 정도 실현 가능성이 있는 미래의 일은 if절에 should를 쓰기도 한다.

  If you **should** run into Matt, tell him that he owes me some money.

A 다음 우리말과 같은 뜻이 되도록 어법상 틀린 부분을 고쳐 쓰시오.

1 내가 너라면 내 마음을 바꾸지 않을 것이다.
I won't change my mind if I were you. 평가원 기출

2 그는 만일 다시 태어나더라도 여전히 자기 자신이기를 바랄 것이다.
If he is to be born again, he would still want to be himself.

3 만일 그러한 일이 발생한다면 나는 경찰에 그것을 신고할 것이다.
If such a thing should happen, I reported it to the police.

B 다음 우리말과 같은 뜻이 되도록 괄호 안의 말을 이용하여 문장을 완성하시오.

1 내가 다시 한 번 기회를 가지게 되면 그것을 놓치지 않을 텐데. (have, miss)
If I ________ a second chance, I ________ it.

2 만일 의사가 당신이 살 날이 6개월 남았다고 말한다면, 당신은 무엇을 할 것인가? (say, do)
If your doctor ________ that you had six months to live, what ________ you ________? 교육청 기출 응용

3 내가 다른 도시로 이사 갈 수 있다면 내 인생이 훨씬 나을 텐데. (be, be)
If I ________ able to move to another city, my life ________ much better. 평가원 기출 응용

C 다음 문장을 가정법 과거 형태로 바꾸어 쓰시오.

1 As I don't have two weeks off, I can't go to Australia.
→ If ________________________.

2 As I don't have enough money, I can't buy the latest cell phone.
→ If ________________________.

3 As I can't buy that beautiful mansion, I can't live there with you.
→ If ________________________.

★ POINT 02 ★★★★

가정법 과거완료

정답 및 해설 p.17

- 쓰임: 과거 사실과 반대되는 일을 상상해서 말할 때 사용하며, '만약 ~했다면 …했을 텐데'라는 의미이다.
- 형태: 〈If+주어+had p.p. ~, 주어+조동사의 과거형+have p.p. …〉

  If I **had got** the job, I **would have earned** a lot of money.

A

다음 문장이 가정법 과거완료 형태가 되도록 괄호 안의 동사를 바꾸어 쓰시오.

1 If I __________ (have) a cell phone, I could __________ (call) you.

2 If I __________ (know) your address, I could __________ (send) you a letter.

3 If he __________ (not, be) drunk, he would __________ (not, have) an accident.

4 If she __________ (be) in your place, she would __________ (not, do) it.

B

다음 우리말과 같은 뜻이 되도록 괄호 안의 말을 이용하여 문장을 완성하시오.

1 내가 그걸 말했다면 너는 충격을 받았을 텐데. (tell, shock)

If I ______________ you that, you ________________. 수능 기출 응용

2 어제 날씨가 춥지 않았다면 낚시하러 갔을 텐데. (be, go)

If it ______________ cold yesterday, I ________________ fishing.

3 네가 전화를 했더라면 내가 그 파티에 가지 않았을 텐데. (call, go)

If you ______________ me, I ________________ to the party.

4 내가 2년 전에 그 주식을 샀다면 돈을 많이 벌었을 텐데. (buy, make)

If I ______________ the stock two years ago, I ________________ a lot of money.

5 그녀가 나와 함께 있지 않았다면 홀로 오래 기다려야 했을 것이다. (be, be)

If she ______________ with me, it ________________ a long wait alone.

평가원 기출 응용

C

다음 문장을 가정법 과거완료 형태로 바꾸어 쓰시오.

1 As it rained, we couldn't go cycling.

→ If ____.

2 As you called, I could wake up early.

→ If ____.

3 As I didn't know his situation, I couldn't help him.

→ If ____.

4 As we didn't take the subway, we couldn't arrive earlier.

→ If ____.

★ POINT 03 ★★★★

혼합가정법

정답 및 해설 p.17

- **쓰임: 과거에 실현되지 않은 일이 현재까지 영향을 미치는 경우에 사용하며, '만약 ~했다면 …할 텐데'라는 의미이다.**
- **형태: 〈If+주어+had p.p. ~, 주어+조동사의 과거형+동사원형 …〉**
  If I **had not missed** my flight, I **would be** in Italy.

A

다음 우리말과 같은 뜻이 되도록 어법상 틀린 부분을 고쳐 쓰시오.

1 만약 네가 내 조언을 들었다면 지금 곤경에 처하지 않았을 텐데.
If you had taken my advice, you are not in trouble now.

2 만약 내가 카메라를 잃어버리지 않았다면 네게 그것을 빌려줄 텐데.
If I have not lost my camera, I could lend it to you.

3 만약 그녀가 어젯밤에 충분히 잤다면 지금 졸리지 않을 텐데.
If she had enough sleep last night, she would not be sleepy now.

B

다음 우리말과 같은 뜻이 되도록 괄호 안의 말을 이용하여 문장을 완성하시오.

1 내가 저녁을 먹었다면 지금 배가 고프지 않을 텐데. (eat, be)
If I ______________ dinner, I ______________ now.

2 너를 만나지 않았더라면 난 지금쯤 집에 있을 거야. (meet, be)
If I ______________ you, I ______________ by now.

3 네가 보스턴으로 이사를 안 갔다면 나는 너와 쇼핑 갈 수 있을 텐데. (move, go)
If you ______________ to Boston, I ______________ shopping with you.

4 만약 내가 불어를 배웠다면 그에게 말할 수 있을 텐데. (learn, speak)
If I ______________ French, I ______________ to him.

5 만약 그녀가 그때 의사의 진료를 받지 않았다면 그녀는 살아 있지 못할 거야. (see, be)
If she ______________ the doctor then, she ______________ alive.

C

다음 문장을 가정법 형태로 바꾸어 쓰시오.

1 As Michael lied to me once, I can't trust him.
→ If ____.

2 As it snowed last night, we can have a snowball fight.
→ If ____.

3 As I didn't bring an umbrella, I can't share it with her.
→ If ____.

POINT 04 ★★★★

가정법 현재

정답 및 해설 p.18

- **쓰임: 현재 또는 미래의 불확실한 가정을 나타낸다. if절에서는 잘 쓰이지 않고, 제안 · 요구 · 주장 · 명령을 나타내는 동사(suggest, demand, insist, order 등) 다음에 오는 that절에서 자주 쓰인다.**
- **형태: 〈(should+) 동사원형〉**

He *demanded* that I **(should) go** to the funeral.
She *insisted* that the meeting **(should) be** postponed.

cf. that절의 내용이 실제로 일어난 일을 나타낼 때는 직설법 시제를 쓴다.
He *insisted* that the woman **was** innocent.

A 다음 우리말과 같은 뜻이 되도록 어법상 틀린 부분을 고쳐 쓰시오.

1 나는 어색한 분위기를 깨기 위해 게임을 하자고 제안했다.
I suggested that we played a game to break the ice.

2 그는 나에게 진실을 말할 것을 요구했다.
He demanded that I told him the truth. 수능 기출 응용

3 Cindy는 Tom이 수학 시험에서 부정행위를 했다고 주장한다.
Cindy insists that Tom cheat on the math exam.

4 그 감독은 Linda가 대회에 참가해야 한다고 주장했다.
The director insisted that Linda participated in the contest. 교육청 기출

B 다음 우리말과 같은 뜻이 되도록 〈보기〉의 말을 이용하여 문장을 완성하시오.

보기	cancel	finish	exercise	show	stimulate	wear

1 그 남자는 내 신분증을 보여 달라고 요구했다.
The man requested that I ______________ my ID card.

2 David는 그 일을 혼자 끝냈다고 주장했다.
David kept insisting that he ______________ the work by himself.

3 의사는 그녀에게 정기적으로 운동하라고 제안했다.
The doctor suggested that she ______________ regularly.

4 그들은 부모가 놀이를 통해 아이들을 자극해야 한다고 주장한다.
They insist that parents ______________ their children through play. 교육청 기출 응용

5 여동생은 내게 정장을 입으라고 권유했다.
My sister recommended that I ______________ a suit.

6 나는 그에게 예약을 취소할 것을 요구했다.
I demanded that he ______________ his reservation.

POINT 05 ★★★★

I wish+가정법

정답 및 해설 p.18

- 〈I wish+가정법 과거/과거완료〉는 현재/과거 사실과 반대되거나 실현 가능성이 희박한 일을 소망할 때 사용하며, '~라면 좋을 텐데/~였다면 좋았을 텐데'라는 의미이다.

  I wish my dad **were** here. (→ I'm sorry that my dad isn't here.)
  I wish I **could win** the prize. (→ I'm sorry that I can't win the prize.)
  I wish I **had bought** this house. (→ I'm sorry that I didn't buy this house.)

A

다음 주어진 문장을 참고하여 빈칸에 알맞은 말을 쓰시오.

1 I'm sorry that I can't swim in the sea.
→ I wish ______________________________. 평가원 기출 응용

2 I'm sorry that she didn't lend me her dress.
→ I wish ______________________________.

3 I'm sorry that I can't climb this mountain often.
→ I wish ______________________________. 수능 기출 응용

4 I'm sorry that Tom didn't apologize to you.
→ I wish ______________________________.

5 I'm sorry that I didn't attend the meeting.
→ I wish ______________________________.

B

다음 우리말과 같은 뜻이 되도록 괄호 안의 말을 이용하여 문장을 완성하시오.

1 내가 그 청바지를 샀더라면 좋았을 텐데. (buy)
I wish I __________ __________ the jeans.

2 이 책이 좀 더 읽기 쉬우면 좋을 텐데. (be)
I wish this book __________ easier to read.

3 나는 대자연 속에서 야영하며 야생동물과 함께하는 것을 즐길 수 있기를 바란다. (can, camp)
I wish I __________ __________ in the wild and enjoy the company of wild animals. 수능 기출 응용

4 어제 우리가 야구 경기를 보러 갔더라면 좋았을 텐데. (go)
I wish we __________ __________ to the baseball game yesterday.

5 아버지와 내가 얘기할 시간이 더 많았더라면 좋았을 텐데. (have)
I wish my father and I __________ __________ more time to talk.

6 그녀는 모든 기억이 자기 머릿속에 영원히 남기를 바랐다. (will, remain)
She wished all the memories __________ __________ in her mind forever. 수능 기출

7 내 여동생이 내게 더 상냥하면 좋을 텐데. (be)
I wish my sister __________ kinder to me.

★ POINT **06** ★★★★

as if+가정법

정답 및 해설 p.18

- **〈as if+가정법 과거/과거완료〉는 각각 주절의 시제와 일치하는 때/주절의 시제보다 앞선 때의 사실과 반대되거나 사실일 가능성이 희박한 일을 가정할 때 사용하며, '마치 ~인 것처럼/마치 ~였던 것처럼'이라는 의미이다.**

  She talks **as if** she **knew** Lauren.
  (→ In fact, she doesn't know Lauren.)
  He treated me **as if** I **had done** something wrong.
  (→ In fact, I hadn't done anything wrong.)

A 다음 주어진 문장을 참고하여 빈칸에 알맞은 말을 쓰시오.

1 In fact, she is not my boss.
→ She talks as if ______________________.

2 In fact, they are not children.
→ Pets greet the aged as if ______________________. 수능 기출 응용

3 In fact, my son didn't enter this school just yesterday.
→ I feel as if ______________________. 수능 기출 응용

4 In fact, Mary doesn't understand my situation.
→ Mary talks as if ______________________.

5 In fact, Mike was sick.
→ Mike looks as if ______________________ at all.

B 다음 우리말과 같은 뜻이 되도록 괄호 안의 말을 이용하여 문장을 완성하시오.

1 그녀는 마치 그리스에 살았던 것처럼 말했다. (live)
She talked ______________________ in Greece.

2 Helen은 마치 그것에 대해 무언가 아는 것처럼 보인다. (know)
Helen looks ______________________ about it.

3 Paul은 자기가 내 남자 친구가 아니었던 것처럼 행동했다. (not, be)
Paul acted ______________________ my boyfriend.

4 그는 마치 내 생각을 읽는 것처럼 나를 바라보았다. (read)
He looked at me ______________________.

5 그는 우리가 전혀 만난 적이 없는 것처럼 행동했다. (never, meet)
He acted ______________________.

6 그날은 마치 정체불명의 무언가가 곧 일어나기라도 할 것처럼 유난히 안개가 심했다. (be)
That day was unusually foggy, __________ something mysterious __________ about to happen. 수능 기출 응용

★ POINT 07 ★★★★

기타 가정법

정답 및 해설 p.18

- **⟨Without[But for] ~+가정법 과거/과거완료⟩는 현재 있는 것을 없다고/과거에 있었던 것을 없었다고 가정할 때 사용하며, '~이 없다면/~이 없었더라면'이라는 의미이다.**

  Without[But for] your advice, I **couldn't finish** the project.
  (= **If it were not for** your advice, ~.)
  Without[But for] your warning, we **would have been** unaware of the danger.
  (= **If it had not been for** your warning, ~.)

- **⟨It is time+가정법 과거⟩는 '이제 ~해야 할 시간이다'라는 의미로, 진작 그렇게 했어야 하는데 하고 있지 않다는 뜻을 내포한다.**

  It is time you **got** out of bed. (= It is time you should get out of bed.)

A 다음 두 문장이 같은 뜻이 되도록 문장을 완성하시오.

1 If it had not been for your help, I couldn't have done it.
→ ______________________, I couldn't have done it. 수능 기출 응용

2 If it were not for the Sun, the Earth would be without life.
→ ______________________, the Earth would be without life.

3 It is time you should finish your lunch.
→ It is time ______________________.

4 Wouldn't life be better without grief? 수능 기출 응용
→ Wouldn't life be better if ______________________?

5 But for your support, I couldn't have succeeded as a writer.
→ If ______________________, I couldn't have succeeded as a writer.

B 다음 우리말과 같은 뜻이 되도록 문장을 완성하시오.

1 내 안경이 없다면 나는 아무것도 못 볼 텐데.
________ ________ ________, I couldn't see anything.

2 이제 네가 그 연례 회의를 위해 떠나야 할 시간이다.
________ ________ ________ ________ ________ for the annual meeting.

3 내 여동생이 없었다면 나는 여기에서 외로웠을 텐데.
________ ________ ________ ________, I would have been lonely here.

4 이제 우리가 다시 일을 해야 할 시간이다.
________ ________ ________ ________ ________ back to work.

5 네 도움이 없었더라면 내 사업을 시작할 수 없었을 텐데.
________ ________ ________, I could not have started my own business.

★ POINT 08 ★★★★

if의 생략 / if절 대용어구

정답 및 해설 p.18

- **if절의 동사가 were, had, should인 경우, if를 생략하고 주어와 동사를 도치시켜 쓰기도 한다.**

  Were I more attractive, she would love me.
  (← If I were more attractive, ~.)
  Had I known what the problem was, I could have fixed it.
  (← If I had known what the problem was, ~.)

- **부정사(구), 부사구 또는 주어인 명사(구) 자체에 가정이나 조건의 의미가 함축되어 있는 경우, if절 없이 가정법을 쓰기도 한다.**

  To hear her sing, you **would fall** in love with her. (← If you heard her sing, ~.)
  With your help, I **could have done** it better. (← If I had had your help, ~.)
  A good student **would not behave** like that. (← If he were a good student, he ~.)

A 다음 두 문장이 같은 뜻이 되도록 문장을 완성하시오.

1 Were it not for all of you, I wouldn't be successful.
→ If ________________________, I wouldn't be successful.

2 I would be happy to pass the exam.
→ I would be happy if ________________________.

3 Given the new project, I would do it very well.
→ If ________________________, I would do it very well.

4 Had he helped her, she would have given him some bread.
→ If ________________________, she would have given him some bread.

수능 기출 응용

5 A great soccer player would have scored a goal.
→ If he ________________________, he would have scored a goal.

B 다음 우리말과 같은 뜻이 되도록 어법상 틀린 부분을 고쳐 쓰시오.

1 네가 우는 걸 보면 Tommy가 슬퍼할 텐데.
Tommy is sad to see you cry.

2 네가 나를 잘 알았다면 그런 말을 하지 않았을 텐데.
You had known me well, you would not have said such a thing. 수능 기출 응용

3 그가 다른 나라에서 태어났다면 그렇게 어린 나이에 죽지 않았을 텐데.
Born in another country, he did not die so young.

4 내가 너라면 희망을 포기하지 않을 텐데.
If were I you, I would not give up hope.

5 이 제안을 수락하려면, 내 가족을 나라 저편으로 이사시켜야 할 것입니다.
Accepting this offer would have required moving my family across the country.
교육청 기출 응용

REVIEW TEST 09 ★

정답 및 해설 p.18

[1-4] 다음 우리말과 일치하도록 빈칸에 알맞은 말을 고르시오.

1

내가 너라면 그에게 내 차를 빌려줄 텐데.
If I ________ you, I would lend him my car.

① am ② is
③ were ④ have been
⑤ had been

2

내가 프랑스에서 태어났다면 좋았을 텐데.
I wish I ________ in France.

① was born ② were born
③ am born ④ would be born
⑤ had been born

3

Amy는 마치 나를 지지하는 것처럼 말한다.
Amy talks as if she ________ me.

① support ② has supported
③ supported ④ was supporting
⑤ had supported

4

내가 그것을 더 빨리 끝냈다면 그 회의에 참석할 수 있었을 텐데.
If I had done it earlier, I ________ the meeting.

① attended ② could attend
③ had attended ④ have attended
⑤ could have attended

[5-8] 다음 두 문장의 뜻이 같도록 빈칸에 알맞은 말을 고르시오.

5

I insisted on him seeing a doctor.
= I insisted that he ________ a doctor.

① see ② sees
③ saw ④ had seen
⑤ seeing

6

I'm sorry that I refused his invitation.
= I wish I ________ his invitation.

① do not refuse ② were not to refuse
③ would not refuse ④ should not refuse
⑤ had not refused

7

If I were more diligent, I would earn more money.
= ________ more diligent, I would earn more money.

① Were ② With
③ Were I ④ I were
⑤ Am I

8

As I didn't join the cooking club, I could not see her more often.
= If I ________ the cooking club, I could have seen her more often.

① join ② joined
③ would join ④ had joined
⑤ could have joined

[9-13] 다음 우리말과 일치하도록 문장을 완성하시오.

9

우리 형이 없었더라면 나는 그 끔찍한 사고에서 살아남을 수 없었을 텐데.
________ ________ ________, I could not have survived the terrible accident.

10

그녀는 마치 자기가 공주인 것처럼 행동한다.
She behaves ________ ________ ________ ________ a princess.

11

내가 그 비행기에 있었더라면 지금 살아 있지 않을 텐데.
If I had been on that flight, I ________ ________ ________ alive now.

12

내가 이 새 차를 살 충분한 돈을 가지고 있다면 좋을 텐데.
I ________ ________ ________ enough money to buy this brand new car.

13

내가 너라면 그녀를 그냥 무시할 텐데.
If I ________ you, I would just ignore her.

[14-15] 다음 문장의 빈칸에 알맞은 말을 고르시오.

14

________ this hat, my face would get very tanned.

① With ② If
③ Were to ④ If it were not for
⑤ If it had not been for

15

The customer demanded that he ________ immediately.

① apologize ② apologizes
③ apologized ④ has apologized
⑤ will apologize

[16-19] 다음 문장 중 어법상 틀린 것을 고르시오.

16

① It is time you went to the concert.
② I were taller, I could be a basketball player.
③ He looked as if he were nervous.
④ A wiser man would do it differently.
⑤ But for her support, I couldn't have made it.

17

① I wish I could earn more money.
② If he should succeed, I would leave this country.
③ If it were not snowing, I will go climbing.
④ If you were to die tomorrow, what would you do?
⑤ My mother insisted that I learn how to swim.

18

① I wish I had musical talent like Mozart.
② If I had told her the truth, she would have panicked.
③ Many people would choose a small house over a big mansion.
④ How would you feel if I am to offer you the sales director position? 수능 기출
⑤ If the racers didn't wear gloves, their hands would get terribly hurt. 교육청 기출 응용

19

① It's time we did something.
② A child would love the product.
③ I had been there, I would have helped.
④ If we lived on a planet where nothing ever changed, there would be little to do. 교육청 기출
⑤ She screamed as if she had lost her mind.

20 다음 문장 중 어법상 옳은 것은?

① I wish you are here with me now.
② What would happen if everything is free?
③ You are already here if you had taken a taxi.
④ He insisted that he not intend to hurt the victim.
⑤ Her parents suggested that she major in linguistics.

[21-22] 다음 글의 빈칸 (A), (B)에 적절한 것끼리 짝지어진 것을 고르시오.

21

I wish I ____(A)____ able to read the story of my life before it actually happens. If I knew how to use the opportunities life gives me, that ____(B)____ really something. 평가원 기출 응용

	(A)	(B)
①	were	is
②	am	would be
③	was	is
④	were	would be
⑤	am	would have been

22 다음 글의 빈칸 (A), (B)에 적절한 것끼리 짝지어진 것은?

____(A)____ the space to grow some food, I would be happy. I've tried to find a local community garden, but the closest one is too far away. I wish the city ____(B)____ more community gardens.

	(A)	(B)
①	I had	built
②	I had	would build
③	Had I	would build
④	Had I	would have built
⑤	I had had	would have built

23 다음 글의 (A), (B), (C)에서 각각 알맞은 것을 고르시오.

My son is in his late thirties, but he behaves as if he (A) (is / were) a teenage boy. I suggested that he (B) (married / should marry) before he is 40, but he didn't even pretend to listen to what I said. I wish my son (C) (acted / had acted) his age and married a nice girl. 평가원 기출 응용

EST

CHAPTER

2010

10

★★★★

관계사

1 주격 관계대명사
2 목적격 관계대명사
3 소유격 관계대명사
4 관계대명사 what
5 관계대명사와 전치사
6 관계부사
7 관계사의 계속적 용법
8 복합관계사

REVIEW TEST 10

정답 및 해설 p.19

★ POINT 01 ★★★★

주격 관계대명사

- **선행사를 수식하는 관계사절의 주어 역할을 하는 관계대명사**

I have a brother **who** likes swimming.
(← I have a brother. + He likes swimming.)
My father bought me a shirt (**which** is) made of cotton.
(← My father bought me a shirt. + It is made of cotton.)

cf. 〈주격 관계대명사+be동사+분사[형용사]〉의 형태인 경우 〈주격 관계대명사+be동사〉는 생략할 수 있다.

선행사	주격 관계대명사
사람	who
사물, 동물	which
사람, 사물, 동물, 사람+사물[동물]	that
관계대명사에 선행사가 포함된 경우	what

cf. 선행사에 형용사의 최상급, 서수, the only, the very, no, some, all, every 등이 포함된 경우 주로 that을 쓴다.
Here are *some* tips **that** may help.

A **다음 문장에서 밑줄 친 부분을 어법에 맞게 고쳐 쓰시오.**

1 There was no one what could help me.
2 That makes me happy is my family.
3 Kate is the only person which heard the bad news.
4 Eat foods who are good for your eyes. 교육청 기출
5 Which is expensive is not necessarily of higher quality.
6 My brother gave me a hat who looks like a fish.

B **다음 두 문장을 관계대명사를 이용하여 한 문장으로 만드시오.**

1 He was wearing a shirt. It was brightly colored.
→ ______________________________
2 Eric had an employee. She was habitually late.
→ ______________________________ 평가원 기출 응용
3 I found a website. It sells picnic tables.
→ ______________________________ 수능 기출 응용
4 The delivery system is convenient for people. They don't have time to go to the library.
→ ______________________________ 교육청 기출 응용
5 It was a movie about a boy and his dog. They lived in the countryside.
→ ______________________________.

POINT 02 ★★★★

목적격 관계대명사

정답 및 해설 p.19

- 선행사를 수식하는 관계사절의 목적어 역할을 하는 관계대명사

He is the man (**whom**) I met at the party yesterday.
(← He is the man. + I met him at the party yesterday.)
I lent him the book (**which**) I bought yesterday.
(← I lent him the book. + I bought it yesterday.)

cf. 목적격 관계대명사는 자주 생략된다.

선행사	목적격 관계대명사
사람	who(m)
사물, 동물	which
사람, 사물, 동물, 사람+사물[동물]	that
관계대명사에 선행사가 포함된 경우	what

cf. 선행사에 형용사의 최상급, 서수, the only, the very, no, some, all, every 등이 포함된 경우 주로 that을 쓴다.
There is *nothing* **that** we can do to change it.

A 다음 괄호 안에서 알맞은 것을 고르시오.

1 I had to give him (which / what) I had.
2 This is the hat (that / what) I knit last year.
3 Kelly is the girl (whom / which) I want to go out with.
4 Ally bought a novel (whom / which) she was looking forward to reading. 교육청 기출 응용

B 다음 문장에서 밑줄 친 부분을 어법에 맞게 고쳐 쓰시오.

1 Jenny didn't like the movie what we saw last week.
2 He is the doctor which I gave a small gift to.
3 I couldn't believe which I had just heard! 수능 기출
4 Early Native Americans had to make everything what they needed. 교육청 기출

C 다음 두 문장을 관계대명사를 이용하여 한 문장으로 만드시오.

1 Swimming is a skill. Anyone can learn it.
→ ______________________ 평가원 기출 응용

2 I like all the books. Sophie wrote them.
→ ______________________

3 This is the woman. I saw her yesterday.
→ ______________________

4 He is the pianist. I support him financially.
→ ______________________

POINT 03 ★★★★

소유격 관계대명사

정답 및 해설 p.19

- **선행사를 수식하는 관계사절의 명사를 꾸며주는 소유격 역할을 하는 관계대명사**

I know a girl **whose** brother is a famous actor.
(← I know a girl. + Her brother is a famous actor.)
This is a website **whose** mission is to provide you with the latest news.
[**of which** the mission = the mission **of which**]
(← This is a website. + Its mission is to provide you with the latest news.)

선행사	소유격 관계대명사
사람	whose
사물, 동물	whose[of which]

A 다음 두 문장을 관계대명사 whose를 이용하여 한 문장으로 만드시오.

1 I have a purse. Its strap is long.
→ ______________________

2 Bordeaux is a region. Its wines are famous.
→ ______________________

3 The teacher noticed a girl. Her name was Serena.
→ ______________________ 평가원 기출 응용

4 I bought a shirt. Its buttons are colorful.
→ ______________________

5 Most publishers will not want to waste time with writers. The writers' material contains too many mistakes.
→ ______________________ 교육청 기출 응용

B 다음 우리말과 같은 뜻이 되도록 주어진 단어를 배열하여 문장을 완성하시오.

1 안경이 빨간색인 저 소녀는 누구니? (are, whose, red, that girl, glasses)
Who is ______________________?

2 그는 작업이 경영사 분야 연구를 중심으로 해온 학자이다. (has centered, a scholar, whose, work)
He is ______________________ on the study of business history. 교육청 기출

3 나는 손잡이가 헐거운 그 큰 냄비를 들어 올렸다. (whose, loose, the big pot, was, handle)
I lifted ______________________.

4 그는 엔진이 고장 난 차를 나에게 보여 주었다. (engine, out of order, whose, the car, was)
He showed me ______________________.

★ POINT 04 ★★★★

관계대명사 what

정답 및 해설 p.20

- **관계대명사 what은 선행사를 포함하며 명사절을 이끈다. the thing(s) that[which]으로 바꾸어 쓸 수 있으며 '~하는 것'이라고 해석한다. what이 이끄는 절은 원칙적으로 단수 취급한다.**

This is **what** I bought for my son's birthday.
(= This is the thing that[which] I bought for my son's birthday.)

A

다음 문장을 밑줄 친 부분에 유의하여 우리말로 해석하시오.

1 What is necessary is a change of perspective.
2 What I like about him is that he is humorous.
3 That's exactly what she told me.
4 I don't believe what they say about Steve.

B

다음 두 문장을 관계대명사 what을 이용하여 한 문장으로 만드시오.

1 That's the thing. I'm thinking of it. 수능 기출 응용
→ ______________________________

2 Thanks a lot for the thing. You've done it for me.
→ ______________________________

3 An artist makes art from the things. He has them around him.
→ ______________________________ 교육청 기출

C

다음 우리말과 같은 뜻이 되도록 주어진 단어를 배열하여 문장을 완성하시오.

1 오늘 할 수 있는 것을 내일로 미루지 마라. (you, what, can, today, do)
Never put off till tomorrow ______________________.

2 내가 정말 원했던 건 사업에서 성공하는 것이었다. (really, I, what, wanted)
______________________ was to succeed in business.

3 과일과 야채를 먹음으로써 신체가 필요로 하는 것을 얻을 수 있습니다. (your, needs, what, body)
You can get ______________________ by eating fruit and vegetables. 교육청 기출 응용

4 너는 내가 전에 말했던 것을 기억하니? (told, what, before, I, you)
Do you remember ______________________?

5 내 딸은 인형처럼 보이는 것을 가리켰다. (a doll, like, what, looked)
My daughter pointed to ______________________.

6 스노보드 타기는 그가 가장 잘하는 것이다. (what, best, does, he)
Snowboarding is ______________________.

정답 및 해설 p.20

POINT 05 ★★★★

관계대명사와 전치사

- **관계대명사가 전치사의 목적어인 경우, 전치사는 관계대명사 바로 앞이나 관계사절의 끝에 올 수 있다.**

  She is the friend **with whom** I live.

  She is the friend (**who(m)[that]**) I live **with**.

  cf. 〈전치사+관계대명사〉의 어순일 때는 who나 that을 쓸 수 없고 관계대명사를 생략할 수도 없다.

  ~~She is the friend **with who[that]** I live.~~

  ~~She is the friend with ✔ I live.~~

A

다음 두 문장이 같은 뜻이 되도록 전치사를 써서 문장을 완성하시오.

1 This is the restaurant. I first met her in the restaurant.

→ This is the restaurant __________ __________ I first met her.

2 Home provides a canvas. We can illustrate who we are on the canvas. 교육청 기출

→ A home provides a canvas __________ __________ we can illustrate who we are.

3 Jay is my only friend. I can open my heart to him.

→ Jay is my only friend __________ I can open my heart __________.

4 The teacher wrote a reply. He answered the questions in the reply. 교육청 기출 응용

→ The teacher wrote a reply __________ __________ he answered the questions.

5 Tim will apply to a college. He can get a scholarship from the college.

→ Tim will apply to a college __________ __________ he can get a scholarship.

6 When did you join the company? You are working for it.

→ When did you join the company __________ you are working __________?

B

다음 문장에서 밑줄 친 부분이 어법상 옳으면 O표 하고, 틀리면 바르게 고쳐 쓰시오.

1 The hotel in which I stayed last night was terrible. 교육청 기출

2 The man with who I was working quit his job.

3 Cocoa beans are seeds from that chocolate is made.

C

다음 우리말과 같은 뜻이 되도록 문장을 완성하시오.

1 그는 경찰이 찾던 그 도둑이다.

He is the thief __________ the police have been looking __________.

2 그녀는 네 명이 앉을 수 있는 벤치를 만들었다.

She made a bench __________ __________ four people can sit.

3 네가 같이 쇼핑을 갔던 소년은 누구니?

Who is the boy __________ __________ you went shopping?

POINT 06 ★★★★

관계부사

정답 및 해설 p.20

- **관계부사 when, where, why, how는 각각 시간, 장소(또는 상황), 이유, 방법의 선행사를 수식하는 관계사절을 이끌며, 관계사절 안에서 부사 역할을 한다.**

  I met James the day **when** I arrived there.
  (← I met James that day. + I arrived there on that day.)
  (= I met James the day **on which** I arrived there.)
  cf. 관계부사는 〈전치사+관계대명사〉로 바꿔 쓸 수 있다.

★ EXAM TIP **how의 경우는 선행사 the way나 관계부사 how 중 하나만 써야 한다.**

This is ~~the way~~ **how** I solved the puzzle.

A

다음 괄호 안에서 알맞은 것을 고르시오.

1 Sunday is a day (why / when) I really try to relax.
2 This is the place (when / where) we write articles. 수능 기출
3 I want to live in a house (that / where) looks over the sea.
4 The smell of candles can affect (how / the way how) you feel. 교육청 기출 응용

B

다음 두 문장이 같은 뜻이 되도록 빈칸을 채우시오.

1 I'll visit the city in which my parents live.
→ I'll visit the city ________ my parents live.
2 Tell me the reason that you didn't eat anything all day.
→ Tell me the reason ________ you didn't eat anything all day.
3 He won't forget the day on which he got his first car.
→ He won't forget the day ________ he got his first car.

C

다음 두 문장을 관계부사를 이용하여 한 문장으로 만드시오.

1 Do you remember the day? We first met that day.
→ ______________________________
2 That's the reason. June broke up with Ted for that reason.
→ ______________________________
3 I like the way. The author portrays the characters in that way.
→ ______________________________
4 Imagine a man is in the situation. He forgot his wedding anniversary in the situation.
→ ______________________________ 교육청 기출 응용

★ POINT **07** ★★★★

관계사의 계속적 용법

정답 및 해설 p.20

- **관계사 앞에 쉼표(,)가 있는 경우를 계속적 용법이라 하며, 이때 관계사절은 선행사에 대한 부가적인 정보를 제공하는 역할을 한다. 계속적 용법의 관계대명사는 〈접속사+대명사〉, 관계부사는 〈접속사+부사〉의 의미를 나타낸다. which는 앞 절 전체를 대신할 수도 있다.**

I like Amy, **who** has a beautiful smile.
(= I like Amy, for she has a beautiful smile.)
We went to Miami beach, **where** we had a good time.
(= We went to Miami beach, and we had a good time there.)

cf. 관계대명사 that, what과 관계부사 why, how는 계속적 용법으로 사용할 수 없다.
Jenny wrote an article, **which[~~that~~]** was difficult for me to understand.

A

다음 괄호 안에서 알맞은 것을 고르시오.

1 He pretended not to hear me, (who / which) was really annoying.

2 One of the boys in the club is Patrick, (who / that) is Sam's cousin.

3 Mr. Johnson, (who / which) likes to fish, goes fishing every weekend.

4 He survived and returned to his hometown, (which / where) he was awarded a medal. 교육청 기출 응용

B

다음 문장에서 밑줄 친 부분을 어법에 맞게 고쳐 쓰시오.

1 Tell me the reason, why you missed the class.

2 I traveled to Australia, when I met an old friend of mine.

3 Every day, you rely on many people, most of which you do not know. 교육청 기출

4 This is the most important crop in the U.S., that produces about half the world's total. 평가원 기출

C

다음 두 문장이 같은 뜻이 되도록 관계사를 이용하여 문장을 완성하시오.

1 I am close with Alice, and she told me her secret.
→ I am close with Alice, ______________________.

2 I met James last night, and he treated me to dinner then.
→ I met James last night, ______________________.

3 I went to Jay's birthday party, and I met Tina there.
→ I went to Jay's birthday party, ______________________.

4 She had a high fever, and it caused her to become deaf.
→ She had a high fever, ______________________. 평가원 기출

5 My train arrived at my destination ten minutes early, and it was perfect.
→ My train arrived at my destination ten minutes early, ______________________
______________. 수능 기출 응용

POINT 08 ★★★★

복합관계사

정답 및 해설 p.20

- 〈관계사+-ever〉: 선행사를 포함한 관계사로, 문맥에 따라 명사절 또는 부사절을 이끈다.

복합관계대명사	whoever	whichever	whatever
명사절 (주어/목적어)	~하는 누구나 (= anyone who)	~하는 어느 것이나 (= anything that)	~하는 무엇이나 (= anything that)
양보의 부사절	누가 ~할지라도 (= no matter who)	어느 것이[을] ~할지라도 (= no matter which)	무엇이[을] ~할지라도 (= no matter what)
복합관계부사	whenever	wherever	however
시간/장소의 부사절	~할 때마다 (= at any time when)	~하는 곳은 어디에나 (= at[in/to] any place where)	-
양보의 부사절	언제 ~할지라도 (= no matter when)	어디에 ~할지라도 (= no matter where)	아무리 ~할지라도 (= no matter how)

cf. 사람인 선행사를 포함하는 복합관계대명사가 관계사절에서 목적어 역할을 할 때는 whomever를 쓰기도 한다.

Whatever you do, finish your homework by 9 o'clock. (= No matter what ~.)

However busy you are, you should attend the conference. (= No matter how ~.)

A 다음 두 문장이 같은 뜻이 되도록 복합관계사를 이용하여 문장을 완성하시오.

1 No matter how hard it is, I can solve it.
→ ____________________, I can solve it.

2 No matter where he goes, I'll follow him.
→ ____________________, I'll follow him.

3 I go to the swimming pool at any time that I'm free.
→ I go to the swimming pool ____________________.

4 You can work on anything that you want.
→ You can work on ____________________. 교육청 기출

5 Anyone who attacks the police will be severely punished.
→ ____________________ will be severely punished.

B 다음 우리말과 같은 뜻이 되도록 복합관계사를 이용하여 문장을 완성하시오.

1 어느 것을 고르든 당신은 만족할 것이다.
_______________ you choose, you will be satisfied.

2 나는 어디를 가든지 연필을 가지고 다니기 시작했다.
I started carrying a pencil with me __________ I went. 수능 기출 응용

3 그 군인이 아무리 용감하다고 해도 그 역시 인간일 뿐이다.
__________ brave the soldier, he is still just a person.

4 그가 무엇을 하든 나는 늘 그를 믿을 것이다.
I'll always believe in him __________ he does.

REVIEW TEST 10 ★

정답 및 해설 p.20

[1-5] 다음 우리말과 일치하도록 빈칸에 알맞은 말을 고르시오.

1

나는 그가 나를 위해 한 일에 감동했다.
I was impressed with ________ he did for me.

① who ② which ③ that
④ how ⑤ what

2

나는 사무실이 시내에 있는 친구가 있다.
I have a friend ________ office is downtown.

① who ② that ③ whose
④ which ⑤ what

3

그것은 내가 생일 선물로 받은 책이다.
It is the book ________ I received for my birthday.

① who ② whom ③ that
④ what ⑤ when

4

이곳이 내가 강아지를 산 애완동물 가게이다.
This is the pet shop ________ I bought my puppy.

① which ② that ③ how
④ when ⑤ where

5

나는 네가 추천하는 사람은 누구나 고용할 것이다.
I will hire ________ you recommend.

① whom ② whose ③ that
④ whomever ⑤ whichever

[6-8] 다음 두 문장의 뜻이 같도록 빈칸에 알맞은 말을 고르시오.

6

The country in which I live is very cold.
= The country ________ I live is very cold.

① which ② that ③ what
④ wherever ⑤ where

7

Eat anything that you want in this restaurant.
= Eat ________ you want in this restaurant.

① that ② whatever ③ when
④ which ⑤ however

8

I have two cousins, and they are in the army.
= I have two cousins, ________ are in the army.

① which ② who ③ what
④ whom ⑤ that

[9-13] 다음 우리말과 일치하도록 문장을 완성하시오.

9

그녀가 내가 보고 싶어했던 그 가수이다.
She is the singer ________ I wanted to see.

10

실종되었던 남자와 그의 차가 강 근처에서 발견되었다.
A man and his car ________ had been missing were found near the river.

11

그녀는 내가 함께 일했던 여자이다.
She is the woman ________ I worked ________.

12

나는 꿈이 호주에서 사는 것인 친구가 있다.
I have a friend ________ dream is to live in Australia.

13

누구든 제일 먼저 오는 사람이 상품을 받을 것이다.
________ comes first will get the prize.

[14-15] 다음 문장의 빈칸에 알맞은 말을 고르시오.

14

This T-shirt, ________ is dirty, is my brother's.

① which ② that ③ of which
④ what ⑤ who

15

I visited Atlanta, ________ I stayed at a five-star hotel.

① which ② that
③ when ④ where
⑤ how

[16-19] 다음 중 밑줄 친 부분이 어법상 틀린 것을 고르시오.

16

① Whichever you choose, I don't care.
② This is Gerry, with whom I went to college.
③ What I'd like to know is not her name.
④ Look at the man who is sitting on the floor!
⑤ The way how he looked at me made me feel comfortable.

17

① That's the reason why he was so upset.
② Which you did for her was very brave.
③ She was the first Asian that climbed the mountain.
④ He lent me his laptop whenever I needed it.
⑤ The festival was held on June 6, when my sister was born.

18

① Try to forget whatever is bothering you.
② However hard I tried, I couldn't get it to work.
③ I can rely on her whenever I need something.
④ Store coffee in a freezer, where has a drier environment. 수능 기출 응용
⑤ The bridge, which is 137 meters long, was built in 1889. 평가원 기출 응용

19

① Find areas in that you excel.
② What really counts is your feelings.
③ Heaven helps those who help themselves.
④ Please refer to the manual whenever you are confused.
⑤ Writing is a tool that will help you adjust to university life. 수능 기출 응용

[20-21] 다음 문장 중 어법상 옳은 것을 고르시오.

20

① English is the only subject whom I like.
② Where's the present what we bought yesterday? 교육청 기출
③ It was an important moment, which impact will always be with her. 교육청 기출 응용
④ You can use which is around you to make tools.
⑤ Ants in groups can do things no single ant can do. 교육청 기출 응용

21

① Challenges we face today is complex.
② Who are the people with who you spend most of your time?
③ They watched a film, after that they were asked to describe it. 교육청 기출 응용
④ He made what many considered an unbelievable decision. 교육청 기출
⑤ They traveled South Africa, which they provided free medical treatment for children. 수능 기출 응용

22 다음 글의 빈칸 (A), (B)에 적절한 것끼리 짝지어진 것은?

Once I passed through the main gate, I could really experience the fair. There were many tents on the right side, ___(A)___ belonged to friends and colleagues. There was also a family space ___(B)___ relations and guests were supplied with delicious food and drinks. 평가원 기출 응용

	(A)	(B)
①	where	where
②	where	which
③	which	where
④	which	whose
⑤	what	why

23 다음 글의 밑줄 친 부분 중 어법상 바르지 못한 것은?

① What often happens is that shoppers end up buying things ② that are not really needed. To solve this problem, just go around with a pen and paper and look at ③ what you are buying. See whether there are other options ④ of which are less expensive or specific to your needs. 평가원 기출 응용

24 다음 글의 (A), (B), (C)에서 어법에 맞는 것을 고르시오.

Much of (A) (what / that) you read suggests more than it says. Writers do not always clearly say (B) (what / how) they want you to know. Frequently, they omit information (C) (what / that) lies beneath the statements they make. 평가원 기출

EST 2010

CHAPTER

11

명사·관사·대명사

POINT 01 ★★★★

셀 수 있는 명사 vs. 셀 수 없는 명사

정답 및 해설 p.21

- **셀 수 있는 명사는 단수형과 복수형(-s[-es])이 있으며, 앞에 관사 a[an], the, 수사 등이 붙는다.**

보통명사	girl, friend, table, potato, dog 등
집합명사	family, committee, staff, crew, class 등

There is **a girl** on the playground. **The two dogs** barked at each other.

- **셀 수 없는 명사는 단수형만 있으며, 앞에 부정관사 a[an]나 수사가 직접 붙지 않는다.**

추상명사	information, honesty, love, courage 등
고유명사	Amy, December, California, Sunday 등
물질명사	rice, money, bread, milk, water, air 등

It takes **courage** to admit you are wrong. He drinks *five glasses of* **water** a day.

cf. 셀 수 없는 명사는 용기나 단위 등으로 양을 나타낸다.

A 다음 괄호 안에서 알맞은 것을 고르시오.

1 We need ten extra (chair / chairs) for the conference.
2 She brings mineral (water / waters) wherever she goes.
3 Do you want to see (play / a play) at the Greenwood Theater? 수능 기출 응용
4 He's truly touched by Julie's (love / loves) for the puppy. 수능 기출
5 I'd like to gather (information / informations) about environmental problems.

B 다음 밑줄 친 부분을 어법에 맞게 고쳐 쓰시오.

1 I'll help him prove his honesties.
2 He baked a loaf of breads in the oven for an hour.
3 We have a few apple tree, so the kids can pick their own apples. 교육청 기출 응용
4 He's going to stay there for two year. 교육청 기출

C 다음 우리말과 같은 뜻이 되도록 〈보기〉의 말을 이용하여 문장을 완성하시오.

보기 apple coin dog luck milk money

1 All the ________ are round in shape.
2 I have two ________, which are brown and white.
3 I don't have any ________ that I can lend you.
4 He took a carton of ________ from the refrigerator.
5 I'm going to the supermarket today to buy some ________. 교육청 기출 응용
6 Jake seems to have had a lot of bad ________ over the last two years.

POINT 02 ★★★★

주의해야 하는 명사

정답 및 해설 p.21

- 집합명사
  - 단수 · 복수 취급이 모두 가능한 집합명사: family, class, committee, staff, audience 등
    His **family** is very rich. (하나의 집합체로 보는 경우)
    My **family** were all safe. (구성원 낱낱으로 보는 경우)
  - 형태는 단수형이지만 항상 복수 취급하는 집합명사: police, people, cattle 등
    The **police** are searching his house.
  - 셀 수 없는 집합명사: furniture, baggage, clothing, machinery, equipment 등
    We'll have to buy **furniture** for the new house.
- 항상 복수형으로 쓰이는 명사: pants, glasses(안경), scissors, jeans 등 쌍을 나타내는 명사
  My **pants** are full of holes.
- 항상 단수 취급하는 명사: 학문·학과명, 질병 이름 등 LINK p.180 수에 유의해야 할 명사 · 대명사
  Economics is interesting to learn.

A 다음 괄호 안에서 알맞은 것을 고르시오.

1 Mathematics (is / are) important in our everyday life.
2 The police (has / have) arrived on the scene. 평가원 기출 응용
3 Some people (is / are) not used to living with discomfort. 수능 기출 응용
4 My father wears (glass / glasses) whenever he reads the newspaper.

B 다음 밑줄 친 부분을 어법에 맞게 고쳐 쓰시오.

1 The cattle is resting in the field.
2 You should wear sturdy shoes and long pant to this event. 교육청 기출 응용
3 Measles are a common disease among children.
4 For the safety of passengers, all baggages are checked.

C 다음 우리말과 같은 뜻이 되도록 문장을 완성하시오.

1 이 위원회는 20명의 회원으로 구성되어 있다.
This __________ __________ composed of 20 members.
2 물리학은 내 전공이지만 나는 그것을 좋아하지 않는다.
__________ __________ my major, but I don't like it.
3 경찰이 실종된 아이를 찾고 있다.
The __________ __________ looking for the missing child.
4 이 가위는 천을 자르는 데 완벽하다.
These __________ __________ perfect for cutting fabric.

★ POINT 03 ★★★★

관사

정답 및 해설 p.21

- **부정관사(a[an])의 쓰임: 막연한 하나, 하나의(= one), 어떤(= a certain), ~마다(= per)**

  I bought **a** notebook at the store. (여러 개 중 아무거나 하나)
  She took **a** day off yesterday. (= one) You're right in **a** sense. (= a certain)
  I take a yoga class twice **a** week. (= per)

- **정관사(the)의 쓰임**

  - **앞에 언급되었거나 서로 알고 있는 것 앞:** I bought a car yesterday, and **the** car is red.
  - **세상에 하나뿐인 것 앞:** There are a lot of stars in **the** sky.
  - **최상급 형용사, 서수, only, same, very가 붙은 말 앞:** She is **the** tallest girl in my class.
  - **구나 절에 의해 수식 받는 명사 앞:** **The** boy whom I like is Japanese.
  - **악기 앞:** I like to play **the** piano.

  cf. 식사나 운동 경기 이름, 교통 · 통신 수단 등을 나타내는 명사 앞이나 시설물, 사물 등이 본래의 목적으로 쓰일 때는 관사를 쓰지 않는다.
  Can you send me your photo by ✔ *e-mail*?
  She goes to ✔ *school* at 8 in the morning.

A 다음 빈칸에 a[an] 또는 the를 쓰고, 관사가 필요 없으면 X표 하시오.

1 __________ sun is slowly getting brighter. 평가원 기출
2 Nina plays __________ flute very well.
3 I bought this computer just __________ year ago. 수능 기출 응용
4 __________ latest models include new systems and features.
5 The subway train didn't move for about __________ hour. 교육청 기출 응용
6 I go to work by __________ bus every morning.
7 I was going to make curry chicken for __________ dinner. 수능 기출
8 Eating is one of __________ greatest ways for people to bond with others. 평가원 기출 응용

B 다음 우리말과 같은 뜻이 되도록 문장을 완성하시오.

1 내 아들은 일찍 잠자리에 들지 않는다.
My son doesn't __________ __________ __________ early.

2 나는 기타 연주하는 법을 배우고 싶다.
I want to learn how to __________ __________ __________.

3 네가 숙제를 마친 다음에 점심을 먹자.
Let's __________ __________ after you finish your homework.

4 그들은 한 달에 한 번 도시에서 바닷가로 여행을 간다.
They make a trip from the city to the beach __________ __________ __________. 평가원 기출 응용

5 어떤 의미에서 Andy는 그것에 대해서 옳았다.
In __________ __________, Andy was right about that.

POINT 04 ★★★★

소유대명사 · 재귀대명사

정답 및 해설 p.21

- **소유대명사: '~의 것'이라는 뜻을 나타내며, 〈소유격+명사〉로 바꾸어 쓸 수 있다.**
  My school uniform is brown, and **his** is navy. (= his school uniform)
  cf. 소유격은 관사, 지시대명사, 부정대명사 등과 나란히 함께 쓰일 수 없기 때문에, 〈한정어(a[an], the, this[that], some 등)+명사+of+소유대명사〉의 순서로 쓰며 이것을 이중소유격이라 한다.
  I'll go there with **a friend of mine**.

- **재귀대명사: 인칭대명사의 소유격 또는 목적격에 -self(단수)나 -selves(복수)를 붙인 것으로, '~ 자신'이라는 뜻을 나타낸다.**
  - **재귀 용법: 주어와 목적어가 동일하여 주어 자신이 동작의 대상이 되는 경우, 동사나 전치사의 목적어로 재귀대명사를 쓴다.**
    He proved **himself** to be innocent.
  - **강조 용법: '혼자서, 직접'의 뜻으로 강조되는 말 뒤나 문장 맨 뒤에 재귀대명사를 써서 의미를 강조한다.**
    I did all the work **myself**.

A 다음 괄호 안에서 알맞은 것을 고르시오.

1 We just got here (us / ourselves).
2 Believe in (you / yourself). 교육청 기출
3 I'd like to buy a necklace like (hers / herself). 교육청 기출
4 I had dinner with (his some friends / some friends of his).

B 다음 우리말과 같은 뜻이 되도록 문장을 완성하시오.

1 그의 사무실은 우리 사무실 바로 옆에 있다.
His office is right next to __________.

2 나는 내 줄넘기를 온라인으로 주문할 거야. 네 것도 주문해 주길 바라니?
I'm going to order my jump rope online. Do you want me to order __________ as well? 교육청 기출 응용

3 그녀는 자신을 따뜻하고 배부르게 하기 위해 돈을 구걸했다.
She begged for money to keep __________ warm and fed. 평가원 기출 응용

4 내 친구 Don은 자기 자신을 음악가라고 여겼다.
My friend Don considered __________ a musician. 평가원 기출

C 다음 우리말과 같은 뜻이 되도록 주어진 단어를 배열하여 문장을 완성하시오.

1 나는 그것을 직접 편집할 기술이 없다. (edit, myself, it)
I don't have the skill to ______________________________. 교육청 기출 응용

2 나는 공원에서 내 학생 중 한 명을 만났다. (a, mine, student, of)
I met ______________________________ at the park.

3 나는 어제 야채를 썰다가 베었다. (chopping, cut, myself)
I ______________________________ vegetables yesterday.

POINT 05 ★★★★

대명사 it의 쓰임

정답 및 해설 p.21

- **비인칭 주어: it은 시간, 요일, 거리, 날씨, 계절 등을 나타내는 문장의 주어로 사용되는데, 이때의 it은 따로 해석하지 않는다.**

  It has been five years since I last saw him.
  How far is **it** from New York to Los Angeles?
  It is going to rain tomorrow.

- **가주어 · 가목적어: it은 뒤에 오는 명사구나 명사절을 대신하여 형식상의 주어 또는 목적어로 사용된다.**

  It is difficult to learn Chinese.
  It is sad that she lost her mother.
  I found **it** hard to concentrate on my studies.

LINK p.58 to부정사의 명사적 용법
LINK p.98 명사절을 이끄는 종속접속사

A

다음 문장에서 어법상 틀린 부분을 고쳐 쓰시오.

1 That will take about 30 minutes to fix it. 수능 기출 응용
2 It is not always easy to getting work done at the office. 수능 기출
3 I think important to make a good first impression.
4 They will be three kilometers from here to the mall.
5 How long does take to get to your office from here?

B

다음 우리말과 같은 뜻이 되도록 주어진 단어를 배열하여 문장을 완성하시오.

1 오후에 비가 올 것이다. (going, to, rain, it, is)
______________________ in the afternoon.

2 너희 집에서 학교까지의 거리는 얼마나 되니? (it, is, from, house, how, your, far)
______________________ to your school?

3 돛은 바다로만 갈 수 있는 나라와 교역하는 것을 가능하게 했다. (it, to trade, possible, made)
The sail ______________________ with countries that could be reached only by sea. 교육청 기출

4 나는 벌써 저녁 7시라는 것을 믿을 수 없다. (already, in, seven, it, the evening, is)
I can't believe that ______________________.

5 당신을 믿는 사람들이 있다는 것은 좋은 일이다. (it, great, is, people, to have)
______________________ who believe in you. 교육청 기출 응용

6 공연 후에 연주자들에게 이것을 주는 것이 관례이다. (give, it, to, is, this, customary)
______________________ to performers after a performance. 수능 기출

7 머지않아 부모님이 돌아오실 것이다. (before, will, it, long, not, be)
______________________ my parents come back.

정답 및 해설 p.22

★ POINT 06 ★★★★

부정대명사 I

- **one: 앞에 언급된 명사와 같은 종류의 불특정한 사람·사물을 가리킬 때 쓰며, 복수명사는 ones로 대신한다.**

  My watch is too old. I want to buy a new **one**.

  cf. 이미 언급된 특정한 것을 가리킬 때는 it을 쓴다.

  I lost my watch. I don't remember where I last had **it**.

- **another: '또 다른 하나'라는 뜻으로 단수명사를 대신하여 쓰이며, 복수형은 없다.**

  I don't like this hat. Show me **another**.

- **other: '다른 것[사람]'이라는 뜻으로 복수형은 others를 쓰며, 정해진 것을 나타낼 때는 앞에 정관사 the를 붙인다.**

  I have two cats. One is white and **the other** is black.

  cf. others가 앞에 관사 the 없이 쓰일 때는 '다른 사람들(= other people)'이라는 뜻을 나타낸다.

★ EXAM TIP

cf. 부정대명사 another, other는 동일한 의미의 형용사로도 쓰인다.

A 다음 괄호 안에서 알맞은 것을 고르시오.

1 I have two sisters. One is tall while (one / the other) is short.

2 This product is cheaper than (ones / the others) in this store.

3 Here are five cards. Pick (it / one) and I'll give (it / one) to you.

4 They replace a broken product with a new (one / other) within a month of its purchase. 교육청 기출

5 This shirt doesn't suit me. Could you show me (another / the other) in this size?

6 Some of the students received many gifts and (another / others) received only a few. 평가원 기출 응용

B 다음 우리말과 같은 뜻이 되도록 어법상 틀린 부분을 고쳐 쓰시오.

1 쿠키를 좀 샀어. 너에게 하나를 줄게.
I bought some cookies. I will give you another.

2 나는 치마 세 벌이 있다. 하나는 검정색, 하나는 파란색, 나머지 하나는 베이지색이다.
I have three skirts. One is black, another is blue, and the others is beige.

3 나는 달걀 한 개를 먹었지만, 아직도 배가 고프다. 한 개 더 먹고 싶다.
I ate an egg, but I'm still hungry. I'd like to eat the other.

4 어떤 사람들은 시골에서 살기를 원하는 반면 또 어떤 사람들은 도시에서 살기를 원한다.
Some people want to live in the country while the others want to live in the city.

★ POINT **07** ★★★★

부정대명사 II

정답 및 해설 p.22

- **all: '모두[모든 것]'라는 뜻으로 all 뒤에 복수명사가 오면 복수동사를, 단수명사가 오면 단수동사를 쓴다.**

  All (of) *the books* I borrowed were interesting.

  cf. all이 '유일한 것(the only thing)'이라는 뜻으로 쓰일 경우에는 단수 취급한다.

  All I want to do is dance.

- **both: '둘 다'라는 뜻으로, 항상 복수 취급한다.**

  Both (of) *the players* are excellent.

- **each: '각자[각각]'라는 뜻으로 개별성을 나타낼 때 쓰이며, 원칙적으로 단수 취급한다.**

  Each of *us* needs to be part of the environmental movement.

  Each *question* has four choices.

cf. 부정대명사 all, both, each는 동일한 의미의 형용사로도 쓰인다. every(모든)는 형용사 용법만 있어 뒤에 단수명사가 오며 원칙적으로 단수 취급한다.

Every *person* wants to have a happy life.

A 다음 괄호 안에서 알맞은 것을 고르시오.

1 (Both / Each) of my parents are tall.

2 Not every teacher (give / gives) weekly exams. 평가원 기출 응용

3 (All / Each) of the companies supports a local charity.

4 (All / Every) of these facts show that dinosaurs and modern reptiles are quite different. 평가원 기출 응용

B 다음 문장에서 밑줄 친 부분을 어법에 맞게 고쳐 쓰시오.

1 Every girls in my class likes the singer.

2 Each of us have a different personality.

3 Both of the man are good at skiing.

4 All the profits from this concert goes to a local orphanage. 교육청 기출 응용

C 다음 우리말과 같은 뜻이 되도록 문장을 완성하시오.

1 그 드라마에 나오는 배우 둘 다 연기를 잘한다.

_______ _______ _______ _______ in the soap opera act well.

2 각각의 제품의 가격은 그 품질에 따라 다르다.

The price of _______ _______ varies according to its quality. 교육청 기출 응용

3 모든 공원은 주말마다 사람들로 혼잡하다.

_______ _______ is crowded with people on weekends.

4 나는 학교에서 만난 사람들 모두 보고 싶다.

I miss _______ _______ _______ _______ I met at school.

★ POINT 08 ★★★★

부정대명사 III

정답 및 해설 p.22

- **either: '둘 중 어느 한 쪽'이라는 뜻으로 보통 단수 취급한다.**

  Does **either** of *your parents* speak English?

- **neither: '둘 중 어느 ~도 아닌'라는 뜻으로 보통 단수 취급한다.**

  Neither of *us* has ever been to Europe.

  cf. 〈(n)either+of+복수(대)명사〉로 쓰이는 경우 일상 영어에서는 복수 취급하기도 한다.

- **none: '아무(것)도 ~않다'라는 뜻으로 셀 수 없는 것을 나타낼 때는 단수 취급하고, 셀 수 있는 것을 나타낼 때는 단수 · 복수 모두 가능한데 보통 복수로 취급하는 경우가 많다.**

  None of *your information* is useful. **None** of *my friends* are[is] single.

cf. 부정대명사 either, neither는 동일한 의미의 형용사로도 쓰인다. no(어떤 ~도 아닌)는 형용사 용법만 있다.

No *one* can do what you've done for me.

A 다음 괄호 안에서 알맞은 것을 고르시오.

1 You can park on (either / none) side of the road.

2 I have three sisters, but (none / neither) of them live in this city.

3 (Either / Neither) of the teams has scored. This game will go into overtime.

B 다음 우리말과 같은 뜻이 되도록 밑줄 친 부분을 고쳐 쓰시오.

1 나의 형 둘 중 어느 누구도 나에게 관심이 없다.
Either of my brothers cares about me.

2 내 친구들 중 누구도 예술에 관심이 없다.
Neither of my friends are interested in art.

3 내 어떤 돈도 불법적으로 획득되지 않았다.
Either of my money was earned illegally.

4 너는 그 두 책 중 한 권이라도 읽었니?
Did you read neither of the books?

C 다음 우리말과 같은 뜻이 되도록 〈보기〉의 말을 이용하여 문장을 완성하시오.

보기	either	neither	none

1 내 고양이 둘 중 어느 것도 밖에 나가는 것을 좋아하지 않는다.
________ ________ ________ ________ likes to go outside.

2 그들 중 그 누구도 음반 업계에서 살아남지 못할 것이다.
________ ________ ________ will survive in the record business. 수능 기출 응용

3 나는 그 두 원피스 중 아무거나 너에게 잘 어울릴 거라고 생각한다.
I think ________ ________ ________ ________ will suit you well.

REVIEW TEST 11 ★

정답 및 해설 p.22

[1-6] 다음 우리말과 일치하도록 빈칸에 알맞은 말을 고르시오.

1

Judy가 직접 우리를 위해 저녁을 준비했다.
Judy ________ prepared supper for us.

① her ② hers ③ herself
④ our ⑤ ourselves

2

Daniel은 나의 유일한 가족이다.
Daniel is ________ only family I have.

① a ② an ③ the
④ either ⑤ neither

3

제가 바닥에 포크를 떨어뜨렸어요. 다른 걸로 가져다주시겠어요?
I dropped my fork on the floor. Could you get me ________?

① either ② one
③ another ④ the other
⑤ others

4

다른 사람의 충고를 듣는 것이 중요하다.
________ is important to listen to others' advice.

① It ② This
③ That ④ One
⑤ Another

5

나는 한 달 동안 파리를 방문할 것이다.
I'll be visiting Paris for ________ month.

① a ② an
③ the ④ each
⑤ every

6

나는 테이블 위에 있는 시계가 내 것이라고 확신한다.
I'm sure that the watch on the table is ________.

① my ② me
③ mine ④ myself
⑤ one

[7-12] 다음 우리말과 일치하도록 문장을 완성하시오.

7

여론의 흐름에 반대되는 말을 하는 데는 많은 용기가 필요하다.
It takes a lot of ________ to speak out against the tide of opinion.

8

그 학교의 모든 학생은 교복을 입어야 한다.
________ ________ in the school has to wear a school uniform.

9

통계학은 내가 학교에서 가장 좋아하는 과목이다.
Statistics __________ my favorite subject in school.

10

어떤 학생들을 제2외국어로 일본어를 배우고, 또 어떤 학생들은 중국어를 배운다.
Some students learn Japanese as a second language and __________ learn Chinese.

11

내 여동생 둘 다 액션 영화 보는 것을 좋아한다.
__________ of my sisters like to watch action movies.

12

나는 그 두 회사 중 어느 쪽도 믿을 만하지 않다고 생각한다.
I think __________ of the two companies is reliable.

[13-15] 다음 문장의 빈칸에 알맞은 말을 고르시오.

13

We'll have __________ dinner at a restaurant in Myeong-dong.

① a ② an ③ the
④ all ⑤ 필요 없음

14

Peter has two hobbies: one is fishing and __________ is cooking.

① other ② the other ③ others
④ another ⑤ some

15

Eric played __________ violin for three hours.

① a ② an ③ the
④ either ⑤ 필요 없음

[16-18] 다음 중 밑줄 친 부분이 어법상 틀린 것을 고르시오.

16

① I went to the stadium <u>by bus</u>.
② I like blue pants more than black <u>ones</u>.
③ None of them <u>are</u> suitable for the job.
④ He taught <u>himself</u> how to use the computer.
⑤ Each of the books on this bookshelf <u>are</u> ten dollars.

17

① All of the glasses on the table <u>are</u> dirty.
② Every person <u>has</u> a different character.
③ Mrs. Wilson is admired for her <u>kindness</u>.
④ The police <u>are</u> looking for him.
⑤ <u>That</u>'ll be rainy and windy tomorrow.

18

① His family <u>are</u> all well.
② Either of the days <u>is</u> fine with me.
③ Can you recommend <u>another</u>?
④ <u>The</u> bright moon is in the sky now.
⑤ They couldn't find fresh <u>waters</u> anywhere.

19 다음 문장 중 어법상 옳은 것은?

① All the shops on the street was closed.
② That was 8 o'clock when we returned.
③ It is very important to eat regularly.
④ This year 3,000 student applied to our university. 교육청 기출
⑤ I watched really touching movie yesterday. 교육청 기출

20 다음 중 대화가 어색한 것은?

① A: You've plugged many things into this outlet. Are you using all of them?
B: Not all of them. 교육청 기출
② A: Surprise! I made this wallet for you.
B: That's unbelievable! Did you really make it yourself? 교육청 기출
③ A: My students are also very excited to visit your school.
B: It's very nice to have a sister school like your. 교육청 기출
④ A: Wow, our living room is just like new.
B: Yeah. It was a good idea to have it painted light green. 교육청 기출
⑤ A: Is there anything I can do to help?
B: No, that's okay. I can handle it myself. 교육청 기출

[21-22] 다음 글의 밑줄 친 부분 중 어법상 바르지 못한 것을 고르시오.

21

Recently, Julie has become interested in cycling. She wants to buy ① a bike, but as new ② ones cost too much, she decides to purchase a used ③ one. She searches several websites to find a good one. She finally finds ④ it she likes. Then she calls the person selling ⑤ it and arranges to meet him. 교육청 기출 응용

22

In the 1650s, people believed that ① flies formed naturally from decaying meat. Through ② an experiment, however, Francesco Redi proved this belief false. He placed ③ the same decaying meat on the bottom of ④ each of the three jars. ⑤ A first jar was left closed. 평가원 기출

[23-24] 다음 글의 (A), (B), (C)에서 각각 알맞은 것을 고르시오.

23

When you're suffering from a cold, you are probably envious of people who (A) (seems / seem) to never get sick. We can't promise you'll never catch (B) (another / the other) cold, but you can increase your chances of staying well with these strategies. Wash your hands five times (C) (a / the) day and leave the windows of your house a little bit open. 평가원 기출 응용

24

There were two fathers that I used to know. Although (A) (both / every) of them worked hard, I noticed that (B) (one / both) of them had a habit of putting his brain to sleep when it came to money matters, and (C) (another / the other) had a habit of exercising his brain. 평가원 기출 응용

EST 2010

CHAPTER 12

★★★★

형용사 · 부사

★ POINT 01 ★★★★

형용사의 쓰임

정답 및 해설 p.22

- **(대)명사 수식: 형용사는 (대)명사를 앞이나 뒤에서 꾸며주는 역할을 한다. 대부분의 경우 명사 앞에서 꾸며주지만, -thing, -body, -one으로 끝나는 대명사의 경우에는 뒤에서 꾸며준다.**

  She is wearing **red** glasses.

  Could you show me something **different**?

- **동사의 보어: 형용사는 주격 보어나 목적격 보어로 쓰여 주어나 목적어의 상태 또는 성질을 나타낸다.**

  I was **angry** at my sister. LINK p.13 2형식 문장

  He found the place **beautiful**. LINK p.16 5형식 문장

cf. 〈the+형용사〉는 '~하는 사람들'이라는 보통명사의 뜻으로 쓰인다.

I believe **the rich** should pay higher taxes.

A 다음 괄호 안에서 알맞은 것을 고르시오.

1 Childhood friends are really (special / specially). 교육청 기출 응용

2 Did you find (anything interesting / interesting anything) in the book?

3 We are raising money to help (a / the) poor.

4 I'd like to introduce you to (someone nice / nice someone).

5 Sometimes we find a piece of writing (hard / hardly) to understand. 교육청 기출

6 A glass of hot milk made me (warm / warmly).

7 New technologies create new interactions and (cultural rules / rules cultural). 교육청 기출

B 다음 우리말과 같은 뜻이 되도록 주어진 단어를 배열하여 문장을 완성하시오.

1 그 실수는 나를 긴장하게 했다. (nervous, me, made, the mistake)

____

2 네 컴퓨터에 뭔가 잘못된 게 있니? (with, wrong, your computer, there, anything, is)

____

3 그는 그 신발이 매우 편안하다는 것을 알게 되었다. (very, he, comfortable, found, the shoes)

____

4 나는 그녀가 살아 있다는 소식을 들어 매우 행복하다. (is, alive, to, that, hear, she, happy)

I am so ______________________________

5 이 병원은 부상당한 사람들로 꽉 차 있다. (this hospital, of, is, wounded, full, the)

____

6 엄마는 우리에게 할 수 있는 특별한 뭔가를 생각해 보라고 말씀하셨다. (do, special, something, to)

Mom told us to think of ______________________________ 수능 기출

POINT 02 ★★★★

수량형용사 I

정답 및 해설 p.23

- **some, any는 '약간의'라는 뜻으로 셀 수 있는 명사와 셀 수 없는 명사 둘 다와 함께 쓰인다. 일반적으로 some은 긍정문에, any는 부정문, 의문문, 조건문에 쓰인다.**

  I'll buy **some** T-shirts today. I don't have **any** cash on me.

  cf. 의문문이라도 긍정의 대답을 기대할 때, 또는 권유나 부탁을 나타낼 때는 some을 쓴다.

  Would you like to have **some** tea?

- **a few(약간의)와 few(거의 없는)는 셀 수 있는 명사 앞에, a little(약간의)과 little(거의 없는)은 셀 수 없는 명사 앞에 쓰인다.**

  Only **a few** students support her. There are **few** trees in this area.

  I added **a little** water to the cup. I have **little** money left.

A 다음 괄호 안에서 알맞은 것을 고르시오.

1 I'll be back in (a little / a few) minutes. 수능 기출 응용

2 I didn't get (any / some) e-mails from you.

3 She brought (any / some) photos to show me.

4 These phones are slow and have very (few / little) functions. 교육청 기출 응용

5 There are hundreds of words that express very (few / little) meaning. 교육청 기출 응용

6 There is still (a little / a few) hope of her winning the championship.

B 다음 우리말과 같은 뜻이 되도록 어법상 틀린 부분을 고쳐 쓰시오.

1 나는 오늘 해야 할 숙제가 좀 있다.

I have any homework to do today.

2 당신의 주문품은 며칠 내로 발송될 것입니다.

Your order will be shipped in a little days.

3 그는 책에 조금의 관심도 없다.

He doesn't have some interest in books.

C 다음 우리말과 같은 뜻이 되도록 문장을 완성하시오.

1 그가 한 말에 동의한 사람은 거의 없었다.

__________ people agreed with what he said.

2 의사는 내게 상한 이가 몇 개 있다고 말했다.

The doctor said that I had __________ bad teeth.

3 맨 위 선반에 약간의 설탕이 있다.

We have __________ sugar on the top shelf. 수능 기출 응용

4 어제는 도로에 교통량이 거의 없었다.

There was __________ traffic on the road yesterday.

POINT 03 ★★★★

수량형용사 II

정답 및 해설 p.23

- **many는 셀 수 있는 명사와, much는 셀 수 없는 명사와 함께 쓰인다.**

  I don't have **many** friends to play with.

  He doesn't have **much** money in his bank account.

- **a lot of[lots of]는 셀 수 있는 명사와 셀 수 없는 명사 둘 다와 함께 쓰인다.**

  She asked me **a lot of[lots of]** questions.

  My uncle drank **a lot of[lots of]** beer yesterday.

A 다음 괄호 안에서 알맞은 것을 고르시오.

1 He collected (much / a lot of) books on classical literature. 평가원 기출 응용

2 Why are you drinking so (many / much) coffee? 수능 기출 응용

3 We put in (many / lots of) effort to finish the project.

4 These days (much / lots of) people use a portable computer or two. 교육청 기출 응용

5 It took her (many / a lot of) courage to drive again after the accident.

6 There are (many / much) children who don't have enough food to survive. 수능 기출 응용

B 다음 밑줄 친 부분을 어법에 맞게 고쳐 쓰시오.

1 Good driving requires many experience. 교육청 기출

2 This table takes up many room.

3 Mark lost much bloods in the car accident.

4 There are much reasons I want to major in French.

5 In Paris, a lot of museum are shut down on either Mondays or Tuesdays.

C 다음 우리말과 같은 뜻이 되도록 괄호 안의 말을 이용하여 문장을 완성하시오.

1 어린 아이에게는 많은 사랑과 관심이 필요하다. (love)

A young child needs ________ ________ ________ ________ and attention.

2 이 치즈 케이크의 칼로리는 얼마입니까? (calorie)

How ________ ________ does this cheesecake have?

3 Alex는 나에게 그녀에 대한 많은 정보를 주지 않았다. (information)

Alex didn't give me ________ ________ about her.

4 이 기계를 작동하는 데는 많은 연료가 필요하다. (fuel)

________ ________ ________ is needed to operate this machine.

5 이 성과 관련된 흥미로운 이야기가 많다. (story)

There ________ ________ ________ ________ connected with this castle.

POINT 04 부사의 쓰임

정답 및 해설 p.23

- 부사는 동사, 형용사, 부사 또는 문장 전체를 수식하며, 때·장소·방법·빈도·정도의 의미를 나타낸다.

Consider this matter **carefully**.

Linda is **very** good at cooking.

He worries **too** much about my health.

Luckily, Jessica was hired by that company.

A 다음 괄호 안에서 알맞은 것을 고르시오.

1 She and her sister got along really (good / well).
2 (Strange / Strangely), I don't look like my brother at all.
3 This farm (actual / actually) helps the city to solve social problems. 평가원 기출
4 (Unfortunate / Unfortunately), few scientists are truly objective. 평가원 기출 응용

B 다음 〈보기〉에서 각 문장의 빈칸에 알맞은 부사를 골라 쓰시오.

보기	hard	loudly	quickly	too	usually	very

1 Jenny studied __________, but didn't get good results.
2 I'll send you the package __________ soon.
3 Jessy __________ works from eight to six.
4 They just kept shouting __________ at the police. 평가원 기출
5 They ran __________ to make it to the front of the line first. 교육청 기출 응용
6 Reading or using a computer for __________ long can lead to tired eyes. 교육청 기출

C 다음 문장에서 부사를 찾아 동그라미 하고, 부사가 수식하는 말에 밑줄을 그으시오.

1 She lifted the chair easily.
2 I think this dress fits me perfectly.
3 Suddenly, she stopped to say hello to her friends. 수능 기출
4 Why does he look so depressed?
5 This medicine I bought yesterday works well.
6 Thank you very much for driving me to the airport.

POINT 05 ★★★★

부사의 위치

정답 및 해설 p.23

- **빈도부사(always, usually, often, sometimes, never 등)는 일반동사 앞 또는 be동사나 조동사 뒤에 위치한다.**

  I **often** dream about having a big house.

  I am **sometimes** late for school.

  cf. usually, often, sometimes는 문두나 문미에도 쓰인다.

  Usually, Brad drives and his wife reads the map.

- **〈타동사+부사〉로 된 동사구의 목적어가 명사인 경우 부사는 목적어의 앞뒤 모두에 올 수 있지만, 목적어가 대명사인 경우 부사는 반드시 목적어 뒤에 와야 한다.**

  I'll turn **off** the lights on the way out.
  [→ turn the lights **off**]

  She found her glasses and put them **on**.
  [→ ~~put **on** them~~]

A 다음 문장에서 어법상 틀린 부분을 고쳐 쓰시오.

1 I don't know how to turn on it.

2 I always will remember you and your family.

3 Without someone to feed us, we never would survive to grow up. 교육청 기출 응용

4 My brother pretends sometimes to be kind to pretty girls.

5 Dinosaurs often are shown in movies as huge monsters. 평가원 기출

6 There were lots of new words, so I had to look up them in a dictionary.

B 다음 우리말과 같은 뜻이 되도록 주어진 단어를 배열하여 문장을 완성하시오.

1 그녀는 캠프의 모닥불을 끄고 자러 갔다. (campfire, the, out, put)
She ______________________ and went to sleep.

2 내 느낌을 말하는 것이 때로는 어렵다. (difficult, say, sometimes, to, is)
It ______________________ how I feel.

3 그는 말할 때 종종 다른 사람의 감정을 상하게 한다. (often, feelings, he, others', hurts)
When he speaks, ______________________. 평가원 기출

4 그것이 작은 화재였기 때문에 그녀가 가까스로 그것을 끌 수 있었다. (put, to, it, managed, out)
Because it was a small fire, she ______________________.

5 그녀는 그에게 더러운 옷을 벗으라고 말했다. (take, clothes, his, off, dirty)
She told him to ______________________.

6 나는 그 기회를 신중하게 고려해 본 후, 그것을 거절하기로 결정했다. (turn, decided, to, down, it) 교육청 기출
After carefully considering the opportunity, I ______________________.

7 한국에서는 한 사람의 생일을 위해 보통 미역국이 요리된다. (is, cooked, usually, seaweed soup)
______________________ for a person on his or her birthday in Korea.
교육청 기출

POINT 06 ★★★★

주의해야 할 부사

정답 및 해설 p.23

- **형용사와 부사의 형태가 같은 경우**

early 형 이른 부 일찍　late 형 늦은 부 늦게　fast 형 빠른 부 빨리　last 형 마지막의 부 마지막으로
high 형 높은 부 높이　enough 형 충분한 부 충분히　long 형 오랜 부 오래　hard 형 열심인 부 열심히

The **early** morning is the best time of day.
She finds it very difficult to get up **early**.

cf. lately는 '최근에', highly는 '대단히, 매우', hardly는 '거의 ~않다'라는 뜻의 부사이다.
I think my son is **highly** intelligent.

- **〈명사+ly〉가 형용사로만 쓰이는 경우**

friendly 형 친절한　lovely 형 사랑스러운　costly 형 값비싼

People who work here are **friendly**.

〈명사+ly〉가 형용사와 부사로 쓰이는 경우

daily 형 매일의 부 매일　weekly 형 매주의 부 매주　monthly 형 매달의 부 매달

A

다음 괄호 안에서 알맞은 것을 고르시오.

1 I haven't seen Matt (late / lately).
2 The cost of houses has soared (high / highly) recently.
3 In big cities, most people (hard / hardly) know their neighbors.
4 Susan is (high / highly) motivated to do well in school.

B

다음 우리말과 같은 뜻이 되도록 문장을 완성하시오.

1 나는 이 주간지 읽는 것을 좋아한다.
I like to read this __________ magazine.

2 그 간호사는 내게 그 알약을 매일 먹으라고 했다.
The nurse told me to take the tablets __________.

3 Sophie는 사랑스러운 여자 쌍둥이를 낳았다.
Sophie gave birth to __________ twin girls.

4 나는 거의 집중할 수가 없었다.
I was __________ able to concentrate.

5 나는 지갑을 마지막으로 가지고 있던 곳이 어디인지 기억이 안 난다.
I can't remember where I had my wallet __________.

6 아빠는 최근에 잠을 잘 주무시지 못하는 것 같다.
My dad doesn't seem to be sleeping well __________. 수능 기출

7 컴퓨터에 대한 이른 노출은 우리의 디지털 세계에 적응하는 데 도움을 준다.
__________ exposure to computers is helpful in adapting to our digital world.
교육청 기출

REVIEW TEST 12 ★

정답 및 해설 p.23

[1-5] 다음 우리말과 일치하도록 빈칸에 알맞은 말을 고르시오.

1

음료에 얼음을 좀 넣으시겠어요?
Would you like __________ ice in your drink?

① few ② little ③ some
④ much ⑤ a lot of

2

Joel은 이 분야에는 경험이 많지 않다.
Joel doesn't have __________ experience in this area.

① little ② few ③ some
④ many ⑤ much

3

나는 그녀가 저녁을 거의 먹지 않아 염려스러웠다.
I was concerned that she __________ ate her dinner.

① hard ② hardly ③ highly
④ late ⑤ lately

4

나는 온라인에서 그 책에 대한 정보를 조금도 찾을 수 없었다.
I couldn't find __________ information about the book online.

① many ② much ③ little
④ few ⑤ any

5

그는 오늘 고객이 많았다.
He had __________ customers today.

① a little ② much ③ a lot of
④ some ⑤ any

[6-11] 다음 우리말과 일치하도록 문장을 완성하시오.

6

밖에 나가기 전에 그것을 입어라.
__________ __________ __________ before you go outside.

7

우리는 때때로 이 백화점에서 쇼핑을 한다.
We __________ __________ at this department store.

8

이 웹사이트는 매일 업데이트된다.
This website is updated __________.

9

오늘 미술사 수업이 늦게 끝났다.
The art history class finished __________ today.

10

남은 사과가 거의 없었다.
There were __________ apples left.

11

나는 Ben이 왜 늘 바쁜지 모른다.
I don't know why Ben __________ __________ __________.

[12-15] 다음 문장의 빈칸에 들어갈 수 없는 말을 고르시오.

12

I spend __________ time with my family.

① few ② little ③ some
④ a lot of ⑤ much

13

I found Billy __________.

① honest ② politely ③ brave
④ friendly ⑤ smart

14

My business was __________ affected by this technology.

① partly ② never ③ deeply
④ hardly ⑤ heavy

15

I feel __________ at night.

① lonely ② sad ③ depressed
④ sleepy ⑤ terribly

[16-19] 다음 중 밑줄 친 부분이 어법상 틀린 것을 고르시오.

16

① We had little snow this winter.
② His rudeness made me angry.
③ I like friendly and outgoing people.
④ The plane is flying high in the sky.
⑤ I'd like to do exciting something with you.

17

① His smile made me happy.
② Did you hear anything interesting at the party?
③ I did a little research on the product.
④ He collected much rare books.
⑤ It's very difficult to please my father.

18

① I have a few questions for him.
② Your leather bag is so pretty.
③ Would you turn off the computer?
④ I worked hardly to achieve my goal.
⑤ I've been working out at home lately.

19

① I often exercise at the gym.
② Can you take the trash out?
③ I'd like to start the interview with some questions from readers. 교육청 기출 응용
④ Programs are intended for those with few or no experience. 교육청 기출
⑤ We offer customers top-quality goods at highly competitive prices. 교육청 기출 응용

[20-21] 다음 문장 중 어법상 옳은 것을 고르시오.

20

① If you like it, you can try on it.
② There are many kinds of hats in the store.
③ It was a wet summer with few sunshine.
④ There must be any ways we can help.
⑤ Much newborn babies throughout the world die within their first month.

21

① The kids hard go to bed early.
② How much cookies do you want?
③ New members are always welcome. 교육청 기출
④ Are you looking for special something for your lovely children?
⑤ Can I keep the book for a little more days?

교육청 기출 응용

[22-23] 다음 글의 밑줄 친 부분 중 어법상 바르지 못한 것을 고르시오.

22

We are committed to safeguarding the privacy of all employees, former and current. If you receive a request for any information regarding a ① former employee, do not provide ② any details of employment. Please ③ pass along the inquiry to Human Resources. If there are ④ some questions about this policy, please feel ⑤ free to contact Human Resources. 교육청 기출 응용

23

My friends believe that I am ① highly gifted in math. Maybe I was born with ② some curiosity about how things work, whether it is a math problem or a magic trick. But from my experiences, I have learned that rapid math is a skill that anyone can learn. And like ③ any useful skill, it takes ④ many time and effort if you wish to become an expert. 평가원 기출 응용

[24-25] 다음 글의 (A), (B), (C)에서 각각 알맞은 것을 고르시오.

24

Nowadays it seems there are (A) (few / little) places to take a walk in the city. Physical activity is so rare that experts suggest you should do (B) (any / some) sort of exercise throughout the day. For example, take (C) (a few / a little) flights of stairs instead of using the elevator.

25

(A) (Many / Much) people argue that knowledge gives you power. Nevertheless, we (B) (sometimes wish / wish sometimes) that we were never informed about many bad things. Do we really need knowledge to be happy? I think knowing more (C) (often can / can often) lead to a life of worry and misery. 평가원 기출 응용

EST CHAPTER 13 2010

비교

1 형용사 · 부사의 비교 변화
2 원급 비교
3 원급 비교 관용 표현
4 비교급 비교
5 비교급 비교 관용 표현
6 최상급 비교
7 최상급 비교 관용 표현
8 원급 · 비교급을 이용한 최상급 표현

REVIEW TEST 13

POINT 01 ★★★★

형용사 · 부사의 비교 변화

정답 및 해설 p.24

- 형용사나 부사는 형태 변화를 통해 '더 ~한[하게], 가장 ~한[하게]'이라는 뜻을 나타낼 수 있다.

1음절 단어	+ -(e)r / -(e)st	short – short**er** – short**est**
〈단모음+단자음〉으로 끝나는 단어	자음을 한 번 더 쓰고+-er / -est	hot – hot**ter** – hot**test**
-y로 끝나는 단어	y를 i로 바꾸고+-er / -est	pretty – pretti**er** – pretti**est**
-ful, -ous, -ing, -ive, -ly 등의 접미사가 붙은 2음절 단어 대부분과 3음절 이상의 단어	단어 앞에+more / most	careful – **more** careful – **most** careful easily – **more** easily – **most** easily

- 비교급과 최상급이 불규칙하게 변하는 단어

good/well – better – best
many/much – more – most
bad/ill – worse – worst
little – less – least

A 다음 괄호 안에서 알맞은 것을 고르시오.

1 I'd like to have a (biger / bigger) office.
2 This is the (hardest / most hard) work I've done.
3 You should have been (carefuler / more careful). 수능 기출
4 Summers are getting (hotter / more hot) as the planet warms.
5 This is the (largest / most large) bank in the United States.
6 I think a round table would be (safer / more safer) for the children. 수능 기출 응용
7 Happy Voice, one of the (popularest / most popular) school clubs, is holding an audition. 교육청 기출 응용

B 다음 우리말과 같은 뜻이 되도록 괄호 안의 말을 이용하여 문장을 완성하시오.

1 Sam은 나보다 더 많은 돈을 번다. (much)
Sam earns ______________ money than I do.
2 두통이 더 심해지고 있다. (bad)
My headache is getting ______________.
3 그 책에서 가장 유용한 정보는 무엇이니? (useful)
What is the ______________ information in the book? 교육청 기출
4 매주 하루씩 종일 쉬는 것이 나를 더 생산적으로 만든다. (productive)
Taking one full day off every week makes me ______________.
5 걷기는 지방을 분해하는 가장 쉬운 방법 중 하나이다. (easy)
Walking is one of the ______________ ways to burn fat.
6 곧 더 나아지기를 바랄게. (well)
I hope you get ______________ soon. 교육청 기출

★ POINT 02 ★★★★

원급 비교

정답 및 해설 p.24

- **〈as+원급+as〉: ~만큼 …한[하게]**

Tim is **as poor as** I am.
Kids don't play **as much as** they used to.
This job is **not as[so] easy as** you think.
cf. 부정형은 〈not as[so]+원급+as〉이다.

A **다음 우리말과 같은 뜻이 되도록 어법상 틀린 부분을 고쳐 쓰시오.**

1 그녀는 Picasso만큼 유명하다.
She is as more famous as Picasso.

2 그 도시는 서울만큼 크다.
The city is big as Seoul.

3 다이아몬드가 당신의 생명만큼 소중하지는 않다.
The diamond is not as precious so your life.

4 이번 여름은 지난여름만큼 덥지 않다.
This summer is not hot as last summer.

5 이 뮤지컬은 내가 그러리라 생각했던 것만큼 환상적이었다.
This musical was as fantastic than I thought it would be.

B **다음 우리말과 같은 뜻이 되도록 괄호 안의 말을 이용하여 문장을 완성하시오.**

1 그 다리는 로마의 다리들만큼 오래되지 않았다. (old)
The bridge is ____________________ the bridges of Rome. 평가원 기출 응용

2 Debbie는 보이는 것만큼 어리지 않다. (young)
Debbie is ____________________ she looks.

3 그의 두 번째 책은 그의 첫 번째 책만큼 인기가 있었다. (popular)
His second book was ____________________ his first book.

4 가이드는 그 운석이 태양계 자체만큼 고대의 것이라고 주장했다. (ancient)
The guide claimed that the meteorite was ____________________ the solar system itself. 교육청 기출 응용

5 이 빨간색 셔츠는 저 노란색 셔츠만큼 싸지 않다. (cheap)
This red shirt is ____________________ that yellow shirt.

6 당신의 차는 생각만큼 많은 것을 운반하지 못한다. (much)
Your car cannot carry ____________________ you think. 수능 기출 응용

★ POINT 03 ★★★★

원급 비교 관용 표현

정답 및 해설 p.24

- **〈as+원급+as possible〉: 가능한 한 ~한[하게]**
  =〈as+원급+as+주어+can〉
  I'd like to receive a reply **as soon as possible**.
  = I'd like to receive a reply **as soon as I can**.
- **〈배수사+as+원급+as〉: ~보다 몇 배 …한[하게]**
  This ring is **twice as expensive as** that one.
  = This ring is **two times more expensive than** that one.
  cf. 〈배수사+비교급+than〉 형태로 쓰기도 한다. 단, twice와 half는 이 형태로 쓸 수 없다.

A 다음 우리말과 같은 뜻이 되도록 주어진 단어를 배열하여 문장을 완성하시오.

1 그는 가능한 한 많이 운동하려고 노력한다. (much, possible, as, as)
He tries to exercise ______________________.

2 미국은 해외 관광에 러시아의 두 배가 넘는 돈을 썼다. (as, twice, Russia, much, as)
The US spent more than ______________________ on international tourism. 교육청 기출 응용

3 제게 가능한 한 빨리 전화 주세요. (as, you, soon, can, as)
Give me a call ______________________.

4 건강을 유지하려면 최대한 많은 물을 마시는 것이 필요하다. (as, possible, water, much, as) 교육청 기출
It is necessary to drink ______________________ to stay healthy.

5 그 책은 저 책보다 세 배 두껍다. (times, than, three, thicker)
The book is ______________________ that one.

B 다음 우리말과 같은 뜻이 되도록 〈보기〉에 주어진 말을 이용하여 문장을 완성하시오.

보기 big hard heavy much often

1 그의 고양이는 내 고양이보다 두 배 무겁다.
His cat is ________ ________ ________ ________ mine.

2 나는 가능한 한 많이 배우도록 최선을 다할 것이다.
I'll do my best to learn ________ ________ ________ ________. 수능 기출

3 그녀의 여행 가방은 그의 것보다 거의 세 배 컸다.
Her suitcase was nearly ________ ________ ________ ________ ________ his.

4 Tony는 다른 학생들보다 테니스를 두 배 열심히 연습한다.
Tony practices tennis ________ ________ ________ ________ the other students.

5 경찰관들은 당신이 사는 지역을 가능한 한 자주 순찰하고 있다.
Police officers are patrolling your area ________ ________ ________ ________ ________. 평가원 기출 응용

★ POINT 04 ★★★★

비교급 비교

정답 및 해설 p.24

- 〈비교급+than〉: ~보다 더 …한[하게]

My room is **cleaner than** yours.
= Your room is **less clean than** mine.
(= Your room is **not as[so] clean as** mine.)

cf. -or로 끝나는 형용사(superior, inferior, prior)는 비교의 의미를 포함하므로 따로 비교 변화를 하지 않으며 뒤에는 than이 아닌 to를 쓴다.
The new model is **superior to** its competitors.

- 비교급 앞에 much, even, far, a lot, still 등이 오면 비교급을 강조하여 '훨씬 더 ~한[하게]'이라는 뜻을 나타낸다.

She is even **more beautiful than** I heard.

cf. very는 비교급을 수식할 수 없다.

A 다음 우리말과 같은 뜻이 되도록 어법상 틀린 부분을 고쳐 쓰시오.

1 Ted는 Susan보다 더 위험하게 운전한다.
Ted drives dangerously than Susan.

2 그의 노트북 컴퓨터는 내 데스크톱 컴퓨터보다 우수하다.
His laptop is superior than my desktop.

3 영상은 말보다 두뇌에 훨씬 큰 영향을 미친다.
An image has a very greater impact on your brain than words. 교육청 기출

B 다음 두 문장이 같은 뜻이 되도록 빈칸에 알맞은 비교급 표현을 쓰시오.

1 Her grades are not as good as mine.
→ My grades are __________ __________ hers.

2 Lucy does not walk as quickly as Sally.
→ Sally walks __________ __________ __________ Lucy.

3 The condition of the bike was not as good as what she had seen on the website.
→ The condition of the bike __________ __________ __________ what she had seen on the website. 교육청 기출 응용

C 다음 우리말과 같은 뜻이 되도록 괄호 안의 말을 이용하여 문장을 완성하시오.

1 이 소파가 저것보다 덜 편안하다. (comfortable)
This couch is ____________________ that one.

2 동물들은 밭을 가는 데 인간보다 훨씬 효율적이었다. (far, efficient)
Animals were ____________________ at plowing than humans. 교육청 기출 응용

3 이곳의 여자들은 남자들보다 더욱 오래 일한다. (even, long)
The women here work ____________________ the men do. 평가원 기출 응용

4 대부분의 공룡들은 오늘날의 파충류들보다 훨씬 컸다. (much, large)
Most dinosaurs were ____________________ the reptiles that live today. 평가원 기출 응용

POINT 05 ★★★★

비교급 비교 관용 표현

정답 및 해설 p.24

- 〈the+비교급, the+비교급〉: ~하면 할수록 더 …하다
  The sooner we finish this job, **the sooner** we can eat dinner.
- 〈비교급+and+비교급〉: 점점 더 ~한[하게]
  The weather is getting **hotter and hotter**.
  cf. more를 붙여 비교급을 만드는 형용사/부사의 경우에는 〈more and more+원급〉으로 나타낸다.
  As he talked, he looked **more and more nervous**.

A 다음 〈보기〉와 같이 비교급을 이용하여 문장을 바꾸어 쓰시오.

보기 As I climbed higher, I became more tired.
→ The higher I climbed, the more tired I became.

1 If you are around the baby more, it will be better for her. 교육청 기출 응용
→ ______________________________

2 As he spent less, he saved more money.
→ ______________________________

3 If the air is drier, you need more water.
→ ______________________________

B 다음 우리말과 같은 뜻이 되도록 괄호 안의 말을 이용하여 문장을 완성하시오.

1 하늘이 점점 더 어두워졌다. (dark)
The sky became ______________.

2 백화점은 점점 더 혼잡해졌다. (crowded)
The department store got ______________.

3 책이 희귀하면 할수록 가격은 더 비싸진다. (rare, expensive)
______________ a book is, ______________ the price.

4 당신이 더 많이 웃을수록 당신의 첫인상은 더 좋아진다. (much, good)
______________ you smile, ______________ your first impression.

5 나는 그의 영어 실력이 점점 더 좋아질 거라고 예상하지 못했다. (good)
I didn't expect that his English would get ______________.

6 옷의 색이 더 밝으면 더 시원할 거라고 생각된다. (pale, cool)
It is thought that ______________ your clothes are, ______________ you'll be. 교육청 기출 응용

★ POINT **06** ★★★★

최상급 비교

정답 및 해설 p.24

- **〈the+최상급〉: 가장 ~한[하게]**

최상급 뒤에 of(~ 중에서)나 in(~ 안에서)을 써서 비교의 범위를 한정해 준다.

Jenny is **the smartest** *of* all the students in my class.

I can run **(the) fastest** *in* my family.

cf. 일상 영어에서는 부사의 최상급에 the를 쓰지 않는 경우도 있다.

- **최상급을 강조할 때는 much, by far, the very 등을 최상급 바로 앞에 쓴다.**

This dictionary is by far **the most useful** of all.

A **다음 괄호 안의 단어를 최상급으로 바꿔 빈칸을 채우시오.**

1 Winter is ______________ time of the year. (cold)

2 Tom swims ______________ of all my classmates. (fast)

3 This model is ______________ one in my shop. (popular) 평가원 기출 응용

4 For me, Monday is ______________ day of the week. (busy)

5 The musical became ______________ ticket in town. (hot) 평가원 기출 응용

6 Of the five countries, Denmark spent ______________ percentage of its GDP on education. (high) 평가원 기출 응용

B **다음 우리말과 같은 뜻이 되도록 어법상 틀린 부분을 고쳐 쓰시오.**

1 소고기 카레가 이 식당에서 가장 맛있는 음식이다.
Beef curry is most delicious food in this restaurant.

2 시리우스는 밤하늘에서 가장 밝은 별이다.
Sirius is the bright star in the night sky.

3 오페라 하우스는 시드니에서 단연 가장 인기 있는 관광 명소이다.
The Opera House is far the most popular tourist attraction in Sydney.

C **다음 우리말과 같은 뜻이 되도록 괄호 안의 말을 이용하여 문장을 완성하시오.**

1 이것이 도쿄에서 가장 높은 빌딩이다. (tall)
This is ________ ________ ________ in Tokyo.

2 실내용 화초는 실내 공기를 거르는 데 단연 최고의 방법이다. (good)
Houseplants are ________ ________ ________ ________ way to filter indoor air. 교육청 기출

3 우리 할아버지는 모든 형제들 중 가장 오래 사셨다. (long)
My grandfather ________ ________ ________ of all his brothers.

4 Joel은 사무실에서 가장 부지런한 직원이다. (diligent)
Joel is ________ ________ ________ employee in the office.

★ POINT 07 ★★★★

최상급 비교 관용 표현

정답 및 해설 p.25

- 〈one of the+최상급+복수명사〉: 가장 ~한 … 중 하나
  Einstein is considered **one of the most important scientists** in history.
- 〈the+최상급+(that)+주어+have ever p.p.〉: '주어'가 지금까지 ~한 것들 중 가장 …한
  This is the **most beautiful lake (that) I've ever seen**.

A 다음 우리말과 같은 뜻이 되도록 주어진 단어를 배열하여 문장을 완성하시오.

1 그것은 내가 지금까지 본 가장 무서운 영화 중 하나였다. (movies, one, scariest, of, the)
It was ______________________ I've ever seen.

2 그녀는 내가 지금까지 만나 본 사람 중 가장 현명하다. (met, ever, wisest, person, the, I've)
She is ______________________.

3 이것이 우리가 지금까지 가져온 것 중 최고의 모임이 될 수도 있다. (ever, we, meeting, had, best, have, the)
This could be ______________________. 수능 기출

4 Paul Auster는 미국에서 최고의 작가 중 한 명이다. (America, in, best, the, one, authors, of)
Paul Auster is ______________________.

5 우리가 할 수 있는 가장 중요한 결정 중 하나는 시간을 어떻게 투자하느냐다. (the, essential, one, most, decisions, of)
______________________ any of us can make is how we invest our time. 교육청 기출

B 다음 우리말과 같은 뜻이 되도록 괄호 안의 말을 이용하여 문장을 완성하시오.

1 이것은 여기에서 가장 맛있는 요리 중 하나이다. (delicious, dish)
This is ______________________ here.

2 Leonardo da Vinci는 지금까지 살았던 가장 학식 있는 사람 중 하나이다. (learned, person)
Leonardo da Vinci was ______________________ that have ever lived. 교육청 기출 응용

3 Google은 세계에서 가장 성공한 회사 중 하나다. (successful, company)
Google is ______________________ in the world.

4 솔직히 말해서 그것은 내가 지금까지 본 최악의 영화 중 하나였다. (bad, see)
To be honest, it was ______________________.

5 빈은 내가 지금까지 가 본 도시 중 가장 아름답다. (beautiful, be)
Vienna is ______________________ to.

6 아이리스는 가장 인기 있는 정원용 꽃 중 하나이다. (popular, garden flower)
The iris is ______________________. 평가원 기출

★ POINT 08 ★★★★

원급 · 비교급을 이용한 최상급 표현

정답 및 해설 p.25

- 원급이나 비교급을 써서 최상급의 의미를 나타낼 수 있다.

Ann is **the cutest** girl in my class.	〈the+최상급〉
→ Ann is **cuter than any other** *girl* in my class.	〈비교급+than any other+단수명사〉
→ Ann is **cuter than all the (other)** *girls* in my class.	〈비교급+than all the (other)+복수명사〉
→ **No girl** in my class is **cuter than** Ann.	〈no+명사+비교급+than〉
→ **No girl** in my class is **as[so] cute as** Ann.	〈no+명사+as[so]+원급+as〉

A 다음 두 문장이 같은 뜻이 되도록 문장을 완성하시오.

1 No actor in Korea is more popular than him.
→ No actor in Korea is ________ ________ ________ him.

2 No book in the market is as comprehensive as this one.
→ No book in the market is ________ ________ ________ this one.

3 Walking is the easiest way to keep ourselves fit. 수능 기출
→ Walking is ________ ________ all the other ways to keep ourselves fit.

4 The country's army is the largest in the world.
→ The country's army ________ ________ ________ any other army in the world.

5 Ethnocentrism is the belief that your culture is better than any other culture.
→ Ethnocentrism is the belief that ________ ________ ________ ________ ________ of all cultures. 수능 기출

B 다음 주어진 단어를 배열하여 문장을 완성하시오.

1 (more, than, crowded, is)
→ In this town, no bakery ____________________ Joe's.

2 (as, New York, as, diverse)
→ No city in the world is ____________________.

3 (any, than, person, faster, other)
→ Helen was promoted ____________________ in the company.

4 (smarter, students, other, than, all, the)
→ My nephew is ____________________ in his class.

5 (other, any, game, more, than)
→ The game has sold ____________________ in history.

6 (all, other, the, better, than, products)
→ This is ____________________ I've tried.

REVIEW TEST 13 ★

정답 및 해설 p.25

[1-5] 다음 우리말과 일치하도록 빈칸에 알맞은 말을 고르시오.

1

나는 Jack만큼 그림을 잘 그릴 수 있다.
I can draw a picture as __________ as Jack.

① good ② better
③ well ④ best
⑤ the best

2

세계에서 가장 긴 강은 어느 것이니?
Which is __________ river in the world?

① long ② longer
③ the longest ④ more long
⑤ the most long

3

Justin은 우리 반의 다른 어떤 소년보다도 인기가 많다.
Justin is __________ than any other boy in my class.

① popular ② popularer
③ the popularest ④ more popular
⑤ the most popular

4

어떤 여자도 우리 어머니보다 더 지혜롭지는 않다.
__________ woman is wiser than my mother.

① Any ② Some ③ No
④ All ⑤ Every

5

그는 나이가 들면 들수록 더 외로워졌다.
__________ he got, the lonelier he became.

① Old ② Older ③ Oldest
④ The older ⑤ The oldest

[6-10] 다음 두 문장의 뜻이 같도록 문장을 완성하시오.

6

This is larger than any other museum in Spain.
= This is __________ __________ museum in Spain.

7

His painting is not as good as Tony's.
= Tony's painting is __________ __________ his painting.

8

No planet is more beautiful than the Earth.
= No planet is __________ __________ __________ the Earth.

9

If you are younger, you will learn a language more quickly.
= __________ __________ you are, __________ __________ __________ you will learn a language.

10

May I talk to the president as soon as possible?
= May I talk to the president as soon as ________ ________?

[11-13] 다음 우리말과 일치하도록 문장을 완성하시오.

11

Sandra는 그날이 다가옴에 따라 점점 더 흥분했다.
Sandra grew ________ ________ ________ excited as the day drew closer.

12

이 디지털 카메라는 네 것보다 두 배 더 비싸다.
This digital camera is ________ ________ ________ ________ yours.

13

그는 세계에서 가장 재능 있는 배우 중 한 명이다.
He is one of ________ ________ ________ ________ in the world.

[14-15] 다음 문장의 빈칸에 들어갈 수 없는 말을 고르시오.

14

Kelly eats ________ faster than Nancy.

① even ② much ③ far
④ very ⑤ a lot

15

I think Davis is the most ________ person in the team.

① big ② popular
③ intelligent ④ hardworking
⑤ important

[16-17] 다음 문장의 빈칸에 알맞은 말을 고르시오.

16

February is ________ month of the year.

① shorter ② shortest
③ the shortest ④ more short
⑤ the most short

17

It was the funniest story I'd ________ heard.

① so ② already ③ well
④ ever ⑤ much

[18-20] 다음 중 밑줄 친 부분이 어법상 틀린 것을 고르시오.

18

① A plane is a lot faster than a bus.
② The man is two times old than I am.
③ My puppy is getting bigger and bigger.
④ Summer is the best season for swimming.
⑤ The seller wanted to close the deal as soon as possible. 교육청 기출 응용

19

① Stay here as quietly as you can.
② This is the tallest tree I've ever seen.
③ Jim is brave than any other boy.
④ A fox is not as large as a wolf.
⑤ Many stars in the universe are thousands of times as hot as the sun. 교육청 기출 응용

20

① The presentation went better than expected. 수능 기출
② We'll leave for Boston as early as possible.
③ I am the youngest employee in my department.
④ It was one of the most exciting movies I've ever seen.
⑤ You can keep the books as longest as you want with no late fee. 교육청 기출

[21-22] 다음 글의 빈칸 (A), (B)에 적절한 것끼리 짝지어진 것을 고르시오.

21

Of the four Korean national parks, Bukhansan was ____(A)____ place to visit. In 2004, there were ____(B)____ as many visitors to Bukhansan as there were to Jirisan. 평가원 기출 응용

	(A)	(B)
①	the most popular	twice
②	more popular	twice
③	the most popular	two
④	popular	twice
⑤	more popular	two

22

The more knowledge we gain, ____(A)____ confusion we obtain to go along with it. The world is simpler in the dark ____(B)____ in the light of day. 평가원 기출 응용

	(A)	(B)
①	more	to
②	more	than
③	the more	as
④	the more	than
⑤	the most	as

[23-24] 다음 글의 밑줄 친 부분 중 어법상 바르지 못한 것을 고르시오.

23

The graph above shows rice exports by four major exporters in 2012 and 2013. ① No other country exported more rice than India in 2012. In both years, Pakistan exported ② the smallest amount of rice of the four countries. In 2012, the amount of rice exported by India was about ③ three times as larger as that exported by Pakistan. In 2013, Thailand exported almost the same amount of rice ④ as Vietnam. 교육청 기출 응용

24

The number of letters sent to Santa in France was ① the largest among the seven countries. And the number of letters sent to Santa in Spain was ② the smallest among them. Great Britain collected ③ as many letters as Finland. The number of letters sent to Santa in Portugal was ④ more large than that of letters sent to Santa in Spain. 평가원 기출 응용

EST CHAPTER 14 2010

CHAPTER 14 전치사

POINT 01 ★★★★

전치사의 쓰임

정답 및 해설 p.26

- 전치사는 목적어(명사(구), 대명사(목적격), 명사절)와 함께 전치사구를 이루어 문장 내에서 형용사나 부사의 역할을 한다.
  - 형용사 역할: 명사를 뒤에서 수식하거나 보어로 쓰인다.
    I got a postcard **from Paris**.　　Sally is **in big trouble**.
  - 부사 역할: 동사, 형용사, 부사, 문장 전체를 수식한다.
    The runner won the race **with ease**.　　I'm good **at all kinds of sports**.
    In short, he betrayed me.

cf. 전치사구가 두 개 이상 연속으로 올 때는 〈장소+방법+시간〉 또는 〈작은 단위+큰 단위〉의 순서로 쓴다.
I'm going **to Jeju by plane on Saturday**.

A 다음 괄호 안에서 알맞은 것을 고르시오.

1 My brother gave it to (my / me) for my birthday. 교육청 기출
2 Danny is fond of (read / reading) comic books.
3 His new apartment is close (my office / to my office).
4 (Instead / Instead of) running away, he walked toward the lion. 교육청 기출 응용
5 Environmental groups say wild animals are in (danger / dangerous).

B 다음 문장에서 전치사구를 찾아 동그라미 하고, 전치사구가 수식하는 말에 밑줄을 그으시오.

1 People who are happy with themselves can make others happy.
2 The plane finally arrived at midnight. 평가원 기출 응용
3 The first flight from Seattle will arrive soon.
4 The ceremony took place at the beginning of February.
5 Unfortunately, holes in socks were common in my family. 평가원 기출 응용
6 To my surprise, it turned out that he didn't commit the crime.

C 다음 우리말과 같은 뜻이 되도록 주어진 단어를 배열하여 문장을 완성하시오.

1 그 나무들의 잎들이 떨어지고 있다. (the, on, trees, the, leaves)
_______________ are falling.

2 David는 고등학교 2학년이다. (second, in, his, year, is)
David _______________ of high school.

3 내 관점으로는, 학생들은 교복을 입어야 한다. (of, from, point, view, my)
_______________, students should wear uniforms.

4 나는 내 고향 도시의 조용한 길에서 혼자 자전거를 타고 있었다. (in, quiet, on, road, a, hometown, my)
I was riding my bicycle alone _______________. 교육청 기출 응용

★ POINT **02** ★★★★

장소 · 방향의 전치사 I

정답 및 해설 p.26

• **장소 · 방향을 나타내는 전치사들의 종류는 다음과 같다.**

at ~에(서)	in ~(안)에	on ~(위)에	by[beside] ~ 옆에	next to ~ 옆에
over ~ 바로 위에	under ~ 바로 아래에	above ~보다 위에	below ~보다 아래에	off ~에서 떨어져서
in front of ~ 앞에	behind ~ 뒤에	around ~ 주위에	into ~ 안으로	out of ~ 밖으로
from ~로부터	to ~까지	toward(s) ~쪽으로	between 〈둘〉 ~ 사이에	among 〈셋 이상〉 ~ 사이에
up ~ 위로	down ~ 아래로	along ~을 따라서	across ~을 가로질러	through ~을 관통하여

A **다음 괄호 안에서 알맞은 것을 고르시오.**

1 Walk (along / up) the stairs to the third floor.
2 There were many people (into / in) the shop.
3 It takes two hours to get to the airport (to / from) here. 수능 기출 응용
4 He looked (around / behind) the restaurant for an empty table.
5 Do you know the distance (among / between) New York and Boston?
6 She picked up a milk carton and poured milk (into / from) the glass.

B **다음 우리말과 같은 뜻이 되도록 〈보기〉에서 알맞은 말을 골라 문장을 완성하시오.**

보기	at	under	on	behind	in front of	out of	by

1 너는 John 옆에 앉을 거니?
Are you going to sit __________ John?

2 나는 내 뒤에서 자전거를 타는 긴 머리의 남자를 발견했다.
I noticed a man with long hair riding __________ me. 교육청 기출 응용

3 알래스카의 얼어붙은 땅 아래에 석유 매장 층이 있다.
Deposits of oil lie __________ the frozen ground of Alaska. 교육청 기출 응용

4 잠시 벤치에 앉는 게 어때?
How about sitting __________ the bench for a while?

5 나는 플라자 호텔에 그를 마중 나갈 것이다.
I'm going to pick him up __________ the Plaza Hotel.

6 갑자기 그녀 앞의 주자가 바닥에 쓰러졌다.
Suddenly, the runner __________ her fell to the ground. 교육청 기출 응용

7 그 마술사는 그의 모자에서 토끼 한 마리를 꺼냈다.
The magician pulled a rabbit __________ his hat.

정답 및 해설 p.26

★ POINT 03 ★★★★

장소 · 방향의 전치사 II

• **at, in, on의 구별**

at	어떤 한 지점(출발지, 도착지 등)이나 비교적 좁은 장소를 나타낼 때 I turned right **at** the end of the street.
in	어떤 것의 내부나 비교적 넓은 장소(국가, 도시 등)를 나타낼 때 My father has lived **in** Chicago all his life.
on	어떤 곳에 접해 있는 것을 나타낼 때 There were a lot of cars **on** the road.

• **on, over, above의 구별**

on	어떤 것의 표면과 닿은 채로 위에 있음을 나타낼 때 He had a band-aid **on** his thumb.
over	어떤 것을 덮는 듯한 느낌으로 바로 위에 있음을 나타낼 때 (↔ under) Do you see the bridge **over** the river?
above	단순히 어떤 것보다 높은 위치에 있음을 나타낼 때 (↔ below) The town stands **above** the river.

A **다음 괄호 안에서 알맞은 것을 고르시오.**

1 Look at the posters (in / on) the wall.

2 A helicopter was circling far (at / above) the large ship.

3 There is light (at / in) the end of the tunnel. 평가원 기출 응용

4 We can see the stars twinkling (in / on) the sky.

5 Applicants must live (at / in) the state of Wisconsin. 교육청 기출 응용

6 A hot air balloon was flying (on / above) the mountain.

7 For more information, you can get a pamphlet (at / in) the reception desk. 교육청 기출

8 Some parents tell their kids to finish all the food (on / above) their plates. 교육청 기출 응용

B **다음 우리말과 같은 뜻이 되도록 괄호 안의 말을 이용하여 문장을 완성하시오.**

1 그녀는 머리 위의 폭신한 구름들을 보았다. (head)
She looked at the fluffy clouds __________ __________ __________.

2 그 천장에 있는 전등이 밝지 않다. (ceiling)
The light __________ __________ __________ is not bright.

3 그녀는 새를 그 새장 안에 넣었다. (cage)
She put the bird __________ __________ __________.

4 James는 그 역에서 여자 친구를 기다리고 있었다. (station)
James was waiting for his girlfriend __________ __________ __________.

★ POINT 04 ★★★★

시간의 전치사 I

정답 및 해설 p.26

• 시간을 나타내는 전치사들의 종류는 다음과 같다.

at 〈시점〉 ~에	in 〈기간〉 ~에, (지금부터) ~ 후에	on 〈특정한 날〉 ~에	before ~ 전에
after ~ 후에	within ~ 이내에	until[till] ~까지(계속)	by ~까지는
through 〈기간〉 ~ 동안 내내	since ~ 이래 (지금까지)	from ~부터	to ~까지
for ~ 동안	during ~ 동안, ~ 중에		

A 다음 괄호 안에서 알맞은 것을 고르시오.

1 The shopping mall closes (at / for) 8 p.m.

2 (After / Within) the operation, his health improved.

3 The hot weather continued (at / through) the summer.

4 The product will be delivered (from / within) 24 hours.

5 You should pay me back (by / for) next Wednesday.

6 My dog hasn't eaten anything (since / until) last night.

7 Can we put off the meeting (since / until) tomorrow?

8 I'm going to stay in Paris (for / until) three weeks.

B 다음 우리말과 같은 뜻이 되도록 〈보기〉에서 알맞은 말을 골라 문장을 완성하시오.

보기 in before until after since from during

1 산업 혁명 기간 중에, 사람들은 공장에서 일주일에 80시간이 넘게 일했다.
__________ the Industrial Revolution, people worked for more than 80 hours a week in factories. 교육청 기출 응용

2 몇 분 후에 내가 다시 전화할게.
I'll call you back __________ a few minutes.

3 그 후로, 그녀는 베스트셀러 소설가가 되었다.
__________ then, she has become a best-selling novelist. 교육청 기출

4 아침 식사 후에 그 문제에 대해 이야기해 보자.
Let's talk about the issue __________ breakfast.

5 그 정원의 벌들은 초봄에서 가을까지 끊임없이 꿀을 생산한다.
The bees in the garden produce a constant supply of honey __________ early spring __________ autumn. 교육청 기출 응용

6 축제 2주 전에, Peter는 감기에 걸렸다.
Two weeks __________ the festival, Peter caught a cold. 수능 기출 응용

★ POINT 05 ★★★★

시간의 전치사 II

정답 및 해설 p.26

- **at, in, on / by, until / for, during의 구별**

at 〈+시각 · 시점〉	**at** 10 o'clock, **at** night, **at** the moment
in 〈+연도 · 계절 · 월 · 오전 · 오후 등 비교적 긴 시간〉	**in** 2020, **in** February, **in** the morning
on 〈+요일 · 날짜 · 특정한 날의 오전 또는 오후〉	**on** Saturday, **on** Thanksgiving Day
by 〈어느 시점까지 동작 완료〉	I have to finish my homework **by** Monday.
until 〈어느 시점까지 동작 · 상태 지속〉	We will stay here **until** the weekend.
for 〈+구체적인 시간 · 기간의 길이〉	My parents have been married **for** 30 years.
during 〈+행사 · 사건 등의 특정 기간〉	He lost his mother **during** the war.

A 다음 괄호 안에서 알맞은 것을 고르시오.

1 He feels cold (at / on) night. 수능 기출 응용
2 I started an online business (at / in) 2017.
3 This book fair will last (by, until) Wednesday.
4 My wife gave birth to a girl (in / on) January 10.
5 The air conditioner keeps us cool (for / during) hot summer days. 교육청 기출 응용
6 Will you keep an eye on my bag (for / during) a minute? 평가원 기출 응용
7 They hope to build the new stadium (by / until) next May.

B 다음 우리말과 같은 뜻이 되도록 문장을 완성하시오.

1 나는 자정에 누군가가 노래 부르는 걸 들었다.
I heard someone singing ________ ________.

2 Paul은 1946년까지 아버지를 만나지 못했다.
Paul did not meet his father ________ ________. 평가원 기출 응용

3 너 오후에 계획이 있니?
Do you have any plans ________ ________ ________?

4 우리는 금요일에 저녁을 먹으러 나갈 것이다.
We will go out for dinner ________ ________. 교육청 기출 응용

5 의사는 그에게 일주일 동안 쉬라고 충고했다.
The doctor advised him to rest ________ ________ ________.

6 독후감은 이달 말까지 이메일로 제출되어야 합니다.
Book reviews should be submitted by e-mail ________ ________ ________ of this month. 교육청 기출 응용

★ POINT 06 ★★★★

원인 · 목적의 전치사

정답 및 해설 p.26

• **원인 · 이유의 전치사**

at 〈감정의 원인〉 ~으로, ~을 알고[보고, 듣고]	I was disappointed **at** his lie.
for ~한 이유로, ~ 때문에	I'm angry with her **for** what she did yesterday.
from ~에서, ~ 때문에	He felt sore **from** exercising too much.
with 〈질병 · 감정의 원인〉 ~으로, ~ 때문에	My uncle is sick **with** lung cancer.
of 〈질병 · 기아 등〉 ~으로, ~ 때문에	He died **of** a heart attack.

• **목적의 전치사**

for ~을 위해서	I made a birthday cake **for** my sister.
on ~의 용건으로, ~차	We went **on** a field trip to the National Museum.

A **다음 괄호 안에서 알맞은 것을 고르시오.**

1 We are tired (at / of) your complaining.

2 We were shocked (at / of) his sudden death.

3 I feel sick (at / from) eating too much dessert.

4 He was absent from school (on / with) a cold.

5 Peter came to see you (at / on) urgent business.

6 She has been suffering (for / from) a pain in her chest.

7 The profits from the event will be used (with / for) cancer research. 평가원 기출 응용

8 Thank you (for / of) agreeing to play the music at my daughter's wedding. 교육청 기출

B **다음 우리말과 같은 뜻이 되도록 〈보기〉에서 알맞은 말을 골라 문장을 완성하시오.**

보기 at for of on with

1 당신은 여기 멕시코에 사업차 오셨나요?
Are you here in Mexico __________ business?

2 나는 오늘 밤 기말고사를 위해 공부해야 한다.
I have to study __________ my final exams tonight. 수능 기출

3 세계 도처에서 매일 사람들이 굶주림으로 죽는다.
All over the world, people die __________ hunger every day.

4 우리는 사태의 갑작스러운 전환에 놀랐다.
We were surprised __________ the sudden turn of events.

5 우리 모두 그녀의 사망 소식에 슬퍼서 울었다.
We all wept __________ sorrow at the news of her death.

POINT 07 ★★★★

수단 · 도구의 전치사

정답 및 해설 p.26

• **수단 · 도구를 나타내는 전치사들의 종류는 다음과 같다.**

with ~을 가지고 〈도구〉	Cut the melon in half **with** a knife.
without ~ 없이	I can't see anything **without** my glasses.
by ~(함)으로써, ~으로 〈교통 · 통신 수단〉	Contact me **by** e-mail or **(by)** cell phone.
in 〈+언어〉 ~으로	The report should be written **in** English.

A 다음 각 문장의 빈칸에 알맞은 말을 〈보기〉에서 골라 쓰시오.

보기		
	in Spanish	by credit card
	with my headphones	by reviewing the last chapter
	without a pair of scissors	by phone or e-mail

1 You can't cut it ________________.

2 Let's begin the class ________________.

3 The book was originally written ________________.

4 I often listen to loud music ________________. 평가원 기출 응용

5 Please sign up for the camp by June 15 ________________. 교육청 기출

6 I had no cash with me, so I paid for the coat ________________.

B 다음 우리말과 같은 뜻이 되도록 문장을 완성하시오.

1 답안은 연필로 작성해야 합니다.
You should write your answers ________ ________ ________.

2 그의 가게는 차로 약 3시간 거리이다.
His shop is about three hours away ________ ________. 수능 기출 응용

3 나는 중국어로 이 단어를 어떻게 말하는지 모른다.
I don't know how to say this word ________ ________.

4 우리는 버스를 타고 대전에 갈 것이다.
We'll go to Daejeon ________ ________.

5 Hanna는 아무 설명 없이 여행 계획을 변경했다.
Hanna changed her travel plans ________ any ________.

6 아이들은 자기 부모의 말을 들음으로써 말하는 법을 배운다.
Children learn to talk ________ ________ ________ their parents.

7 아침을 거를 때, 당신은 연료 없이 달리려고 하는 자동차와 같다.
When you skip breakfast, you are like a car trying to run ________ ________. 교육청 기출

정답 및 해설 p.26

★ POINT 08 ★★★★

기타 전치사

• **관련 · 주제의 전치사**

about 〈일반적인 내용〉 ~에 대하여	I'd like to know more **about** you.
on 〈전문적인 내용〉 ~에 대하여	She gave a lecture **on** Shakespeare.
of ~에 대하여	This is a story **of** a young girl with a terminal illness.

• **찬반의 전치사**

for ~에 찬성하는	Are you **for** or **against** this plan?
against ~에 반대하는	

A **다음 괄호 안에서 알맞은 것을 고르시오.**

1 I worry (on / about) my father's health.
2 I'm sure Tina went (for / on) his proposal.
3 You can write a review (on / against) any type of book. 교육청 기출
4 A lot of people in my country are (about / against) the war.

B **다음 우리말과 같은 뜻이 되도록 문장을 완성하시오.**

1 그것은 상식에 어긋난다.
It goes __________ common sense. 평가원 기출
2 모든 학생들이 내 의견에 찬성했다.
All of the students went __________ my opinion.
3 남북 전쟁에 대한 이 책을 읽은 적이 있니?
Have you ever read this book __________ the Civil War?
4 그 고객은 우리의 서비스에 대해 불평하고 있다.
The customer is complaining __________ our service.

C **다음 각 문장의 빈칸에 알맞은 말을 〈보기〉에서 골라 쓰시오.**

보기 of on against for

1 Who will you vote ________in the upcoming general election?
2 Why are you ________ the policy?
3 Her description ________ the accident was not reliable.
4 I bought a textbook ________ modern Japanese history.

REVIEW TEST 14 ★

정답 및 해설 p.26

[1-5] 다음 우리말과 일치하도록 빈칸에 알맞은 말을 고르시오.

1

나는 여름에 종종 아이스크림을 먹는다.
I often eat ice cream ___________ the summer.

① at ② in ③ on
④ for ⑤ within

2

그는 그 아름다운 강을 따라 운전했다.
He drove ___________ the beautiful river.

① across ② through
③ around ④ along
⑤ from

3

Donna는 세 달째 영어를 배우고 있다.
Donna has been learning English ___________ three months.

① in ② for
③ during ④ through
⑤ since

4

Sally의 아버지는 그녀의 미니스커트를 보고 놀랐다.
Sally's father was surprised ___________ her miniskirt.

① at ② for ③ on
④ from ⑤ with

5

너는 그 책들을 내일까지 반납해야 한다.
You should return the books ___________ tomorrow.

① to ② by ③ till
④ since ⑤ through

[6-8] 다음 두 문장의 빈칸에 공통으로 들어갈 말을 고르시오.

6

- I'm going to check out ___________ noon.
- Did you have a good time ___________ the party?

① in ② at ③ on
④ from ⑤ for

7

- He is an expert ___________ North Korean issues.
- Would you pass me the cup ___________ the table?

① of ② in ③ on
④ about ⑤ under

8

- We are all ___________ his proposal.
- Tom was punished ___________ cheating on the exam.

① at ② with ③ from
④ for ⑤ against

[9-12] 다음 우리말과 일치하도록 빈칸에 알맞은 전치사를 쓰시오.

9

그는 Mary와 Amy 사이에 앉게 되어 기뻤다.
He was happy to sit __________ Mary and Amy.

10

나는 내가 그것을 5월 6일에 주문한 것을 기억한다.
I remember I ordered it ________ May 6th.

11

그녀는 문 뒤에 누군가가 숨어있다는 것을 몰랐다.
She didn't know someone was hiding ________ the door.

12

Sandra는 이번 달 말까지 집에 없을 것이다.
Sandra won't be at home __________ the end of this month.

[13-16] 다음 문장의 빈칸에 알맞은 것을 고르시오.

13

She broke the lock __________ a knife.

① in ② for ③ from
④ to ⑤ with

14

We'll visit Hong Kong _________ the Christmas holiday.

① in ② within ③ from
④ during ⑤ since

15

I went to my grandmother's house __________ train.

① in ② for ③ by
④ at ⑤ to

16

You can stay in the room __________ tomorrow afternoon.

① by ② to ③ during
④ until ⑤ since

[17-19] 다음 중 밑줄 친 부분이 어법상 틀린 것을 고르시오.

17

① An airplane is flying below the clouds.
② What is that black thing under the desk?
③ The new railroad passes through our town.
④ I don't know why they are against his plan.
⑤ He said he hoped to arrive there until nine.

18

① With the noise, I couldn't concentrate.
② He goes to Singapore at business twice a year.
③ I'm thinking of buying a new watch. 교육청 기출 응용
④ How about taking a walk after lunch?
⑤ It was evening when I landed in Malaysia. 교육청 기출 응용

19

① The event will last for an hour. 교육청 기출 응용
② Our center is open Monday through Friday. 평가원 기출
③ There's a lot of traffic in Saturdays. 평가원 기출 응용
④ The books will be shipped within two days.
⑤ I don't want to make a mistake in front of people. 평가원 기출

20 다음 글의 (A), (B), (C)에서 각각 알맞은 것을 고르시오.

Two days later (A) (at / in) dawn I heard the lookout shout, "Land!" Everyone who was well enough to stand crowded on deck. (B) (Along / Through) the gray mist we saw it; a dark outline (C) (among / between) sea and sky. 수능 기출 응용

[21-23] 다음 글의 밑줄 친 부분 중 어법상 바르지 못한 것을 고르시오.

21

A: Hey, Danny. How are you?
B: I'm fine, but a little confused. I'm ① in the library, but none of our group members are here.
A: What? We're not meeting ② until Thursday.
B: Really? I thought we were supposed to meet here ③ on 12:30 this afternoon.
A: We were going to, but we changed the date because we needed more time ④ for individual work. 수능 기출 응용

22

*① On early 19th century London, a young man named Charles Dickens had a strong desire to be a writer. But everything seemed to be ② against him. He had so little confidence in his ability to write that he mailed his writings secretly ③ at night to editors so that nobody would laugh ④ at him. Story ⑤ after story was refused. 교육청 기출 응용

23

Theodore Taylor, born ① in North Carolina ② on 1921, was the author of more than 50 books ③ for young adult readers. At age 13 he wrote a column ④ on high school sports ⑤ for a local newspaper. 평가원 기출 응용

[24-25] 다음 글의 빈칸 (A), (B)에 적절한 것끼리 짝지어진 것을 고르시오.

24

Dice are small cubes. Each side has a different number of dots ___(A)___ it, ranging from one to six. In the past, people used them ___(B)___ fortunetelling, not for games. 수능 기출 응용

	(A)	(B)
①	on	of
②	over	in
③	in	in
④	over	for
⑤	on	for

25

A dilemma tale is an African story form that ends with a question. The question asks the listeners to choose ___(A)___ several alternatives. By encouraging active discussion, a dilemma tale invites its audience to think ___(B)___ right and wrong. 평가원 기출

	(A)	(B)
①	among	for
②	among	about
③	in	on
④	in	about
⑤	for	on

EST CHAPTER 2010

15

일치 · 화법

POINT 01 ★★★★

수의 일치 I

정답 및 해설 p.27

- **수에 유의해야 할 명사 · 대명사**
  - each, every ~, -thing, -body, -one은 단수 취급한다. LINK p.140-141 부정대명사
  - 학문 · 학과명이나 병명은 -s로 끝나도 단수 취급한다. LINK p.135 주의해야 하는 명사
  - 〈the+형용사〉는 '~한 사람들'이라는 뜻으로 복수 취급한다.

  Somebody is waiting for you outside.
  Physics is the subject that I like most.
  The wounded were sent to a hospital.

- **접속사로 연결되어 하나의 주어를 이루는 경우**
  - 〈both A and B〉는 복수형 동사를 취한다. LINK p.97 상관접속사
  - 〈either A or B〉, 〈neither A nor B〉, 〈not only A but also B(= B as well as A)〉는 B에 동사의 수를 일치시킨다.

  Both Simon and I love playing tennis. **Neither my sister nor I** am shy.
  The coach, as well as the players, is ready.

A 다음 괄호 안에서 알맞은 것을 고르시오.

1 The homeless (is / are) in need of help.
2 (Is / Are) there anything we can do? 수능 기출
3 Each of us (needs / need) people in our lives who encourage us. 교육청 기출
4 Mathematics (was / were) one of my favorite subjects in high school.

B 다음 문장에서 어법상 틀린 부분을 고쳐 쓰시오.

1 Either he or you needs to fix it.
2 Betty as well as I live near the school.
3 It was a small accident and nobody were hurt. 평가원 기출 응용
4 Diabetes are the fastest growing disease in the world.

C 다음 우리말과 같은 뜻이 되도록 괄호 안의 말을 이용하여 문장을 완성하시오.

1 나는 누군가가 거리를 따라 오고 있는지를 보려고 뒤를 힐끗 보았다. (come)
I glanced behind me to see if ________ ________ ________ down the street. 교육청 기출

2 Sally뿐 아니라 나도 농구 선수이다. (be)
________ ________ Sally ________ ________ I ________ a basketball player.

3 모두에게 행복할 만한 일이 있다. (have)
Everyone ________ something to be happy about. 교육청 기출

4 Roy와 Jenny 둘 다 출판사에서 일한다. (work)
________ Roy ________ Jenny ________ for a publishing company.

POINT 02 ★★★★

수의 일치 II

정답 및 해설 p.27

- ★ EXAM TIP 주어가 긴 경우
  - 동명사구가 주어일 때는 단수 취급한다.
  - 형용사구나 형용사절이 주어를 수식할 때는 수식 받는 주어에 동사의 수를 일치시킨다.

  Reading comic books is my hobby.

  The pine trees *on the hill* are large.

  The man *to whom you should talk* is Eric Stone.

- 부분 · 수량을 나타내는 어구가 붙는 경우
  - 〈a number of+복수명사〉는 '많은 ~'이라는 뜻으로 복수 취급한다.
  - 〈all[most, half, some, the rest, 분수] of+명사〉는 뒤에 오는 명사의 수에 동사의 수를 일치시킨다.

  A number of shops are not going to be open tomorrow.

  Most of my money is spent on clothes and shoes.

  cf. 〈the number of+복수명사〉는 '~의 수'라는 뜻으로 단수 취급한다.

  The number of students is decreasing each year.

A 다음 괄호 안에서 알맞은 것을 고르시오.

1 The earrings on the desk (is / are) mine.

2 All of the furniture (is / are) in great condition.

3 I don't know where the rest of my money (is / are).

4 Most of his landscapes (was / were) done in shades of black. 교육청 기출

5 Eating breakfast (is / are) important for your health.

6 The blanket with flower patterns (looks / look) nice. 교육청 기출

7 A number of people (was / were) gathering around the famous singer.

B 다음 우리말과 같은 뜻이 되도록 괄호 안의 말을 이용하여 문장을 완성하시오.

1 게임을 하는 것이 아이들에게 항상 나쁜 것은 아니다. (play, be)

________ ________ ________ not always bad for kids.

2 참가자의 수는 20명으로 제한된다. (limit)

The number of participants ________ ________ ________ 20. 수능 기출

3 물을 제외하면 체중의 절반은 단백질이다. (half, be)

________ ________ your body's weight ________ protein, excluding water.

4 그 학생들 중 3분의 2가 아시아 국가 출신이다. (third, come)

________ ________ ________ the students ________ from Asian countries.

5 함께 아침 식사를 하는 가족들은 자주 친근한 대화를 한다. (eat, have)

________ ________ ________ breakfast together often ________ nice conversations. 평가원 기출 응용

★ POINT 03 ★★★★

시제 일치의 원칙

정답 및 해설 p.27

- **주절의 시제가 현재일 때, 종속절의 시제에는 제한이 없다.**

I think she **lived** a happy life. (나는 그녀가 행복한 삶을 **살았다고** 생각한다.)
I think she **lives** a happy life. (나는 그녀가 행복한 삶을 **산다고** 생각한다.)
I think she **will live** a happy life. (나는 그녀가 행복한 삶을 **살 거라고** 생각한다.)

- **주절의 시제가 과거일 때, 종속절에는 과거 또는 과거완료시제가 쓰인다.**

I thought she **had lived** a happy life. (나는 그녀가 행복한 삶을 **살았다고** 생각했다.)
I thought she **lived** a happy life. (나는 그녀가 행복한 삶을 **산다고** 생각했다.)
I thought she **would live** a happy life. (나는 그녀가 행복한 삶을 **살 거라고** 생각했다.)

A

다음 문장에서 주절의 시제를 과거로 바꿀 때 빈칸에 알맞은 말을 쓰시오.

1 She tells me that we will be able to use electricity that day. 교육청 기출 응용
→ She told me that ____________________.

2 Michael says that I have to do the job for him.
→ Michael said that I ____________________.

3 Does he realize what his family means to him?
→ Did he realize what his family ____________________?

4 Kate doesn't know that I have found a job.
→ Kate didn't know that I ____________________.

5 My parents are talking to the teacher who caught me cheating.
→ My parents were talking to the teacher who ____________________.

B

다음 우리말과 같은 뜻이 되도록 괄호 안의 말을 이용하여 문장을 완성하시오.

1 나는 버스에 지갑을 두고 내렸다는 걸 알았다. (find, leave)
I __________ I __________ __________ my wallet on the bus.

2 너는 그녀가 언제 돌아올지 아니? (know, return)
Do you __________ when she __________ __________?

3 나는 그가 왜 그 제안을 받아들였는지 이해가 안 된다. (understand, accept)
I __________ __________ why he __________ that offer.

4 나는 네가 역사학을 공부하고 싶어 하는 줄 알았어. (think, want)
I __________ __________ __________ __________ __________ history. 교육청 기출

5 우리 수학 선생님이 그 시험에 문제가 좀 있다고 말씀하셨다. (say, have)
Our math teacher __________ the test __________ some problems. 평가원 기출 응용

6 내 친구들은 모두 Jack이 꽤 매력적이라고 생각한다. (think, be)
All my friends __________ that Jack __________ quite attractive.

★ POINT 04 ★★★★

시제 일치의 예외

정답 및 해설 p.27

- **종속절이 현재에도 유효한 일반적 진리, 과학적 사실 등을 나타낼 때는 주절의 시제에 관계없이 종속절에 현재시제를 쓴다.**

  We learned that the earth **rotates** once a day.

  cf. 주절이 과거시제라도 직업, 나이, 특성, 현재 관습 등과 같이 현재에도 사실인 내용일 경우, 종속절의 시제로 현재와 과거시제 모두 쓸 수 있다.
  I heard that Max **gets[got]** up at five every morning.

- **종속절이 역사적 사실을 나타낼 때는 주절의 시제에 관계없이 종속절에 과거시제를 쓴다.**

  The teacher said that the Second World War **ended** in 1945.

A 다음 괄호 안에서 알맞은 것을 고르시오.

1 My five-year-old son learned that the sun (set / sets) in the west.

2 The teacher said that water (freezes / froze) at 0 degrees Celsius.

3 My brother didn't understand that one and two (makes / made) three.

4 Did you know that West and East Germany (are united / were united) in 1990?

5 Mr. Smith taught us that Mexico (gained / had gained) its independence in the early 1800s.

B 다음 우리말과 같은 뜻이 되도록 괄호 안의 말을 이용하여 문장을 완성하시오.

1 나는 그분이 칭찬이 항상 도움이 되는 건 아니라고 말씀하셨을 때 놀랐어. (helpful)
I was surprised when he said praise ________ ________ ________. 평가원 기출

2 너는 우림이 빠르게 사라지고 있다는 걸 알았니? (disappear)
Did you know that the rainforests ________ ________ rapidly?

3 지구가 태양 주위를 돈다는 걸 누가 발견했니? (move around)
Who discovered that the Earth ________ ________ ________ ________?

4 그들은 프랑스 혁명이 1789년에 일어났다는 것을 알고 있었다. (break out)
They knew that the French Revolution ________ ________ ________ ________.

5 너는 Tom이 Rebecca와 사귀고 있다는 얘기를 들었니? (go out with)
Did you hear that Tom ________ ________ ________ ________ Rebecca?

6 그는 매주 일요일에 그 양로원에서 일한다고 말했다. (work)
He said that he ________ at the nursing home every Sunday. 평가원 기출 응용

7 나는 John F. Kennedy가 미국의 35번째 대통령이었다는 것을 배웠다. (be)
I learned that John F. Kennedy ________ ________ ________ ________ of the United States.

★ POINT 05 ★★★★

평서문의 화법 전환

정답 및 해설 p.27

- **직접화법의 평서문을 간접화법으로 바꾸는 방법**

Tony said, "I am hungry."
→ Tony **said (that) he was hungry**.

① 전달동사 say는 그대로 쓰고, say to는 tell로 바꾼다.
② 쉼표(,)와 인용부호(" ")를 없애고, 인용문을 that절로 바꾼다.
③ that절의 인칭대명사를 전달자의 입장에 맞게 바꾼다.
④ that절의 시제를 전달동사의 시제에 일치시킨다.
⑤ 필요하다면 that절의 형용사나 부사 등을 전달하는 시점과 입장에 맞게 바꾼다.

cf. 화법 전환 시 바뀌는 대표적인 형용사 · 부사

- now → then, at the time
- this → that
- yesterday → the day before, the previous day
- here → there
- today → that day
- ago → before
- tomorrow → the next[following] day

A 다음 문장을 간접화법은 직접화법으로, 직접화법은 간접화법으로 바꿀 때 빈칸에 알맞은 말을 쓰시오.

1 The weather forecaster said, "It will be cloudy and rainy." 교육청 기출 응용
→ The weather forecaster said that ____________ cloudy and rainy.

2 He told her that he wanted to be on time. 평가원 기출 응용
→ He said to her, "____________ on time."

3 James said, "I have to study for the exam this week."
→ James said that ____________ for the exam ________.

4 My grandmother tells me that I should eat healthy food.
→ My grandmother says to me, "____________ healthy food."

B 다음 문장을 간접화법으로 바꾸어 쓰시오.

1 He said to me, "I feel better today."
→ He told me ________________________.

2 Jill said to me, "I would like to eat pizza."
→ Jill told me ________________________.

3 David told me, "I hung out with my friends here."
→ David told me________________________.

4 The actress said, "I will participate in a volunteer program for the blind." 교육청 기출 응용
→ The actress said________________________.

5 Mike said, "I bought this book yesterday."
→ Mike said ________________________. 수능 기출 응용

★ POINT 06 ★★★★

의문문 · 명령문의 화법 전환

정답 및 해설 p.28

- **직접화법의 의문문을 간접화법으로 바꾸는 방법**
  - **의문사가 있는 의문문: 전달동사를 ask 등으로 바꾸고, 인용문은 〈의문사+주어+동사〉의 순서로 쓴다.**

    He said to me, "Where do you live?" → He **asked** me **where I lived**.
  - **의문사가 없는 의문문: 전달동사를 ask 등으로 바꾸고, 인용문은 〈if[whether]+주어+동사〉의 순서로 쓴다.**

    Amy said, "Are you busy?" → Amy **asked if[whether] I was busy**.
- **직접화법의 명령문을 간접화법으로 바꾸는 방법**
  - **전달동사를 tell, order, advise, ask 등으로 바꾸고, 인용문의 동사를 to부정사로 바꾼다.**

    I said to my son, "Go to bed early." → I **told** my son **to go** to bed early.

cf. 부정 명령문은 to부정사 앞에 not을 쓴다.

A 다음 우리말과 같은 뜻이 되도록 어법상 틀린 부분을 고쳐 쓰시오.

1 Amy는 여동생에게 몇 시냐고 물었다.
Amy asked her sister what time was it.

2 나는 그에게 그 책을 읽어 본 적이 있냐고 물었다.
I asked him if he has read the book.

3 그녀에게 그것에 대해 걱정하지 말라고 말해 줘.
Please tell her don't worry about it. 교육청 기출

B 다음 문장을 괄호 안의 동사를 이용하여 간접화법으로 바꾸어 쓰시오.

1 Margo said to him, "Stop smoking." (order) 수능 기출 응용
→ ____________________

2 I said to Grandfather, "What are you looking at?" (ask) 교육청 기출
→ ____________________

3 He said to me, "Don't play the violin after 7 p.m." (tell) 수능 기출 응용
→ ____________________

4 I say to my son, "Treat older people with respect." (tell)
→ ____________________

5 She asked me, "Have you been to New York?" (ask)
→ ____________________

6 My teacher said to me, "Finish the book by tomorrow." (tell)
→ ____________________

7 Susan said to me, "Who lent you the camera?" (ask)
→ ____________________

REVIEW TEST 15 ★

정답 및 해설 p.28

[1-4] 다음 두 문장의 빈칸에 들어갈 말이 순서대로 바르게 짝지어진 것을 고르시오.

1

• Most of the survivors ________ children.
• Each of them ________ something to do.

① was - has ② were - have
③ was - is ④ were - has
⑤ were - are

2

• Every student ________ wearing a hat.
• Mathematics ________ the most difficult subject for me.

① were - are ② was - is
③ were - is ④ was - are
⑤ has - is

3

• Both Jerry and Sally ________ quite shy.
• Speaking ill of others ________ bad.

① are - is ② are - are ③ is - is
④ is - are ⑤ are - were

4

• Not only you but also he ________ my close friend.
• A number of balloons ________ rising into the sky.

① are - is ② are - are ③ is - is
④ is - are ⑤ are - were

[5-8] 다음 우리말과 일치하도록 빈칸에 알맞은 말을 고르시오.

5

나는 Steven이 승진할 것을 알았다.
I knew that Steven ________ promoted.

① is ② was ③ will be
④ had been ⑤ would be

6

Sylvia는 나에게 그녀를 도와줄 수 있는지 물었다.
Sylvia asked me ________ I could help her.

① how ② why ③ that
④ what ⑤ whether

7

그녀는 남동생에게 그의 지저분한 차를 닦으라고 말했다.
She told her brother ________ his dirty car.

① clean ② cleaning
③ cleaned ④ to clean
⑤ being cleaned

8

나는 Jeff가 탁자 위의 꽃병을 깨뜨린 걸 안다.
I know that Jeff ________ the vase on the table.

① break ② breaks
③ broke ④ breaking
⑤ will break

[9-12] 다음 두 문장의 뜻이 같도록 문장을 완성하시오.

9

I said to him, "What did you have for lunch?"
= I asked him ______________________.

10

Nancy said, "I don't know what to do."
= Nancy said that ____________________.

11

Her friend said to her, "Don't eat too much chocolate."
= Her friend advised her ______________
______________________.

12

He said to me, "Are you single?"
= He asked me ______________________.

[13-17] 다음 우리말과 일치하도록 괄호 안의 말을 이용하여 문장을 완성하시오.

13

실직자들은 가능한 한 빨리 새로운 직장을 얻길 원한다. (want)
The unemployed __________ to get a new job as soon as possible.

14

나는 그가 10년 동안 그 회사에서 일했었다고 들었다. (work)
I heard that he __________ __________ for the company for 10 years.

15

네 정원에 있는 꽃들이 아름답다. (be)
The flowers in your garden __________ beautiful.

16

내 여동생뿐 아니라 나도 브라질에 가 봤다. (be)
I as well as my sister __________
__________ to Brazil.

17

Donna는 내게 집을 페인트칠해 본 적이 있느냐고 물었다. (paint)
Donna asked me __________ __________
__________ ever __________ a house.

[18-21] 다음 중 밑줄 친 부분이 어법상 틀린 것을 고르시오.

18

① I heard that he would move to Toronto.
② Chris goes to church every Sunday with his brother.
③ A number of soldiers were wounded in the war.
④ A woman asked me where the nearest bus stop was.
⑤ The man who is carrying two bags are very kind.

19

① Most of the birds were black.

② Both Linda and Paul like to play chess.

③ I told him to be more polite to me.

④ I heard that the criminal had been arrested.

⑤ The documentary said humans first take on the moon in 1969.

20

① I asked how much it was.

② I didn't know you liked hiking. 교육청 기출

③ This picture of mountains looks great. 교육청 기출 응용

④ The commander told his men to be careful.

⑤ Most of the things that could improve the situation was out of our control. 교육청 기출 응용

21

① Either he or you are wrong.

② He asked me if I missed him.

③ Each of its ears is a different size. 교육청 기출

④ Talking to my friends make me feel better.

⑤ I could not tell what kind of bird it was. 교육청 기출

22 다음 글의 (A), (B), (C)에서 각각 알맞은 것을 고르시오.

Tom received a call. The caller (A) (said / told) him that he had won a free night's stay at a hotel. All he needed to do was pay the tax. The caller asked him (B) (giving / to give) a credit card number. So he gave his credit card number to the caller. Later, he found that the hotel (C) (has / had) no plan to offer a free night's stay. 평가원 기출 응용

[23-24] 다음 글의 빈칸 (A), (B)에 적절한 것끼리 짝지은 것을 고르시오.

23

Later, the police realized that they ___(A)___ made a terrible mistake. Neither the man nor the woman ___(B)___ a thief. They were just French onion sellers. 평가원 기출 응용

	(A)	(B)
①	have	were
②	had	was
③	had	were
④	has	was
⑤	have	is

24

Eating delicious food together ___(A)___ the way we make relationships strong. Food is more than calories and nutrients for the body; it is something that ___(B)___ the soul rich as well. 평가원 기출 응용

	(A)	(B)
①	is	makes
②	is	make
③	are	make
④	are	makes
⑤	is	making

EST CHAPTER 2010

16

특수 구문

POINT 01 ★★★★

부정 표현

정답 및 해설 p.29

- 부사 hardly[scarcely, barely](거의 ~아닌)와 seldom[rarely](좀처럼 ~않는)은 부정의 의미를 포함하고 있으므로 not과 같은 부정어와 함께 쓰지 않는다.

  My father **rarely** expresses his emotions.

  ~~She couldn't **hardly** believe what she saw.~~

- 부분 부정: all, every, always 등이 not과 함께 쓰여 '모두[언제나] ~인 것은 아니다'라는 의미를 나타낸다. 이때 주로 〈not ~ all[every, always]〉의 어순으로 쓴다.

  Not all the money in the fund is used wisely.

- 전체 부정: no, none, neither, never 등은 '아무도[둘 다, 결코] ~않다'라는 의미를 나타낸다. LINK p.141 부정대명사

  No one was injured in the accident.

A

다음 〈보기〉에서 알맞은 말을 골라 대화를 완성하시오.

보기 every hardly nobody

1 A: That guy is waving at us. Is he a close friend?
B: No, I __________ know him.

2 A: I'm sorry I was absent again. I had a stomachache.
B: Stop lying. __________ believes you anymore.

3 A: Why don't you go play soccer with your friends, Sam?
B: Mom, I don't like playing soccer. Not __________ boy enjoys sports.

B

다음 우리말과 같은 뜻이 되도록 주어진 단어를 배열하여 문장을 완성하시오.

1 우리 아들이 항상 일찍 잠자리에 드는 건 아니다. (does, always, go, bed, to, not)
My son ________________________ early.

2 우리 둘 다 아직 결혼할 생각이 없다. (us, neither, wants, of)
________________________ to get married yet.

3 영어에서 문자들은 그 소리와 거의 일치하지 않는다. (match, their, seldom, sounds)
In English, letters ________________________. 평가원 기출 응용

C

다음 우리말과 같은 뜻이 되도록 문장을 완성하시오.

1 모든 학생들이 대학 교육비를 감당할 수 있는 것은 아니다.
__________ __________ __________ are able to afford a university education.

2 내 다른 옷가지 중 어느 것도 마르지 않았다.
__________ __________ my other clothing was dry. 교육청 기출

3 나는 그렇게 인상적인 연설을 전에 결코 들어본 적이 없다.
I __________ __________ __________ such an impressive speech before. 수능 기출 응용

POINT 02 ★★★★ 생략

정답 및 해설 p.29

- **문맥상 없어도 의미 파악이 가능한 부분이나 반복되는 부분은 생략되는 경우가 많다.**
  He is not as active as Nancy **(is)**.
  Jane gets up at six and **(Jane)** eats breakfast at seven.
  I didn't help him because he didn't ask me to **(help him)**.
- **접속사 when, while, if, though 등이 이끄는 부사절의 주어가 주절의 주어와 일치하는 경우, 부사절의 〈주어+be동사〉는 종종 생략된다.**
  I study best *when* **(I am)** at the library.

A 다음 문장에서 생략할 수 있는 부분을 괄호로 묶으시오.

1 Sue doesn't go out much, and Mina doesn't go out much either.
2 Sue is much more friendly than Julie is.
3 I'll go and I'll return these books right away. 수능 기출 응용
4 Though he was sad, he pretended to be cheerful. 평가원 기출 응용
5 My brother gave me a cap and gave my sister a pair of sneakers.
6 Productivity improvements are as important to the economy as they are important to the individual company. 교육청 기출 응용

B 다음 〈보기〉와 같이 문장에서 생략된 부분을 찾아 표시하고, 생략된 말을 쓰시오.

보기 그녀는 재즈 댄스보다 라틴 댄스를 좋아한다.
She prefers Latin^(dance) to Jazz dance.

1 Michael은 너보다 훨씬 똑똑하다.
Michael is a lot smarter than you.

2 나는 그가 내게 화가 나 있다고 생각했지만, 그렇지 않았다.
I thought he was angry at me, but he wasn't.

3 빨래를 할 때 세제를 추가하는 것을 잊지 마라.
While doing the laundry, don't forget to add some soap.

4 원한다면 소리를 키워라.
Turn up the volume if you want to.

5 나는 배가 고팠지만 오후 6시 이후에 아무것도 먹지 않았다.
Though hungry, I didn't eat anything after 6 p.m.

6 Anna는 Kate보다 기타를 잘 친다.
Anna plays the guitar better than Kate.

7 3D 인쇄의 비용은 낮아지고 있고, 품질은 좋아지고 있다.
The cost of 3D printing is getting lower and the quality better. 교육청 기출 응용

POINT 03

동격

정답 및 해설 p.29

- 명사 · 대명사의 의미를 보충하거나 다르게 바꾸어 말하기 위해서 뒤에 다른 명사(상당어구)나 명사절 등을 덧붙이는 경우가 있는데, 이 관계를 동격이라고 한다.

I like Emma, my sister's friend.

We hit on the idea of asking viewers to donate money.

The news that the president would visit France was announced.

The question of whether the Internet should be regulated is controversial.

A 다음 문장에서 밑줄 친 부분과 동격인 어구를 찾아 밑줄을 그으시오.

1 I heard the news that Mike and Susan are getting married.

2 Some people disagree with the idea of exposing young children to computers. 교육청 기출 응용

3 Some residents express concern that tourists cause traffic congestion. 수능 기출 응용

4 We are studying Neptune, the farthest known planet in our solar system.

5 The book is based on the belief that human beings are essentially selfish.

B 다음 〈보기〉에서 알맞은 말을 골라 빈칸을 채우시오.

보기			
	the problem	the claim	Abraham Lincoln
	the fact	my boss	the world-famous photographer

1 __________ that he lied to me made me upset.

2 Mr. Johnson, __________, is out of the office now.

3 I hope you are enjoying the exhibition of the works of Steve Kim, __________ __________. 교육청 기출

4 We greatly admire __________, the 16th president of America.

5 __________ that we have recently entered the Information Age is wrong. 수능 기출 응용

6 We'll discuss __________ of whether Tom is suitable for the position of manager.

C 다음 문장을 밑줄 친 부분에 유의하여 우리말로 해석하시오.

1 We live in Asia, the largest continent in the world.

2 She is excited at the thought of seeing Brian.

3 Sandy Brown, our swimming coach, retired last month. 교육청 기출 응용

4 Mike gave his opinion that watching TV a lot is bad for teens.

5 He wasn't discouraged by the fact that he had no experience.

6 Dublin, Ireland's capital city, has a population of 1.3 million.

★ POINT 04 ★★★★

도치 I

정답 및 해설 p.29

- **자동사가 쓰인 문장에서 장소의 부사구가 강조되어 문장 앞에 오는 경우, 〈부사구+동사+주어〉의 어순으로 쓴다.**

  Here **comes the bus**!
  V S

  Under the bed **lay my cat**.
  V S

- **so, neither가 앞 문장의 내용을 받아서 문장 앞에 오는 경우, 긍정문 뒤에는 〈so+동사+주어〉, 부정문 뒤에는 〈neither+동사+주어〉의 어순으로 쓰여 '~도 또한 그렇다[그렇지 않다]'라는 뜻을 나타낸다.**

  The food was terrible and *so* **was the service**. (= ~ the service was terrible, too.)
  V S

  I can't go further. — *Neither* **can I**. (= I can't go further, either.)
  V S

A

다음 문장을 부사구를 강조하여 바꿀 때 빈칸에 알맞은 말을 쓰시오.

1 Rows of delicious-looking chocolate bars were right in front of his eyes.
→ Right in front of his eyes ______________________________. 수능 기출

2 An old castle stands on the top of the hill.
→ On the top of the hill ______________________________.

3 A small box wrapped in gold paper lay on the table.
→ On the table ______________________________.

B

다음 대화에서 어법상 틀린 부분을 고쳐 쓰시오.

1 A: I'm still very sleepy. B: So do I.

2 A: I will go to the swimming pool today. B: So I will.

3 A: Kelly didn't do her homework at all. B: So did I.

C

다음 우리말과 같은 뜻이 되도록 so 또는 neither를 사용하여 문장을 완성하시오.

1 나는 요리를 못하는데 그도 그렇다.
I am not good at cooking, and ____________________.

2 Peter는 수영을 잘 못하는데 나도 그렇다.
Peter can't swim well, and ____________________. 평가원 기출 응용

3 Ted는 그 댄스 동아리에 가입할 거고 나도 그렇다.
Ted will join the dance club, and ____________________.

4 나는 노트북 컴퓨터를 사고 싶은데 내 여동생도 그렇다.
I want to buy a laptop, and ____________________. 수능 기출 응용

정답 및 해설 p.29

★ POINT 05 ★★★★

도치 II

- **부정의 뜻이 있는 말(not, never, little, hardly, seldom, rarely, only 등)가 강조되어 문장 앞에 오는 경우, 〈부정어+조동사+주어+본동사〉의 어순으로 쓴다. 일반동사의 경우 do동사가 대신 앞으로 나간다.**

Not only **is he** a great singer but he is also an amazing lawyer.
Never **have I heard** such a strange story.
Hardly **did she dream** that she would become a supermodel.

A 다음 문장을 부정어를 강조하여 바꿀 때 빈칸에 알맞은 말을 쓰시오.

1 Max could rarely meet Jennifer.
→ Rarely ______________________ Jennifer.

2 I never imagined that it would snow in April.
→ Never ______________________ that it would snow in April. 수능 기출 응용

3 She had seldom seen a child with so much talent.
→ Seldom ______________________ with so much talent.

B 다음 밑줄 친 부분을 어법에 맞게 고쳐 쓰시오.

1 Seldom visits John his parents.

2 Never has watched he such an interesting musical.

3 Only recently humans have created various languages and alphabets. 교육청 기출 응용

4 Little did I dreamed that my team would win the championship.

5 Hardly he could know that it would be his last chance to see her.

C 다음 우리말과 같은 뜻이 되도록 주어진 단어를 이용하여 문장을 완성하시오.

1 그들은 전에 캐나다에 가 본 적이 없다. (be)
Never ______________________ before.

2 그것은 비쌀 뿐만 아니라 전혀 불필요하다. (be)
Not only ______________________, but it is totally unnecessary.

3 나는 아침 후로 거의 쉬지 못했다. (have)
Hardly ______________________ any rest since morning.

4 그녀는 자기에게 가족이 얼마나 중요한지 거의 깨닫지 못했다. (realize)
Little ______________________ how important her family was to her.

5 나는 집에 도착하고서야 버스 정류장의 벤치에 지갑을 놓고 온 것을 깨달았다. (realize)
Not until I got home ______________________ that I had left my purse on the bench at the bus stop. 교육청 기출 응용

POINT 06 ★★★★

강조

정답 및 해설 p.29

- 문장의 내용이 사실임을 강조하기 위해 본동사 앞에 do동사를 써서 '(정말) ~하긴 하다'라는 뜻을 나타낸다.

  He **does like** wearing blue jeans.
  I **did make** a chocolate cake for you.

- 〈It is[was] ~ that ...〉 강조 구문: It is[was]와 that 사이에 강조하는 말을 두고 나머지를 that 이하에 써서 '…한 것은 바로 ~이다'라는 뜻을 나타낸다.

  (← My sister gave me this necklace.)
  It was this necklace **that** my sister gave me.
  It was my sister **that[who]** gave me this necklace.
  cf. 강조하는 말이 사람이면 that 대신 who를 쓰기도 한다.

A 다음 문장을 밑줄 친 부분을 강조하여 바꿀 때 빈칸에 알맞은 말을 쓰시오.

1 This spaghetti tastes good.
→ This spaghetti ________________.

2 However unnoticeably, maps reflect the world views of their makers. 수능 기출 응용
→ However unnoticeably, ________________ of their makers.

3 Julie looked depressed yesterday.
→ Julie ________________.

4 We're supposed to leave at 9 o'clock. 수능 기출 응용
→ It is ________________.

5 I met Sarah on the street by accident.
→ It was ________________.

6 Kate dropped by a store to buy a new skirt. 평가원 기출 응용
→ It was ________________.

B 다음 우리말과 같은 뜻이 되도록 주어진 단어를 배열하여 문장을 완성하시오.

1 Tom은 예의 없는 식사 태도를 가지고 있긴 하다. (bad, does, table manners, have)
Tom ________________.

2 내가 매일 저녁 산책을 하는 것은 바로 이 공원에서다. (that, take a walk, I, it, in this park, is)
________________ every evening.

3 Andrew가 큰 실수를 한 것은 바로 그때였다. (was, that, then, it, Andrew, a big mistake, made)
________________. 평가원 기출

4 어제 경찰차를 들이받은 것은 바로 Dean이었다. (Dean, the police car, was, who, it, crashed into)
________________ yesterday.

REVIEW TEST 16 ★

정답 및 해설 p.30

[1-5] 다음 우리말과 일치하도록 빈칸에 알맞은 말을 고르시오.

1

아무리 감사의 말씀을 드려도 부족할 것 같아요.
Never __________ you enough.

① I can thank ② I can't thank
③ can thank I ④ can I thank
⑤ can't I thank

2

나는 정말로 극장 앞에서 너를 기다렸다.
I __________ wait for you in front of the theater.

① am ② is ③ do
④ does ⑤ did

3

Robert는 개를 좋아하지 않고 나도 그렇다.
Robert doesn't like dogs, and __________.

① so am I ② so do I
③ neither will I ④ neither am I
⑤ neither do I

4

내가 Jessica와 함께 간 곳은 바로 Mark의 결혼식이었다.
It was Mark's wedding __________ I went to with Jessica.

① what ② when ③ that
④ who ⑤ which

5

숲 속에 오두막 한 채가 서 있었다.
In the woods __________.

① a cabin stood ② a cabin did stand
③ did a cabin stand ④ stood a cabin
⑤ a cabin stands

[6-10] 다음 우리말과 일치하도록 문장을 완성하시오.

6

항상 네가 하고 싶은 대로만 할 수는 없다.
You __________ __________ do as you like.

7

지하철역에서 내 가방을 훔친 것은 바로 이 남자였다.
__________ was this man __________ stole my bag in the subway station.

8

너는 Peter의 다리가 부러졌다는 소식을 들었니?
Did you hear the news __________ Peter broke his leg?

9

그 두 사람 중 누구도 시험 공부를 열심히 하지 않았다.
__________ of them studied hard for the exam.

10

그는 정말 의사의 진찰을 받아야 한다.
He __________ have to see a doctor.

[11-14] 다음 대화의 빈칸에 알맞은 말을 고르시오.

11

A: I'm not very hungry now.
B: ____________________

① So am I. ② So do I.
③ So I am. ④ Neither am I.
⑤ Neither do I.

12

A: Dan can run 100 meters in 12 seconds.
B: ____________________

① So can I. ② So do I.
③ So I can. ④ Neither can I.
⑤ Neither I can't.

13

A: I think David should be more careful.
B: ____________________

① So am I. ② So do I.
③ So I am. ④ Neither do I.
⑤ Neither I do.

14

A: You didn't finish the report, did you?
B: __________, but I forgot to submit it.

① I did finish it ② I finish it
③ I do finished it ④ did I finish it
⑤ do I finish it

[15-17] 다음 밑줄 친 부분을 강조하여 문장을 바꾸어 쓰시오.

15

I want to have a great sense of humor.
→ ________________________________

16

Jake showed me how to swim.
→ ________________________________

17

He continued only after some time.
→ ________________________________

[18-21] 다음 중 밑줄 친 부분이 어법상 틀린 것을 고르시오.

18

① Hardly ate she vegetables.
② None of my friends had a car.
③ It was in winter that I first met Dave.
④ Mr. Clinton, my teacher, is very generous.
⑤ I did promise her that I wouldn't be late again.

19

① Not all the windows were open.
② Will you help me if you can?
③ Scarcely could I see anything.
④ Jim, one of my best friends, is very smart.
⑤ It was an earring what I lost at the mall.

20

① He is not always polite.
② Into the office came my boss.
③ Though rich, she is unhappy.
④ Little did I imagine I would win the lottery.
⑤ Your guess which Betty is from Canada is wrong.

21

① It was Sarah who asked for help.
② Along the street a little girl walked.
③ When faced with a problem, we instinctively seek to find a solution. 교육청 기출 응용
④ Is there any chance that we will get a seat?
⑤ None of the participants were aware of the purpose of the experiment.

22 다음 문장 중 어법상 옳은 것은?

① I hate the idea that going to the dentist.
② There some dark clouds were in the sky.
③ I did felt sorry for what happened to him.
④ Rarely have I a chance to work with such a celebrity.
⑤ Not all residents attribute environmental damage to tourism. 수능 기출

[23-24] 다음 글의 빈칸 (A), (B)에 적절한 것끼리 짝지어진 것을 고르시오.

23

Claudius made a rule ___(A)___ no young man could marry until he had served a certain number of years in the army. It was a priest, Valentine, ___(B)___ broke the rule and performed secret marriages for many young couples. 평가원 기출 응용

	(A)	(B)
①	of	that
②	that	which
③	that	who
④	which	who
⑤	of	when

24

At one of the tables in a restaurant ___(A)___ in a stroller. Her mother is feeding her from a jar of baby food. Not only ___(B)___ interested in her food, but she is also interested in everything else that is going on. 평가원 기출 응용

	(A)	(B)
①	are a baby	is the baby
②	is a baby	does the baby
③	a baby is	the baby is
④	is a baby	is the baby
⑤	a baby is	does the baby

지은이

NE능률 영어교육연구소

NE능률 영어교육연구소는 혁신적이며 효율적인 영어 교재를 개발하고 영어 학습의 질을 한 단계 높이고자 노력하는 NE능률의 연구조직입니다.

문제로 마스터하는 고등영문법

펴 낸 이 주민홍
펴 낸 곳 서울특별시 마포구 월드컵북로 396(상암동) 누리꿈스퀘어 비즈니스타워 10층
(주)NE능률 (우편번호 03925)
펴 낸 날 2017년 9월 15일 개정판 제1쇄
2024년 5월 15일 제23쇄
전 화 02 2014 7114
팩 스 02 3142 0356
홈페이지 www.neungyule.com
등록번호 제 1-68호
I S B N 979-11-253-1726-5 53740
정 가 12,000원

NE 능률

고객센터

교재 내용 문의 : contact.nebooks.co.kr (별도의 가입 절차 없이 작성 가능)
제품 구매, 교환, 불량, 반품 문의 : 02-2014-7114
☎ 전화문의는 본사 업무시간 중에만 가능합니다.

NE능률 교재 MAP

문법 구문

아래 교재 MAP을 참고하여 본인의 현재 혹은 목표 수준에 따라 교재를 선택하세요.
NE능률 교재들과 함께 영어실력을 쑥쑥~ 올려보세요!
MP3 등 교재 부가 학습 서비스 및 자세한 교재 정보는 www.nebooks.co.kr 에서 확인하세요.

초1-2

초3
- 그래머버디 1
- 초등영어 문법이 된다 Starter 1

초3-4
- 그래머버디 2
- 초등영어 문법이 된다 Starter 2
- 초등 Grammar Inside 1
- 초등 Grammar Inside 2

초4-5
- 그래머버디 3
- Grammar Bean 1
- Grammar Bean 2
- 초등영어 문법이 된다 1
- 초등 Grammar Inside 3
- 초등 Grammar Inside 4

초5-6
- Grammar Bean 3
- Grammar Bean 4
- 초등영어 문법이 된다 2
- 초등 Grammar Inside 5
- 초등 Grammar Inside 6

초6-예비중
- 능률중학영어 예비중
- Grammar Inside Starter
- 원리를 더한 영문법 STARTER

중1
- 능률중학영어 중1
- Grammar Zone 입문편
- Grammar Zone 워크북 입문편
- 1316 Grammar 1
- 문제로 마스터하는 중학영문법 1
- Grammar Inside 1
- 열중 16강 문법 1
- 쓰기로 마스터하는 중학서술형 1학년
- 중학 천문장 1

중1-2
- 능률중학영어 중2
- 1316 Grammar 2
- 문제로 마스터하는 중학영문법 2
- Grammar Inside 2
- 열중 16강 문법 2
- 원리를 더한 영문법 1
- 중학영문법 총정리 모의고사 1
- 중학 천문장 2

중2-3
- Grammar Zone 기초편
- Grammar Zone 워크북 기초편
- 1316 Grammar 3
- 원리를 더한 영문법 2
- 중학영문법 총정리 모의고사 2
- 쓰기로 마스터하는 중학서술형 2학년
- 중학 천문장 3

중3
- 능률중학영어 중3
- 문제로 마스터하는 중학영문법 3
- Grammar Inside 3
- 열중 16강 문법 3
- 중학영문법 총정리 모의고사 3
- 쓰기로 마스터하는 중학서술형 3학년

예비고–고1
- 문제로 마스터하는 고등영문법
- 올클 수능 어법 start
- 천문장 입문

고1
- Grammar Zone 기본편 1
- Grammar Zone 워크북 기본편 1
- Grammar Zone 기본편 2
- Grammar Zone 워크북 기본편 2
- 필히 통하는 고등 영문법 기본편
- 필히 통하는 고등 서술형 기본편
- 천문장 기본

고1-2
- 필히 통하는 고등 영문법 실력편
- 필히 통하는 고등 서술형 실전편
- TEPS BY STEP G+R Basic

고2-3
- Grammar Zone 종합편
- Grammar Zone 워크북 종합편
- 올클 수능 어법 완성
- 천문장 완성

고3

수능 이상/ 토플 80-89 · 텝스 600-699점
- TEPS BY STEP G+R 1

수능 이상/ 토플 90-99 · 텝스 700-799점
- TEPS BY STEP G+R 2

수능 이상/ 토플 100 · 텝스 800점 이상
- TEPS BY STEP G+R 3

고등학생을 위한 문법 연습의 길잡이

문제로 마스터하는 고등영문법

MASTER

정답 및 해설

NE 능률

고등학생을 위한 문법 연습의 길잡이

문제로 미스터하는 고등영문법

MASTER

정답 및 해설

CHAPTER 01

문장의 이해

★ POINT 01 구와 절 p.10

A **1** 구 **2** 절 **3** 절 **4** 절 **5** 구 **6** 절 **7** 구

B **1** 형용사구 **2** 명사구 **3** 명사구
4 형용사구 **5** 부사구

C **1** 명사절 **2** 명사절 **3** 부사절
4 형용사절 **5** 부사절

★ POINT 02 문장의 종류 p.11

A **1** the movie starts → does the movie start
2 did he → didn't he
3 finish you → you finish
4 Not waste → Don't waste
5 Do → Be **6** is → isn't

B **1** inspiring the lecture was
2 a pretty girl she is
3 lovely those flowers are

★ POINT 03 1형식 문장 (S+V) p.12

A **1** We (S) stayed (V) **2** She (S) waited (V)
3 We (S) walked (V) **4** They (S) are (V)
5 The lion (S) recovered (V)
6 Linda (S) lives (V) **7** is (V) a small park (S)

B **1** His room is just above mine.
2 Her dog died last month.
3 There are many cars on the road.
4 They will be here for three days.
5 David and I talked for hours.
6 The pilates lesson starts at seven in the evening.

★ POINT 04 2형식 문장 (S+V+C) p.13

A **1** deep **2** a photographer **3** a mystery
4 disappointed **5** sweet

B **1** interesting **2** unfair **3** anxious
4 smart **5** sour **6** true

C **1** He is getting worse.
2 All of them look serious.
3 The cat's fur feels very soft.
4 Cindy became a member of our club.

★ POINT 05 3형식 문장 (S+V+O) p.14

A **1** dinner **2** to eat a hamburger
3 his phone number **4** this book
5 thousands of people

B **1** I introduced Billy to my friends.
2 He laid his coat on the bed.
3 The museum hosts many exhibits.
4 Nate reminds me of my father.
5 We like to eat spicy food.
6 Tonya resembles her mother in many ways.
7 He was reading a novel in his room.
8 She spent too much money on this trip.

★ POINT 06 4형식 문장 (S+V+O_1+O_2) p.15

A **1** He sent me a letter from Greece.
2 Mike made his daughter a small bed.
3 I will get a notebook for you.
4 Her mother gave a bundle of lilies and roses to her.

B **1** me a lovely lunch 또는 a lovely lunch for me
2 to my children **3** for his brother

C **1** give, to me **2** made, for her
3 will send you **4** pass me **5** lent, to him

★ POINT 07 5형식 문장 (S+V+O+C) I p.16

A **1** I feel my spirit lifted
2 have made my life a living hell
3 calls him an angel
4 elected Mr. Martin their mayor
5 leave Kate alone
6 appointed him president of the company

B **1** make people sleepy
2 found the exam easy **3** kept me awake
4 leave the door open
5 named their baby Violet

★ POINT 08 5형식 문장 (S+V+O+C) II p.17

A **1** to save **2** happen **3** complain **4** to leave

B **1** asked him to send me the download link
2 allowed me to use her pen

3 want me to give you a hand
4 told me to respect others

C 1 expect her to be 2 ordered guards to put
3 had her do

REVIEW TEST 01

p.18

1 ④ 2 ③ 3 ① 4 ③ 5 ② 6 ⑤ 7 ④ 8 ① 9 ⑤
10 ① 11 fresh 12 How 13 There is 14 to 15 ⑤
16 ④ 17 ⑤ 18 ④ 19 ⑤ 20 ③ 21 ④ 22 ⑤
23 (A) When (B) check (C) stayed in 24 ③ 25 ⑤

1 3형식 문장에서 동사가 buy면 〈buy+직접목적어(+for+간접목적어)〉의 형태가 된다.

2 5형식 문장에서 ask는 to부정사를 목적격 보어로 취한다.

3 명령문으로, 형용사 patient를 보어로 취하는 동사원형 Be가 알맞다.

4 5형식 문장에서 지각동사 see는 원형부정사나 현재분사를 목적격 보어로 취한다.

5 감탄문이고 뒤에 〈a[an]+형용사+명사+주어+동사〉가 있으므로 앞에 What이 와야 한다.

6 〈보기〉와 ⑤는 〈주어+동사+목적어(+수식어)〉의 3형식 문장이다. (① 2형식, ② 1형식, ③④ 5형식)

7 〈보기〉와 ④는 〈주어+동사+간접목적어+직접목적어〉의 4형식 문장이다. (① 2형식, ②③⑤ 3형식)

8 〈보기〉와 ①은 〈주어+동사(+수식어)〉의 1형식 문장이다. (② 3형식, ③⑤ 5형식, ④ 2형식)

9 긍정문 뒤에는 부정형 부가의문문이 와야 하는데, went가 일반동사의 과거형이므로 didn't she가 알맞다.

10 yes/no 의문문이고, 조동사 can이 쓰였으므로 Yes, I can. 또는 No, I can't.가 대답이 될 수 있다.

11 2형식 문장에서 감각동사 뒤에는 형용사가 보어로 온다.

12 감탄문이고 뒤에 〈형용사+주어+동사〉가 있으므로 앞에 How가 와야 한다.

13 '~이 있다'라는 뜻을 나타내는 〈There+be동사+주어 ~〉의 1형식 문장으로, 주어인 a bus stop이 단수형이므로 There is가 알맞다.

14 3형식 문장에서 동사가 give면 〈give+직접목적어(+to+간접목적어)〉의 형태가 된다.

15 5형식 문장에서 사역동사 make는 원형부정사를 목적격 보어로 취한다.

16 뒤에 형용사가 나오므로 주격 보어를 취하는 동사가 올 수 있다.

17 동사 discuss는 타동사이므로 전치사 없이 목적어 the problem이 바로 와야 한다.

18 부정명령문은 동사원형 앞에 Don't 또는 Never를 쓴다.

19 rob은 rob A of B의 형태로 쓰인다.

20 ① 감탄문이고 뒤에 〈형용사+주어+동사〉가 있으므로 What 대신 How를 써야 한다. ② 1형식 문장으로 주어가 복수명사인 Kids이므로 동사는 learn이 되어야 한다. ④ 보어 자리에는 형용사가 오므로 magically를 magical로 고쳐 써야 옳다. ⑤ 지각동사 see는 원형부정사나 현재분사를 목적격 보어로 취하는 동사다.

21 ① 명령문은 동사원형으로 시작한다. ② tell은 목적격보어로 to부정사를 취하는 동사다. ③ 일반동사가 쓰인 문장의 의문문이므로 Were 대신 Did를 써야 한다. ⑤ ask는 목적격 보어로 to부정사를 취하는 동사다.

22 ① 3형식 문장에서 동사가 give면 〈give+직접목적어(+to+간접목적어)〉의 형태가 된다. ② 이 문장에서 walk는 1형식 동사이므로 목적어를 바로 취할 수 없다. ③ 의문사가 있는 의문문에서는 의문사가 문장 앞으로 나온다. ④ 5형식 문장이므로 목적어 뒤에 바로 목적격 보어가 나와야 한다.

23 (A) 의문사를 필요로 하는 의문문인데, B의 대답으로 보아 시간을 나타내는 의문사 When이 알맞다. (B) 사역동사 let은 원형부정사를 목적격 보어로 취하므로 check이 알맞다.
(C) 1형식 문장으로, 동사 stayed 뒤에 장소를 나타내는 수식어구 in room 606이 와야 한다.

24 동사 remind는 목적어 다음에 전치사 of가 이끄는 구가 나오므로 me 다음에 of가 와야 한다.

25 (A) 3형식 문장으로 빈칸에는 목적어가 와야 하는데, 동사 like는 to부정사와 동명사 둘 다를 목적어로 취할 수 있다.
(B) 5형식 문장으로 빈칸에는 목적격 보어가 와야 하는데, 동사 allow는 to부정사를 목적격 보어로 취한다.

CHAPTER 02 시제

★ POINT 01 현재시제·과거시제

p.22

A 1 heard 2 is 3 was

B 1 bought 2 died 3 holds 4 is 5 was

C 1 got 2 participated
3 comes 4 doesn't have

★ POINT 02 미래시제 p.23

A **1** will **2** am going to
3 will **4** will **5** am going to

B **1** am going to see **2** am going to sell
3 will be **4** am going to visit
5 am going to give birth to

★ POINT 03 미래를 나타내는 현재형·진행형 p.24

A **1** don't **2** get **3** will be able to

B **1** O **2** will look after **3** get some rest
4 O **5** returns **6** O

C **1** the meeting will be held
2 I get there
3 it rains tomorrow

★ POINT 04 진행형 p.25

A **1** is reading **2** will be waiting for
3 was talking to **4** am studying
5 will be enjoying **6** was listening to

B **1** feel **2** has **3** will be hiking
4 is growing **5** was doing

C **1** while I was sleeping **2** I am having pizza
3 He will be working

★ POINT 05 현재완료 I (계속·경험) p.26

A **1** has never used **2** have been
3 hasn't[has not] heard

B **1** has never broken **2** have liked
3 Have you read **4** has been
5 have you stayed

C **1** has worked at this restaurant since 2014
2 has run the business for ten years

★ POINT 06 현재완료 II (완료·결과) p.27

A **1** has moved
2 has passed
3 has left
4 have just arrived

B **1** 우리는 막 그의 제안을 받아들였다. (완료)
2 나는 가방을 버스에 두고 내린 것 같다. (결과)
3 Max는 어디에 머물지 아직 결정하지 못했다. (완료)
4 불이 꺼져서, 방이 매우 춥다. (결과)
5 자동차 공유 운동이 전 세계에서 나타났다. (결과)

C **1** has gone to Canada
2 has left his wallet at home
3 have forgotten Amy's cell phone number

★ POINT 07 과거 vs. 현재완료 p.28

A **1** quit **2** have just finished **3** ran into
4 had **5** did you buy **6** has taught

B **1** did he get a haircut **2** visited
3 has been **4** caused **5** has lost
6 have passed **7** have never heard
8 has gone out

★ POINT 08 과거완료·미래완료·완료진행형 p.29

A **1** had been **2** had never seen
3 will have studied **4** had lived
5 will have been waiting **6** have been using

B **1** had already started
2 will have finished
3 had never spoken

C **1** had been using my computer
2 will have been teaching English
3 have been working on the project for two months

REVIEW TEST 02 p.30

1 ④ **2** ③ **3** ⑤ **4** ⑤ **5** ④ **6** ③ **7** ② **8** ③ **9** ③
10 ② **11** ⑤ **12** ① **13** ② **14** ① **15** ③ **16** ② **17** ④
18 ② **19** ⑤ **20** ④ was snowing **21** ② moved
22 ④ **23** ② **24** ②

1 어제부터 먹지 않은 상태가 현재에도 이어지고 있으므로 현재완료를 써야 한다.

2 과거 시점에 진행 중이던 일에 관해 묻고 있으므로 과거진행형을 써야 한다.

3 예정된 미래의 일을 나타내므로 〈be going to+동사원형〉을 써야 한다.

4 두 시간 전부터 현재까지 계속 자고 있으므로 현재완료진행

형이 알맞다.

5 미래의 어떤 시점까지 완료될 일을 나타내므로 미래완료가 알맞다.

6 공항에 도착한 과거 시점을 기준으로 그때까지 완료된 일을 나타내므로 과거완료가 알맞다.

7 종속절에 과거시제가 쓰이고, 주절에 과거진행형이 오는 것이 자연스럽다.

8 A가 최근의 경험을 묻고 있으므로 현재완료가 오는 것이 적절하다. 또한 특정한 과거 시점을 나타내는 부사구(last night)와 현재완료는 함께 쓸 수 없다.

9 과거에 시작한 공부를 현재에도 계속하고 있으므로 현재완료(계속)가 알맞다.

10 과거에 가입한 동아리를 이미 탈퇴해서 현재는 가입되어 있지 않으므로 과거시제를 써야 한다.

11 ①~④의 현재완료형은 경험을, ⑤의 현재완료형은 결과를 나타낸다.

12 ①의 현재완료형은 완료를, ②~⑤의 현재완료형은 계속을 나타낸다.

13 과거를 나타내는 부사구(five years ago)가 있으므로 과거시제가 알맞다.

14 조건을 나타내는 부사절에서는 미래를 표현하는 데 현재시제가 쓰인다.

15 과거의 특정 시점을 기준으로 그 전에 있었던 일이므로 과거완료를 써야 한다.

16 feel이 감정을 나타내므로 진행형으로 쓸 수 없다.

17 전치사 since는 '~부터 죽'이라는 의미이므로 특정 시점을 나타내는 과거 시제와 함께 쓰지 않는다.

18 특정 과거 시점을 나타내는 last ~는 현재완료와 함께 쓰지 않는다.

19 과거의 특정 시점인 when I got there 이전에 일어난 일을 나타내므로 과거완료를 써야 한다.

20 특정한 과거 시점을 나타내는 부사절(when I came ...)이 있으므로 현재완료진행형은 적절하지 않으며, 과거진행형인 was snowing으로 고쳐야 한다.

21 특정한 과거 시점을 나타내는 부사구(last spring)가 있으므로 현재완료형은 쓸 수 없다.

22 과거에서 현재까지 계속된 일을 나타내므로 현재완료형 has gotten을 써야 한다.

23 특정한 과거 시점을 나타내는 부사절(When I told you ...)이 있으므로 과거시제인 gave가 적절하다.

24 (A) 내일 두 번째 결혼식을 거행할 예정이므로 미래의 예정을 나타내는 현재진행형이 적절하다. (B) 미래의 예정을 나타내는 〈be going to+동사원형〉이 적절하다.

CHAPTER 03 조동사

★ POINT 01 can, be able to, could (능력 · 가능) p.34

A **1** be able to **2** can **3** can
4 be able to **5** can **6** be able to

B **1** was able to **2** be able to **3** could
4 be able to **5** be able to **6** was able to

C **1** be able to make **2** could write
3 be able to see **4** will be able
5 be able to eat **6** will be able

★ POINT 02 can, could (가능성 · 허가 · 요청) p.35

A **1** 3월에는 매우 추울 수 있다.
2 언제든 우리를 보러 와도 돼!
3 전문가들도 실수를 할 수 있다.
4 당신의 강의 노트를 빌릴 수 있을까요?
5 이제 내 노트북 컴퓨터를 사용해도 돼.
6 사무실에서는 휴대전화를 사용할 수 없습니다.
7 내 얼굴에 파우더를 좀 더 발라 줄래?
8 이 쿠폰을 회원 카드와 함께 사용할 수 있을까요?

B **1** (2) **2** (3) **3** (2)

C **1** Can[Could] you recommend **2** can rest
3 can cause

★ POINT 03 may, might (추측 · 허가) p.36

A **1** It may rain.
2 I may not be able to finish it today.
3 She might be sick.
4 No, you may not.
5 May I ask your price range?

B **1** may have **2** May I have **3** might not work out
4 may leave **5** may be

★ POINT 04 must, have to (의무 · 추측) p.37

A **1** have to do
2 don't have to go 또는 need not go
3 must sign

B **1** must **2** have to **3** must **4** must **5** have to

C **1** have to **2** can't **3** must **4** don't need to
5 had to **6** must not **7** will have to

★ POINT 05 should, ought to (충고·제안) p.38

A **1** should **2** ought not to **3** should not
4 ought to **5** should **6** ought to

B **1** ought to keep **2** should not run around
3 ought to bring **4** should not focus
5 should wear **6** ought to see a doctor
7 should not try

★ POINT 06 had better, would rather (충고·선택) p.39

A **1** You'd better not skip **2** I'd rather go
3 I'd better get started

B **1** had better hurry up **2** would rather stay
3 had better wear **4** would rather study
5 had better start **6** had better see

C **1** had better not hang **2** would rather not go
3 had better keep **4** would rather watch
5 would rather go on a trip

★ POINT 07 used to, would (습관) p.40

A **1** used to be an actor **2** used to go out
3 used to be a fire station **4** used to go camping

B **1** used to **2** used to **3** used to
4 used to **5** would **6** would

C **1** Helen은 종종 지칠 때까지 울곤 했다.
2 Patrick은 사업차 태국을 방문하곤 했다.
3 나는 어린아이일 때 이 집에 살았었다.
4 그는 그저 버스를 보러 버스 정거장에 가곤 했다.
5 Laura는 예전에 키에 대한 콤플렉스가 있었다.

★ POINT 08 조동사+have p.p. p.41

A **1** may → must **2** must not → cannot[can't]
3 must → should

B **1** must have trained very hard
2 should have called you earlier
3 may[might] have seen the movie

C **1** should not have broken up
2 can't have forgotten
3 may[might] have seen
4 must have changed
5 may[might] have met
6 should have slept

REVIEW TEST 03 p.42

1 ③ **2** ② **3** ④ **4** ⑤ **5** ① **6** ② **7** ④ **8** ①
9 had better not tell **10** may[might] have lied
11 would rather have **12** don't have[need] to pay 또는 need not pay **13** ③ **14** ④ **15** ③ **16** ④
17 ④ **18** ③ **19** ③ **20** ④ **21** ⑤ **22** ④ **23** ①
24 (A) should (B) can't (C) are able to **25** ⑤

1 과거에 지속되던 상태를 나타낼 때는 used to를 사용한다.

2 must는 '~임에 틀림없다'라는 추측의 의미를 나타낸다.

3 '~하지 않는 게 좋을 것이다'라는 충고의 의미를 나타내므로 had better not이 알맞다.

4 '~했어야 했다'라는 과거 사실에 대한 후회를 나타내므로 〈should have p.p.〉가 알맞다.

5 may는 '~해도 된다'라는 허가의 의미를 나타낸다.

6 must가 '~해야 한다'라는 의무를 나타낼 때, have to로 바꾸어 쓸 수 있다.

7 would는 '~하곤 했다'라는 의미로, 과거의 습관을 나타낸다.

8 can't[cannot]는 '~일 리가 없다'라는 강한 부정의 추측을 나타낼 때 쓴다.

9 '~하지 않는 게 좋을 것이다'라는 충고의 의미를 나타내므로 〈had better not+동사원형〉을 쓴다.

10 '~했을지도 모른다'라는 과거 사실에 대한 불확실한 추측을 나타내므로 〈may[might] have p.p.〉를 쓴다.

11 선택의 상황에서 '(그보다는) ~하고 싶다'라는 의미를 나타내는 〈would rather+동사원형〉이 알맞다.

12 '~할 필요가 없다'라는 불필요의 의미를 나타내므로 〈don't have to[don't need to, need not]+동사원형〉을 쓴다. '~하면 안 된다'라는 의미의 must not을 쓰지 않도록 주의한다.

13 '~하지 않아야 한다'라는 충고·제안의 의미를 나타내는 shouldn't가 적절하다.

14 '~임에 틀림없다'라는 강한 추측의 의미를 나타내는 must가 적절하다.

15 문맥상 '~일 리가 없다'라는 강한 부정의 추측을 나타내는 can't가 적절하다.

16 would rather 다음에는 동사원형이 와야 한다.

17 ought to의 부정형은 ought not to이다.

18 〈should have p.p.〉는 과거 사실에 대한 후회를 나타내며, 부정형은 〈should not have p.p.〉이다.

19 '~하는 게 좋을 것이다'라는 충고의 의미를 나타내는 had better를 써야 한다.

20 요청의 의미를 나타내는 Can을 써야 한다.

21 조동사 두 개를 연달아 쓸 수 없으므로 will have to로 미래의 의무를 나타낸다.

22 '~임에 틀림없다'라는 의미의 강한 추측을 나타내는 must가 알맞다.

23 조동사 두 개를 연달아 쓸 수 없으므로 will be able to로 미래의 능력을 나타낸다.

24 문맥상 (A)에서는 should(~해야 한다), (B)에서는 can't(~할 수 없다), (C)에서는 are able to(~할 수 있다)를 쓰는 것이 자연스럽다.

25 문맥상 (A)에는 '~할 필요가 없다'라는 의미의 don't have to가, (B)에는 '~할 수 있다'라는 의미의 can이 들어가야 자연스럽다.

CHAPTER 04 수동태

★ POINT 01 수동태의 기본 개념 p.46

A 1 made 2 was punished 3 is included
4 was impressed by 5 resembles

B 1 Cleopatra was bitten by a snake.
2 I was blinded by the flame.
3 These beautiful pictures were drawn by a famous artist.
4 This museum is visited by thousands of people each day.

C 1 were destroyed by
2 was invented by
3 was selected

★ POINT 02 4형식 문장의 수동태 p.47

A 1 got 2 was sent to 3 was written to
4 was given to 5 was made for

B 1 was taught Korean by a friend
was taught to me by a friend
2 was offered a new position (by him)
was offered to me (by him)
3 was sent a thank-you note (by me)
was sent to her (by me)
4 was told the story of the company (by them)
was told to me (by them)
5 was made for her by Robert
6 was bought for my mother (by me)

★ POINT 03 5형식 문장의 수동태 I p.48

A 1 The project is considered a failure.
2 He was called a genius.
3 I was told to stop playing the piano.
4 I was asked to paint a picture on the wall.
5 The 18th century is called the golden age of botanical painting.

B 1 keeps the room warm
is kept warm by the stove
2 advised me to get some exercise
was advised to get some exercise (by him)
3 made the actress famous
was made famous by the movie
4 warned them not to enter the building
were warned not to enter the building (by the police)

★ POINT 04 5형식 문장의 수동태 II p.49

A 1 bark → to bark
2 believing → to believe
3 to swim → swim[swimming]

B 1 I was made to pay for the damage (by the clerk).
2 I was made to work overtime (by my boss).
3 Pam was heard to cry in her dorm room.
4 He was made to apologize to me (by his mother).
5 The suspect was seen to argue with the victim (by a witness).

C 1 was made to stay
2 was heard to say
3 was seen to take a walk

★ POINT 05 수동태의 여러 가지 형태 p.50

A **1** The Alps are being destroyed by tourists.
2 Something must be done to help those people.
3 My laptop is being repaired now.
4 Students should be accompanied by an adult.
5 Plastics can be used in place of natural materials.
6 This oil has been used for cooking for centuries.

B **1** will be delivered **2** was being held
3 must be kept **4** will be picked
5 can be given **6** has been influenced

★ POINT 06 주의해야 하는 수동태 I p.51

A **1** Don't let your promise be broken.
2 His visit was put off until Tuesday.
3 My clothes were made fun of by Jennifer.
4 Two deer were run over by a speeding car.
5 The children are taken care of by their grandmother.
6 The director is looked up to by many of the employees.

B **1** be wasted
2 was spoken ill of
3 be finished
4 was laughed at
5 should not be looked down on

★ POINT 07 주의해야 하는 수동태 II p.52

A **1** is said that this country is the land of opportunity
2 is believed that a broken mirror is a sign of bad luck
3 was reported that the criminal was tall and thin

B **1** is thought that all life is precious
2 are said to be popular among men this season
3 is considered that James Dean is one of the greatest actors of all time

C **1** is said that he looks younger
2 is believed to be from
3 is said to have been
4 is thought to have

★ POINT 08 by 이외의 전치사를 쓰는 수동태 p.53

A **1** in[with] **2** with **3** of **4** with

B **1** in → of **2** of → with **3** with → in **4** of → at

C **1** am satisfied with
2 was worried about
3 am pleased with
4 is interested in
5 is composed of

REVIEW TEST 04 p.54

1 ③ **2** ③ **3** ⑤ **4** ② **5** ③ **6** ④ **7** ③ **8** ④ **9** ①
10 ② **11** ① **12** ② **13** ⑤ **14** was made for us
15 to get more rest **16** is believed that **17** ⑤ **18** ②
19 ⑤ **20** ① **21** ④ **22** ① was cut into **23** ⑤
24 ① **25** (A) is bought (B) used (C) should be kept

1 사물이 주어이고 미래의 일을 나타내므로 〈will be p.p.〉의 미래형 수동태가 알맞다.

2 "People say that baseball is one of the most popular sports."에서 that절의 주어가 수동태 문장의 주어가 되면 that절의 동사는 to부정사로 바뀐다.

3 '~에 대해 걱정하다'라는 뜻의 be worried about이 알맞다.

4 사역동사 make의 목적격 보어로 쓰인 원형부정사는 수동태에서 to부정사로 바뀐다.

5 진행형의 수동태는 〈be동사+being p.p.〉의 형태로 쓴다.

6 지각동사의 목적격 보어로 쓰인 원형부정사는 수동태에서 to부정사가 되어야 한다.

7 긍정명령문의 수동태는 〈Let+목적어+be p.p.〉의 형태이다.

8 현재완료의 수동태는 〈have[has] been p.p.〉의 형태로 쓴다.

9 4형식 문장의 직접목적어를 주어로 하여 수동태 문장을 쓸 때, 대부분의 동사는 간접목적어 앞에 to를 쓴다.

10 조동사가 있는 문장의 수동태는 〈조동사+be p.p.〉의 형태로 쓴다.

11 be filled with는 '~로 가득 차다', be pleased with는 '~로 기쁘다'라는 뜻이다.

12 be disappointed in[with]은 '~에 실망하다', be interested in은 '~에 흥미가 있다'라는 뜻이다.

13 4형식 문장의 직접목적어를 주어로 해 수동태 문장을 쓸 때,

대부분의 동사는 간접목적어 앞에 to를 쓴다. “They say that large turtles live for hundreds of years.”에서 that절의 주어가 수동태 문장의 주어가 되면, that절의 동사는 to부정사로 쓴다.

14 4형식 문장의 직접목적어를 주어로 하여 수동태 문장을 쓸 때, 동사가 make이면 간접목적어 앞에 for를 쓴다.

15 5형식 문장을 수동태로 바꿀 때 목적격 보어는 〈be p.p.〉 뒤에 그대로 쓴다.

16 that절이 목적어인 문장의 수동태는 〈It+be동사+p.p.+that ~〉의 형태로 쓸 수 있다.

17 4형식 문장의 직접목적어를 주어로 하여 수동태 문장을 쓸 때, 동사가 buy이면 간접목적어 앞에 for를 쓴다.

18 사역동사 make의 목적격 보어로 쓰인 원형부정사는 수동태에서 to부정사로 바뀐다.

19 주어 Central America가 동사 hit의 대상이므로 문맥상 수동태인 〈have[has] been p.p.〉의 형태가 적절하다.

20 ② 진행형의 수동태는 〈be동사+being p.p.〉의 형태로 쓰므로 review를 reviewed로 고쳐 써야 옳다. ③ 명령문의 수동태는 〈Let+목적어+be p.p.〉의 형태로 쓰므로 exposed를 be exposed로 고쳐 써야 옳다. ④ 4형식 문장의 직접목적어를 주어로 하여 수동태 문장을 쓸 때, 동사가 give이면 간접목적어 앞에 to를 쓴다. 따라서 for를 to로 고쳐 써야 옳다. ⑤ 4형식 문장의 간접목적어를 주어로 하여 수동태 문장을 쓸 때는 전치사를 쓰지 않는다.

21 ① '~로 가득 차 있다'라는 뜻으로는 be filled with를 쓴다. ② 5형식 문장을 수동태로 바꿀 때, 지각동사의 목적격 보어로 쓰인 원형부정사는 to부정사로 바뀐다. ③ 주어 study가 동사 publish의 대상이므로 문맥상 수동태인 〈be p.p.〉의 형태가 적절하다. ⑤ 조동사가 있는 문장의 수동태는 〈조동사+be p.p.〉의 형태로 쓴다.

22 문맥상 주어 old money가 동사 cut의 대상이므로 수동태가 적절하다.

23 지각동사의 목적격 보어는 수동태에서 to부정사로 바뀌므로 was seen to hit이 되어야 한다.

24 “People believed that the Goddess Sedna had separated the land animals from the sea animals.”를 수동태로 바꿔 쓸 때 that절의 주어가 수동태 문장의 주어로 나오면 that절의 동사는 to부정사로 쓴다.

25 (A) 주어 Coffee가 동사 buy의 대상이므로 수동태가 알맞다. (B) 조동사가 있는 문장의 수동태 may be kept와 and로 연결되는 어구이므로 used가 알맞다. (C) 주어 opened cans of coffee가 동사 keep의 대상이므로 수동태가 알맞다.

★ CHAPTER 05 부정사

★ POINT 01 to부정사의 명사적 용법 Ⅰ – 주어·목적어·보어 p.58

A **1** To learn **2** to buy **3** is to become

B **1** to win **2** to help **3** to travel **4** to go

C **1** I decided to buy a new car.
2 Our aim is to please the customers.
3 It is good for your health to avoid salty foods.
4 The company wants to enter the Asian market.

★ POINT 02 to부정사의 명사적 용법 Ⅱ – 의문사+to부정사 p.59

A **1** where to stay **2** where to turn for help
3 when to get off **4** how to help her

B **1** how to change **2** where to buy
3 when to quit **4** what to do
5 what to eat **6** how to get there
7 who(m) to hire

★ POINT 03 to부정사의 형용사적 용법 Ⅰ – 명사 수식 p.60

A **1** to live in **2** to show
3 something to tell **4** time to go

B **1** to play with **2** evidence to prove
3 anything to eat **4** to get to know

C **1** received a list of gifts to choose from
2 have twelve customers to serve
3 was his turn to give a speech
4 give me a chair to sit on
5 needs someone to look after her kids
6 made the decision to marry him
7 miss this opportunity to improve your writing

★ POINT 04 to부정사의 형용사적 용법 Ⅱ – be+to부정사 p.61

A **1** is to start **2** was to be seen
3 was to become **4** are to arrive
5 is to be held

B 1 are to have a pop quiz tomorrow
2 is not to be found anywhere
3 were to fall in love
4 are not to miss the deadline again
5 are to get there by noon
6 are to keep the place clean

★ POINT 05 to부정사의 부사적 용법 I – 목적·결과 p.62

A 1 to study Chinese 2 to fail 3 to return

B 1 (in order[so as]) to make
2 (in order[so as]) not to upset
3 to find
4 (in order[so as]) to write up
5 to find

C 1 나는 시간을 낭비하지 않으려고 택시를 탔다.
2 나는 내 꿈을 이루기 위해 어떤 일이라도 할 것이다.
3 나는 집에 돌아와서 내 베개가 갈가리 찢긴 것을 발견했다.
4 Samuel은 자라서 따뜻하고 관대한 사람이 되었다.
5 Tim은 남동생을 방문하려고 Seattle로 갔다.

★ POINT 06 to부정사의 부사적 용법 II – 원인·판단의 근거·조건 p.63

A 1 나는 나쁜 소식을 듣게 되어 유감이다.
2 Simon은 아이들이 안전하다는 것을 알고 안심했다.
3 정부에 대항하여 목소리를 내다니 그 사람들은 용감했다.
4 그녀가 말하는 걸 들으면, 너는 그녀가 전문가라고 생각하게 될 것이다.
5 Jessica는 너의 이메일을 받으면 기뻐할 것이다.

B 1 glad to hear
2 disappointed to lose
3 kind to lend
4 excited to watch
5 wise to refuse

C 1 was sorry to see his best worker go
2 was very nice to drive me home in her car
3 was surprised to hear that Hans had moved to Mexico
4 hear her speak Japanese, you would take her for a Japanese
5 was disappointed to find the gallery closed

★ POINT 07 to부정사의 부사적 용법 III – 형용사·부사 수식 p.64

A 1 tall enough to reach 2 too tired to clean
3 so kind, she lent 4 so poor, he couldn't buy

B 1 too busy to eat lunch
2 very difficult to use
3 low enough to see the animals below
4 too young to understand the novel

C 1 나는 그것을 시도할 정도로 용감하지 않다.
2 Steven은 함께 어울리기가 어려웠다.
3 지금은 너무 늦어서 그의 아버지께 전화를 드릴 수 없다.
4 이 도시는 밤에 혼자 걸어 다니기 위험하다.
5 그 의자는 앉아서 돌아다니기 쉬워 보인다.

★ POINT 08 독립부정사 p.65

A 1 To make matters worse
2 To tell (you) the truth
3 To be honest 4 To begin with
5 so to speak 6 Strange to say
7 to be sure

B 1 말하자면 그는 내 역할 모델이다.
2 이상한 이야기지만 나는 지하철을 타 본 적이 없다.
3 우선 나는 닭고기 수프를 먹고 싶다.
4 Will은 확실히 믿을 만하지만, 가끔 무례할 때가 있다.
5 설상가상으로 우리의 간판선수는 다리가 부러졌다.
6 사실대로 말하면 나는 그 일을 맡고 싶지 않다.
7 솔직히 그 스테이크는 너무 질겨서 자를 수조차 없었다.

★ POINT 09 to부정사의 의미상 주어 p.66

A 1 for 2 for 3 of 4 of 5 for 6 for 7 of

B 1 of you to help 2 of her to expect
3 you to participate in 4 of him to quit
5 for me to buy 6 for her to do

★ POINT 10 to부정사의 부정·시제·태 p.67

A 1 not to 2 to be invited 3 never to
4 to have been 5 to be accepted 6 to finish

B 1 to be considered
2 to have been chosen
3 to have been 4 to be sent
5 not to bother 6 never to open
7 not to use

★ POINT 11 목적격 보어로 쓰이는 to부정사 p.68

A **1** allowed my kids to have
2 gets me to clean **3** warned him to stop

B **1** forces us to act **2** want me to be
3 asked her to turn on
4 doesn't allow me to use
5 tells me to stay away **6** advised me to leave

C **1** 판사는 그를 석방하라고 명령했다.
2 그들은 그녀를 강으로 뛰어들게 했다.
3 의사는 나에게 설탕과 소금을 피하라고 한다.
4 선생님은 그에게 다시는 늦지 말라고 경고했다.
5 우리는 여러분이 이 프로그램을 이용하기를 권장합니다.
6 그녀는 아이가 식사 전에 쿠키를 먹도록 허락하지 않는다.

★ POINT 12 목적격 보어로 쓰이는 원형부정사 p.69

A **1** coming **2** wash **3** to bring
4 laugh **5** to have 6 leave
7 touch **8** know

B **1** beat[beating] **2** look **3** apply for
4 bark[barking] **5** (to) lower

C **1** makes me work out
2 saw her park[parking]
3 let me stay up

REVIEW TEST 05 p.70

1 ① **2** ③ **3** ② **4** ③ **5** ④ **6** ② **7** ③ **8** ④
9 to be elected **10** sing[singing] **11** what to say
12 to fix **13** ① **14** ② **15** ④ **16** ④ **17** ① **18** ④
19 ⑤ **20** ⑤ **21** ⑤ **22** ⑤ **23** ② **24** ④ **25** ②

1 make 등의 사역동사는 목적격 보어로 원형부정사를 쓴다.

2 It이 가주어로 쓰였으므로 진주어로는 to부정사가 들어가는 것이 적절하다.

3 to부정사가 나타내는 때가 술어동사의 시제와 같으므로 〈to-v〉를 쓴다.

4 사람에 대한 평가를 나타내는 형용사가 be동사의 보어로 사용되는 경우, to부정사의 의미상 주어는 〈of+목적격〉을 써서 나타낸다.

5 문맥상 〈where+to-v(어디로[어디에서] ~해야 할지)〉가 decided on의 목적어가 되어야 한다.

6 〈enough to-v〉는 '~할 만큼 충분히 …하다'라는 뜻이다.

7 〈too ~ to-v〉는 '너무 ~해서 …할 수 없다'라는 뜻이다.

8 to부정사가 나타내는 때가 술어동사의 시제보다 앞서므로 완료형 to부정사 〈to have p.p.〉가 적절하다.

9 to부정사의 의미상 주어인 I가 동사 elect의 대상이므로 〈to be p.p.〉의 형태가 적절하다.

10 지각동사의 목적격 보어로는 원형부정사나 현재분사를 쓴다.

11 〈what+to-v(무엇을 ~해야 할지)〉가 know의 목적어 역할을 한다.

12 to fix가 형용사처럼 someone을 뒤에서 수식한다.

13 사역동사 let은 목적격 보어로 원형부정사를 쓴다.

14 to부정사의 의미상 주어는 보통 to 앞에 〈for+목적격〉을 써서 나타낸다.

15 운명을 나타내는 〈be+to-v〉 구문이며, to부정사의 부정은 to 앞에 not[never]을 쓴다.

16 ④의 to go는 앞의 명사 a promise를 수식하는 to부정사의 형용사적 용법으로, 나머지는 부사적 용법으로 쓰였다.

17 ①은 결과를 나타내는 to부정사의 부사적 용법으로, 나머지는 명사적 용법으로 쓰였다.

18 수식 받는 명사가 부정사구 안에 있는 전치사의 목적어가 되는 경우 전치사를 빠뜨리지 않도록 주의한다. (← to live in a new apartment)

19 started의 목적어로는 to부정사 또는 동명사가 오므로 spread를 to spread 또는 spreading으로 고쳐 써야 옳다.

20 learn 뒤에 목적어로 to부정사가 와야 하므로 use를 to use로 고쳐 써야 옳다.

21 ① want 뒤에 목적어로 to부정사가 와야 하므로 buy를 to buy로 고쳐 써야 옳다. ② needs 뒤에 목적어로 to부정사가 와야 하므로 be를 to be로 고쳐 써야 옳다. ③ 완료형 to부정사는 〈to have p.p.〉의 형태로 써야 하므로 to having been을 to have been으로 고쳐 써야 옳다. ④ 사람에 대한 평가를 나타내는 형용사가 be동사의 보어로 사용되는 경우, to부정사의 의미상 주어는 〈of+목적격〉을 써서 나타내므로 for you를 of you로 고쳐 써야 옳다.

22 ① 감정의 원인을 나타내는 to부정사가 와야 하므로 learn을 to learn으로 고쳐 써야 옳다. ② 판단의 근거를 나타내는 to부정사가 와야 하므로 of make를 to make로 고쳐 써야 옳다. ③ allow는 목적격 보어로 to부정사를 취하므로 take를 to take로 고쳐 써야 옳다. ④ 목적을 나타내는 to부정사가 와야 하므로 to beautifying을 to beautify로 고쳐 써야 옳다.

23 ②는 to부정사의 형용사적 용법으로 앞의 One way를 수식한다. 나머지는 모두 명사적 용법으로 쓰였다.

24 time을 수식하는 형용사적 용법의 to부정사 to learn이 되어야 한다.

25 (A) 지각동사 see는 목적격 보어로 원형부정사나 현재분사를 취하므로 come[coming]이 알맞다. (B) want는 목적어로 to부정사를 취하는 동사이므로 to live가 알맞다.

CHAPTER 06 동명사

★ POINT 01 동명사의 역할 p.74

A **1** Sitting **2** writing **3** investing

B **1** Finding a well-paying job
2 licking his hand **3** assisting the disabled

C **1** Being late is not a good habit.
2 I finished writing my final report.
3 Eating too much chocolate makes you fat.
4 My favorite pastime is playing video games.
5 He was ashamed of cheating on the math test.

★ POINT 02 동명사 vs. to부정사 I p.75

A **1** calling **2** to build **3** helping
4 to see **5** gathering **6** to give **7** watching

B **1** to support **2** watching **3** to provide
4 playing 5 teaching

C **1** decided to dye **2** denied committing
3 put off doing

★ POINT 03 동명사 vs. to부정사 II p.76

A **1** telling **2** sitting[to sit] **3** to be
4 to take **5** to say **6** making[to make]
7 complaining[to complain]

B **1** gave up eating **2** Try to participate
3 remembers locking **4** regret to say
5 forgot to bring **6** likes going[to go]

★ POINT 04 동명사의 의미상 주어 p.77

A **1** his[him] being **2** his[him] talking
3 her being **4** our[us] arriving
5 her daughter('s) majoring

B **1** him lying to me
2 my asking your e-mail address
3 the accused being guilty
4 you having a talent for music
5 me succeeding as a designer
6 people taking his picture

★ POINT 05 동명사의 부정·시제·태 p.78

A **1** being rejected **2** buying
3 having been treated **4** drinking
5 being elected **6** not having finished

B **1** not having told 또는 not telling
2 being 또는 having been **3** recognizing
4 not waiting for 또는 not having waited for
5 being criticized
6 bringing 또는 having brought
7 being given 또는 having been given

★ POINT 06 동명사를 사용한 관용 구문 p.79

A **1** fish → fishing **2** sit → sitting
3 to take → taking **4** see → seeing
5 to travel → traveling

B **1** is worth reading **2** no use apologizing
3 having difficulty[trouble] choosing
4 looks forward to seeing
5 spent three hours repairing
6 am busy getting ready
7 cannot[can't] help doubting

REVIEW TEST 06 p.80

1 ② **2** ④ **3** ② **4** ⑤ **5** ③ **6** ④ **7** ④ **8** ⑤
09 being caught **10** your[you] being **11** not calling
12 having lied **13** ③ **14** ④ **15** her being so sick
16 Gossiping about people **17** having met **18** ③
19 ① **20** ④ **21** ③ **22** ① **23** ④ **24** ③
25 (A) treating (B) surviving (C) to do

1 avoid는 동명사를 목적어로 취한다.

2 '~할 것을 잊어버렸다'라는 의미를 나타내려면 forgot 다음에 to-v가 와야 한다.

3 ⟨look forward to v-ing⟩는 '~하는 것을 고대하다'라는 뜻이다.

4 동명사가 나타내는 때가 술어동사의 시제보다 앞서므로 ⟨having p.p.⟩의 형태를 쓸 수 있다.

5 전치사의 목적어 자리이므로 v-ing가 알맞다.

6 ⟨be used to v-ing⟩는 '~하는 것에 익숙하다'라는 뜻을 나타낸다.

7 plan은 to부정사를 목적어로 취한다.

8 give up은 동명사를 목적어로 취한다.

9 문맥상 수동형이 되어야 하므로 ⟨being p.p.⟩의 형태가 적절하다.

10 전치사 of의 목적어가 필요하므로 being이 알맞고, 문장의 주어와 동명사의 주어가 일치하지 않으므로 being 앞에는 의미상 주어(소유격 또는 목적격)가 와야 한다.

11 동명사의 부정은 동명사 앞에 부정어를 써서 나타낸다.

12 동명사가 술어동사의 시제보다 앞서므로 ⟨having p.p.⟩의 형태를 쓸 수 있다.

13 ⟨can't help v-ing⟩는 '~하지 않을 수 없다'라는 뜻을 나타낸다.

14 전치사 of의 목적어 자리이고, 동명사의 의미상 주어 Kelly가 동사 admit의 대상이므로 ⟨being p.p.⟩의 형태가 적절하다.

15 문장의 주어와 동명사의 주어가 일치하지 않으므로 동명사 being 앞에 의미상 주어(소유격 또는 목적격)를 밝혀야 한다.

16 동명사구가 문장에서 주어 역할을 하여 Gossiping about people이 되어야 한다.

17 that절이 나타내는 때가 술어동사의 시제보다 앞서므로 완료형인 ⟨having p.p.⟩ 형태로 바꿔 쓸 수 있다.

18 refuse는 to부정사를 목적어로 취하므로 to answer가 와야 한다.

19 ⟨feel like v-ing⟩는 '~하고 싶다'라는 뜻을 나타낸다.

20 finish는 동명사를 목적어로 취한다.

21 ① '~하지 않을 수 없다'라는 뜻의 관용 표현은 ⟨cannot help v-ing⟩이므로 cry를 crying으로 고쳐 써야 옳다. ② decide는 to부정사를 목적어로 취하므로 not taking을 not to take로 고쳐 써야 옳다. ④ 전치사의 목적어 자리에는 동명사를 쓰므로 be를 being으로 고쳐 써야 옳다. ⑤ 문맥상 Keep ... ahead가 문장의 주어가 되어야 하므로 Keep을 Keeping 또는 To keep으로 고쳐 써야 옳다.

22 ② want는 to부정사를 목적어로 취하므로 winning을 to win으로 고쳐 써야 옳다. ③ be동사의 보어 자리이므로 construct를 constructing 또는 to construct로 고쳐 써야 옳다. ④ plan은 to부정사를 목적어로 취하므로 doing을 to do로 고쳐 써야 옳다. ⑤ 전치사의 목적어 자리에는 동명사를 쓰므로 to manage를 managing으로 고쳐 써야 옳다.

23 (A) learn은 to부정사를 목적어로 취한다. (B) '~하는 것을 멈추다'라는 의미를 나타내려면 stop 다음에 v-ing가 와야 한다. ⟨stop to-v⟩는 부사적 용법으로 '~하기 위해서 멈추다'라는 뜻이다.

24 that절의 주어 자리이므로 동명사 starting이 되어야 한다.

25 (A) ⟨be worth v-ing⟩는 '~할 가치가 있다'라는 뜻을 나타낸다. (B) 전치사 of의 목적어 자리이고, 의미상 주어를 목적격 대명사로 나타냈으므로 동명사가 와야 한다.
(C) decide는 to부정사를 목적어로 취한다.

CHAPTER 07 분사

★ POINT 01 분사의 쓰임 p.84

A 1 Winning 2 wearing 3 taken
4 written 5 a bear eating

B 1 called Anne
2 surrounded by a lot of people
3 working in American homes
4 wandering around the cars

C 1 satisfied with my presentation
2 have their parking tickets stamped
3 her sleeping baby

★ POINT 02 현재분사 vs. 과거분사 p.85

A 1 stealing 2 locked 3 used 4 closed
5 hurt 6 barking 7 deserted 8 selling

B 1 burning 2 removed 3 cheating
4 crying 5 broken 6 looking

★ POINT 03 감정을 유발하는 v-ing vs. 감정을 느끼는 p.p p.86

A 1 boring 2 excited 3 surprising
4 shocked 5 exciting 6 embarrassed

B 1 confusing 2 interested 3 exciting
4 bored 5 satisfying 6 disappointed

C 1 interesting 2 pleased 3 confused
4 disgusting 5 amazed

★ POINT 04 분사구문의 형태 p.87

A 1 Being busy
2 Playing badminton yesterday
3 Going straight ahead
4 Joining the drama club together
5 Traveling by car
6 Wanting to make a good impression

B 1 Seeing this 2 Not having money
3 Playing basketball 4 Being late
5 Turning left

★ POINT 05 분사구문의 의미 p.88

A 1 나는 집에서 TV를 보다가 잠이 들었다.
2 규칙적으로 운동을 하기 때문에 그는 전혀 살이 찌지 않는다.
3 Breaden은 웃으며 통로를 따라 걸었다.
4 인터넷 검색을 하다가 그녀는 내 블로그를 찾아냈다.
5 오빠와 싸우다가 그 여자아이는 울기 시작했다.

B 1 Being with you
2 Always telling the truth
3 Not wearing contact lenses

C 1 As I was only twelve
2 while I tested their weight
3 When she received the phone call
4 If you behave like that

★ POINT 06 분사구문의 시제와 태 p.89

A 1 Having watched the comedy show
2 Looking for work in Tokyo
3 Having seen the movie before
4 (Being) Stuck in an elevator
5 Having slept for three hours last night
6 (Being) Used sparingly

B 1 (Being) Faced 2 Waiting 3 Having worked
4 Having lost 5 Having finished

★ POINT 07 독립 분사구문 p.90

A 1 There being nothing to do
2 Our class being canceled
3 Her thoughts wandering
4 The plane starting to land
5 It being very hot these days
6 The marketing director complaining

B 1 Frankly speaking 2 Judging from
3 Speaking of John Grisham 4 Considering that

★ POINT 08 〈with+(대)명사+분사〉 구문 p.91

A 1 closed 2 turned 3 watering
4 running 5 reading 6 tapping

B 1 my mouth shut 2 its cover removed
3 the TV turned on 4 her hair combed
5 his feet bleeding 6 with their names written

REVIEW TEST 07 p.92

1 ③ 2 ③ 3 ⑤ 4 ② 5 ④ 6 ② 7 ③ 8 ④ 9 ⑤
10 surprising 11 Not eating 12 the radio turned on
13 Generally speaking 14 ② 15 ③ 16 ③ 17 ①
18 ④ 19 ⑤ 20 ② 21 ④ 22 ② 23 ②
24 (A) walking (B) barking (C) running

1 '~한 감정을 느끼게 되는'이라는 수동의 뜻이므로 과거분사 satisfied가 알맞다.

2 지각동사 heard의 목적어(her name)와 목적격 보어가 수동의 관계이므로 과거분사 called가 적절하다.

3 분사구문의 시제가 주절의 시제보다 앞서므로 〈having p.p.〉의 형태가 알맞다.

4 능동이나 진행의 의미를 나타낼 때는 현재분사를 쓴다.

5 수동이나 완료의 의미를 나타낼 때는 과거분사를 쓴다.

6 부사절의 주어와 주절의 주어가 일치하므로 주어를 생략하고 분사구문을 만든다. 부사절의 시제가 주절의 시제와 일치하므로 분사는 〈v-ing〉 형태로 쓴다.

7 부사절의 주어와 주절의 주어가 일치하지 않을 때는 부사절의 주어를 그대로 남겨 두고 분사구문을 만든다. 부사절의 시제가 주절의 시제와 일치하므로 분사는 〈v-ing〉 형태로 쓴다.

8 문맥상 이유(~해서)의 의미를 나타내므로 As가 적절하다.

9 주절의 시제보다 이전에 일어난 일이므로 완료형 분사구문 Having been이 적절하다.

10 '~한 감정을 유발하는'이라는 능동의 의미이므로 현재분사가

알맞다.

11 분사구문의 부정은 분사 앞에 부정어를 쓴다.

12 〈with+(대)명사+분사〉에서 명사와 분사가 수동의 관계이므로 과거분사를 써야 한다.

13 〈generally speaking〉은 관용적으로 쓰이는 분사구문으로, '일반적으로 말해서'라는 뜻이다.

14 문맥상 '~하고 있는'이라는 능동 · 진행의 의미를 갖는 현재분사가 알맞다.

15 〈judging from〉은 '~로 판단하건대'라는 뜻의 비인칭 독립 분사구문이다.

16 〈with+(대)명사+분사〉 구문에서 명사와 분사가 능동의 관계이므로 현재분사가 알맞다.

17 사역동사 have의 목적어(my hair)와 목적격 보어가 수동의 관계이므로 과거분사인 cut이 와야 한다.

18 '~한 감정을 유발하는'이라는 능동의 의미이므로 현재분사인 disappointing이 쓰여야 한다.

19 접속사와 주어를 대신하는 분사구문이 나와야 한다.

20 의미상 주어인 people이 '~한 감정을 느끼게 되는'이라는 수동의 의미이므로 과거분사 satisfied로 고쳐 써야 옳다.

21 (A) 앞에 Having been이 생략된 분사구문이다. (B) '~한 감정을 느끼게 되는'이라는 수동의 의미이므로 과거분사 frustrated가 알맞다.

22 (A) 지각동사의 목적어(David)와 목적격 보어가 능동의 관계이므로 동사원형 play 또는 현재분사 playing이 알맞다. (B) '~한 감정을 유발하는'이라는 능동의 의미이므로 현재분사 satisfying이 알맞다.

23 주절의 시제보다 한 시제 앞서고 능동의 의미이므로, Having watched가 와야 한다.

24 (A) 부사절 as I walked towards the fence에서 접속사와 주어를 생략하고 동사를 현재분사 walking으로 바꿔 분사구문으로 나타낼 수 있다. (B) 능동 · 진행의 의미를 가지는 현재분사 barking이 알맞다. (C) 지각동사의 목적어와 목적격 보어가 능동의 관계이므로 동사원형 run 또는 현재분사 running이 알맞다.

★ CHAPTER 08 접속사

★ POINT 01 등위접속사 p.96

A **1** and **2** but **3** so **4** or **5** or

B **1** or you'll be punished **2** and you'll be fitter

3 or you'll be late for the meeting

C **1** and get some sleep

2 three or four days a month

3 but it has better customer reviews

4 so people drive everywhere

★ POINT 02 상관접속사 p.97

A **1** either writer or director

2 neither recognized her nor remembered her name

3 not only in science but also in math

4 both a checking account and a savings account

B **1** is → are **2** plays → play **3** are → is

C **1** either, or **2** neither, nor

3 not only, but also **4** both, and

★ POINT 03 명사절을 이끄는 종속접속사 I – that p.98

A **1** He hopes ✔ he will be rich.

2 They believe ✔ I'm highly gifted.

3 It's a relief ✔ your injury is not serious.

4 It is amazing ✔ she survived the accident.

5 My concern is ✔ he only stays in his room ....

6 The best thing about driverless cars is ✔ people won't ....

B **1** that friends are important

2 that I have no money

3 that she committed the crime

4 that he has been missing

5 that he doesn't love me

C **1** Owen이 대학을 마치지 않았다는 것은 사실이다.

2 문제는 우리가 그 시험에 대비하기에 충분한 시간이 없다는 것이다.

3 저는 저희의 영업 시간이 다음 달부터 변경될 것이라고 알려야만 합니다.

★ POINT 04 명사절을 이끄는 종속접속사 II – if, whether p.99

A **1** if **2** Whether **3** whether **4** if **5** if

B **1** that **2** whether **3** that **4** Whether

C **1** if I wanted more tea

2 if she is interested in knitting

3 whether you go with me

4 whether Steven will be elected mayor
5 whether I can trust the information

★ POINT 05 접속사 역할을 하는 의문사 p.100

A 1 Do you know where the closest library is?
2 Who do you think will be there?
3 I'd like to know when my order will be shipped.
4 I don't remember when the concert took place.
5 He isn't sure which camera he should buy.
6 What do you believe the best solution is?

B 1 which graph I'll use
2 where we are and what we are
3 when you were born
4 where she got the lamp
5 why he has been absent from school

★ POINT 06 부사절을 이끄는 종속접속사 I (시간) p.101

A 1 When 2 Since 3 while

B 1 우리가 가까이 갈수록 그 탑은 더 커 보였다.
2 그가 수영을 하는 동안 나는 저녁으로 피자를 준비했다.
3 Diane은 매일 아침 화장을 하면서 노래를 부른다.
4 나는 Nate가 열 살 때부터 그와 알고 지낸다.
5 Carol은 머리 위의 간판을 보았을 때 그녀의 친구를 기다리고 있었다.

C 1 As my turn came 2 while you are working
3 since Mary left me 4 When he was young

★ POINT 07 부사절을 이끄는 종속접속사 II (시간) p.102

A 1 until 2 by the time
3 the moment 4 by the time

B 1 Every time 2 until
3 As soon as 4 by the time

C 1 As soon as Robert arrived home
2 until Lewis died in 1963
3 by the time you get here
4 every time I open the file
5 The moment I saw her

★ POINT 08 부사절을 이끄는 종속접속사 III (조건) p.103

A 1 Unless it is raining hard
2 if parents don't invest precious time in them
3 if it's not next Monday 4 Unless he comes

B 1 Unless → If 또는 aren't → are
2 If → Unless 또는 take → don't take
3 as soon as → as long as

C 1 If you need further information
2 Unless we make a reservation
3 Unless you're ready by six
4 as long as you keep trying

★ POINT 09 부사절을 이끄는 종속접속사 IV (양보) p.104

A 1 if 2 Even if 3 Whether
4 While 5 Even though

B 1 Even though I explained my situation
2 Though the teacher was patient
3 Even if this project fails
4 While I got an A in English
5 Although I was very hungry

★ POINT 10 부사절을 이끄는 종속접속사 V (기타) p.105

A 1 네가 집에 일찍 갈 수 있도록 그 일을 도와줄게.
2 내 플래너는 내가 그러지 않아도 되도록 내 일정을 기억한다.
3 라디오 소리가 너무 커서 나는 공부에 집중할 수 없다.
4 그녀는 너무 기분이 상해서 내 사과를 받지 않고 집에 갔다.

B 1 so, that 2 so that, can[may] 3 such a, that

C 1 The car is so old that
2 so that the children can sleep
3 so that he could visit
4 such a good film that

REVIEW TEST 08 p.106

1 ④ 2 ④ 3 ③ 4 ④ 5 ② 6 ⑤ 7 ① 8 ⑤ 9 ① 10 As 11 Even though 12 so that 13 why she was late 14 ① 15 ③ 16 ② 17 ① 18 ② 19 ④ 20 ② 21 ④ 22 ③ 23 ③ 24 (A) When (B) if

1 명사절을 이끌며 '~인지 아닌지'라는 뜻을 나타내는 접속사 whether가 알맞다.
2 '만약 ~할지라도'라는 양보의 의미를 나타내는 접속사 Even if가 알맞다.
3 〈neither A nor B〉는 'A도 B도 아니다'라는 뜻이다.
4 명사절을 이끌며 '~하는 것'이라는 뜻을 나타내는 접속사 that이 알맞다.
5 '~인 반면에'라는 뜻을 나타내는 접속사 while이 알맞다.
6 〈not only A but also B〉는 'A뿐만 아니라 B도'라는 뜻으로,〈B as well as A〉와 같다.
7 〈both A and B〉는 'A와 B 둘 다'라는 뜻이다.
8 the moment와 as soon as는 '~하자마자'라는 뜻이다.
9 unless는 '~하지 않는 한'이라는 뜻으로 if ~ not과 같다.
10 '~함에 따라'라는 뜻을 나타내는 접속사 As가 알맞다.
11 '비록 ~이지만'이라는 뜻을 나타내는 접속사 Even though가 알맞다.
12 '~하도록'이라는 뜻을 나타내는 접속사 〈so that ~〉이 알맞다.
13 간접의문문의 어순은 〈의문사+주어+동사〉이다.
14 if는 명사절을 이끌어 '~인지 아닌지'라는 뜻으로, 부사절을 이끌어 '만약 ~한다면'이라는 뜻으로 쓰인다.
15 since는 '~이래로(시간), ~이기 때문에(이유)'라는 뜻을 나타낸다.
16 while은 '~하는 반면(양보), ~하는 동안(시간)'이라는 뜻을 나타낸다.
17 주절이 do you think[guess, believe, imagine]인 경우, 의문사절의 의문사가 문장 맨 앞에 와야 한다.
18 〈not only A but also B〉는 의미상 강조하는 B에 동사의 수를 일치시키므로 likes가 와야 한다.
19 조건을 나타내는 부사절에서는 현재형을 써서 미래의 일을 나타낸다.
20 간접의문문의 어순은 〈의문사+주어+동사〉이므로 what the box contained로 고쳐 써야 옳다.
21 (A) '~하도록'이라는 의미를 나타내는 〈so that ~〉이 알맞다. (B) 문맥상 '~하는 동안'이라는 의미를 나타내는 while이 알맞다.
22 (A) '너무 ~해서 …하다'라는 의미의 〈so+형용사+that ...〉 구문이 되도록 so가 와야 한다. (B) 문맥상 조건을 나타내는 if(만약 ~한다면)가 알맞다.
23 means의 목적어 역할을 하는 명사절을 이끌며 '~하는 것'이라는 의미를 나타내는 that이 와야 한다.
24 문맥상 (A)에는 '~할 때'라는 뜻의 When이, (B)에는 '만약 ~한다면'이라는 뜻의 if가 알맞다.

★ CHAPTER 09

가정법

★ POINT 01 가정법 과거 p.110

A 1 won't → wouldn't 2 is to → were to
3 reported → would report

B 1 had, would not miss 2 said, would, do
3 were, would be

C 1 I had two weeks off, I would[could] go to Australia
2 I had enough money, I would[could] buy the latest cell phone
3 I could buy that beautiful mansion, I would [could] live there with you

★ POINT 02 가정법 과거완료 p.111

A 1 had had, have called 2 had known, have sent
3 had not been, not have had
4 had been, not have done

B 1 had told, would have been shocked
2 had not been, would have gone
3 had called, would not have gone
4 had bought, would have made
5 had not been, would have been

C 1 it had not rained, we would[could] have gone cycling
2 you hadn't called, I couldn't have woken up early
3 I had known his situation, I would[could] have helped him
4 we had taken the subway, we would[could] have arrived earlier

★ POINT 03 혼합가정법 p.112

A 1 are not → would not be
2 have → had 3 had → had had

B 1 had eaten, would not be hungry
2 hadn't met, would be home
3 had not moved, could go
4 had learned, could speak
5 had not seen, would not be

C 1 Michael had not lied to me once, I could trust him
2 it had not snowed last night, we could not have a snowball fight
3 I had brought an umbrella, I could share it with her

★ POINT 04 가정법 현재 p.113

A 1 played → (should) play 2 told → (should) tell
3 cheat → cheated
4 participated → (should) participate
B 1 (should) show 2 (had) finished
3 (should) exercise 4 (should) stimulate
5 (should) wear 6 (should) cancel

★ POINT 05 I wish+가정법 p.114

A 1 I could swim in the sea
2 she had lent me her dress
3 I could climb this mountain often
4 Tom had apologized to you
5 I had attended the meeting
B 1 had bought 2 were 3 could camp
4 had gone 5 had had 6 would remain
7 were

★ POINT 06 as if+가정법 p.115

A 1 she were my boss
2 they were children
3 my son had entered this school just yesterday
4 she understood my situation
5 he hadn't been sick
B 1 as if she had lived
2 as if she knew something
3 as if he had not been
4 as if he read my thoughts
5 as if we had never met
6 as if, were

★ POINT 07 기타 가정법 p.116

A 1 Without[But for] your help
2 Without[But for] the Sun
3 you finished your lunch
4 it were not for grief
5 it had not been for your support
B 1 Without my glasses 2 It is time you left
3 But for my sister 4 It is time we got
5 Without your help

★ POINT 08 if의 생략 / if절 대용어구 p.117

A 1 it were not for all of you
2 I passed the exam
3 I were given the new project
4 he had helped her
5 had been a great soccer player
B 1 is → would be
2 You had → Had you 또는 If you had
3 did not die → would not have died
4 If were I you → Were I you 또는 If I were you
5 would have required → would require

REVIEW TEST 09 p.118

1 ③ 2 ⑤ 3 ③ 4 ⑤ 5 ① 6 ⑤ 7 ③ 8 ④
9 Without my brother 10 as if she were 11 would not be 12 wish I had 13 were 14 ④ 15 ① 16 ②
17 ③ 18 ④ 19 ③ 20 ⑤ 21 ④ 22 ③ 23 (A) were (B) should marry (C) acted

1 가정법 과거에서 if절의 동사가 be동사일 때, 주어의 인칭과 수에 상관없이 were를 쓴다.
2 과거 사실과 반대되는 소망을 나타내므로 〈I wish+가정법 과거완료〉의 형태가 알맞다.
3 as if 뒤에서 주절의 시제와 일치하는 때의 사실과 반대되는 일을 나타내므로 가정법 과거인 supported가 알맞다.
4 과거 사실과 반대되는 일을 가정하는 가정법 과거완료이므로, 주절의 동사는 〈조동사의 과거형+have p.p.〉가 알맞다.
5 제안 · 요구 · 주장 · 명령을 나타내는 동사 뒤에 오는 that절에 동사는 〈(should +) 동사원형〉 형태를 쓴다.
6 I wish 뒤에서 과거에 이루지 못한 소망을 나타내므로 가정법 과거완료인 〈had not p.p.〉가 알맞다.
7 if절의 동사가 were, had, should인 경우 if를 생략할 수 있는데, 이때 주어와 동사가 도치된다.
8 과거 사실과 반대되는 일을 가정하고 있으므로 가정법 과거

완료를 쓰며, 따라서 if절의 동사는 〈had p.p.〉가 알맞다.

9 과거에 있었던 것을 없었다고 가정할 때 〈Without ~+가정법 과거완료〉를 쓸 수 있다.

10 〈as if+가정법 과거〉는 현재 사실과 반대되거나 사실일 가능성이 희박한 일을 가정할 때 사용하며, '마치 ~인 것처럼'이라는 뜻이다.

11 과거에 실현되지 않은 일이 현재까지 영향을 미치는 경우이므로 〈If+주어+had p.p. ~, 주어+조동사의 과거형+동사원형 …〉의 혼합가정법을 쓴다.

12 현재 사실과 반대되는 일을 소망할 때 〈I wish+가정법 과거〉를 쓴다.

13 현재 사실과 반대되는 일을 가정하는 가정법 과거가 되어야 하는데, be동사이므로 주어의 인칭과 수에 관계없이 were를 쓴다.

14 주절이 가정법 과거이고, 문맥상 '~이 없다면'이라는 뜻을 나타내므로 If it were not for가 알맞다.

15 제안 · 요구 · 주장 · 명령을 나타내는 동사 뒤에 오는 that절에 동사는 〈(should +) 동사원형〉 형태를 쓴다.

16 if절의 동사가 were, had, should인 경우, if가 생략되면 주어와 동사가 도치된다.

17 가정법 과거에서 주절의 동사는 〈조동사의 과거형+동사원형〉이므로 will go는 would go가 되어야 한다.

18 과거형 조동사 would를 통해 실현 가능성이 희박한 미래의 일을 가정하고 있음을 알 수 있으므로 조건절에는 were to를 써야 한다.

19 if절의 동사가 were, had, should인 경우, if가 생략되면 주어와 동사가 도치된다.

20 ① 현재 사실과 반대되는 일을 소망하는 〈I wish+가정법 과거〉 구문이므로 are를 were로 고쳐 써야 옳다. ② 현재 사실과 반대되는 가정을 하고 있으므로 조건절의 is를 were로 고쳐 써야 옳다. ③ if절의 동사가 〈had p.p.〉인 혼합 가정법 문장이므로, 주절의 동사는 〈조동사의 과거형+동사원형〉인 would be로 고쳐 써야 옳다. ④ 문맥상 that절의 내용이 이미 일어난 일을 나타내므로 직설법 시제인 had not intended로 고쳐 써야 옳다.

21 (A) 현재 사실과 반대되거나 실현 가능성이 희박한 일을 소망할 때 〈I wish+가정법 과거〉를 쓴다.
(B) 가정법 과거를 써서 if절에 과거형 동사가 왔으므로, 주절의 동사는 〈조동사의 과거형+동사원형〉이 알맞다.

22 (A) 현재 사실과 반대되는 일을 가정하고 있으므로 가정법 과거를 쓰는데, if가 생략되면 주어와 동사가 도치된다.
(B) 현재 사실과 반대되는 일을 소망하는 것이므로 〈I wish+가정법 과거〉를 쓴다.

23 (A) 현재 사실과 반대되는 일이므로 〈as if+가정법 과거〉가 와야 하는데, if절의 동사가 be동사이므로 were가 알맞다.
(B) 제안 · 요구 · 주장 · 명령을 나타내는 동사 뒤에 오는 that절에 동사는 〈(should +) 동사원형〉 형태를 쓴다.
(C) 현재 사실과 반대되는 일을 소망하는 〈I wish+가정법 과거〉 형태가 되어야 한다.

CHAPTER 10 관계사

★ POINT 01 주격 관계대명사 p.122

A 1 that[who] 2 What 3 that[who]
4 which[that] 5 What 6 which[that]

B 1 He was wearing a shirt which[that] was brightly colored.
2 Eric had an employee who[that] was habitually late.
3 I found a website which[that] sells picnic tables.
4 The delivery system is convenient for people who[that] don't have time to go to the library.
5 It was a movie about a boy and his dog that lived in the countryside.

★ POINT 02 목적격 관계대명사 p.123

A 1 what 2 that 3 whom 4 which

B 1 which[that] 2 who(m)[that]
3 what 4 that[which]

C 1 Swimming is a skill which[that] anyone can learn.
2 I like all the books that[which] Sophie wrote.
3 This is the woman who(m)[that] I saw yesterday.
4 He is the pianist who(m)[that] I support financially.

★ POINT 03 소유격 관계대명사 p.124

A 1 I have a purse whose strap is long.
2 Bordeaux is a region whose wines are famous.
3 The teacher noticed a girl whose name was Serena.
4 I bought a shirt whose buttons are colorful.
5 Most publishers will not want to waste time with writers whose material contains too many

mistakes.

B **1** that girl whose glasses are red
2 a scholar whose work has centered
3 the big pot whose handle was loose
4 the car whose engine was out of order

★ POINT 04 관계대명사 what p.125

A **1** 필요한 것은 관점의 변화다.
2 그에 대해 내가 좋아하는 점은 그가 재미있다는 것이다.
3 그게 바로 그녀가 내게 말한 것이다.
4 나는 그들이 Steve에 대해 말하는 것을 믿지 않는다.

B **1** That's what I'm thinking of.
2 Thanks a lot for what you've done for me.
3 An artist makes art from what he has around him.

C **1** what you can do today
2 What I really wanted
3 what your body needs
4 what I told you before
5 what looked like a doll
6 what he does best

★ POINT 05 관계대명사와 전치사 p.126

A **1** in which **2** on which **3** that[who(m)], to
4 in which **5** from which **6** that[which], for

B **1** O **2** whom **3** which

C **1** who(m)[that], for **2** on which
3 with whom

★ POINT 06 관계부사 p.127

A **1** when **2** where **3** that **4** how

B **1** where **2** why **3** when

C **1** Do you remember the day when we first met?
2 That's the reason why June broke up with Ted.
3 I like how the author portays the characters.
4 Imagine a man is in the situation where he forgot his wedding anniversary.

★ POINT 07 관계사의 계속적 용법 p.128

A **1** which **2** who **3** who **4** where

B **1** the reason why **2** where **3** whom **4** which

C **1** who told me her secret
2 when he treated me to dinner
3 where I met Tina
4 which caused her to become deaf
5 which was perfect

★ POINT 08 복합관계사 p.129

A **1** However hard it is **2** Wherever he goes
3 whenever I'm free **4** whatever you want
5 Whoever attacks the police

B **1** Whichever[Whatever] **2** wherever **3** However
4 whatever

REVIEW TEST 10 p.130

1 ⑤ **2** ③ **3** ③ **4** ⑤ **5** ④ **6** ⑤ **7** ② **8** ②
9 who(m)[that] **10** that **11** who(m)[that], with
12 whose **13** Whoever **14** ① **15** ④ **16** ⑤ **17** ②
18 ④ **19** ① **20** ⑤ **21** ④ **22** ③ **23** ④
24 (A) what (B) what (C) that

1 선행사를 포함하는 관계대명사 what이 알맞다.

2 관계사가 관계사절에서 선행사 a friend의 소유격 역할을 하므로 whose가 알맞다.

3 사물인 선행사를 수식하며 관계사절의 목적어 역할을 하는 관계사로 that이 알맞다.

4 선행사 the pet shop이 관계사절 안에서 장소를 나타내는 부사 역할을 하므로 관계부사 where가 알맞다.

5 사람인 선행사를 포함하며 '~하는 사람은 누구나'라는 의미를 나타내는 목적격 복합관계대명사 whomever가 알맞다.

6 장소의 선행사(The country)를 수식하는 관계사절을 이끌며 관계사절 안에서 부사(전치사+명사) 역할을 하는 where가 알맞다.

7 anything that은 선행사를 포함하는 복합관계대명사 whatever(~하는 것은 무엇이나)로 바꿔 쓸 수 있다.

8 선행사가 사람이며 계속적 용법이므로 주격 관계대명사 who가 알맞다.

9 사람인 선행사를 수식하며 관계사절의 목적어 역할을 하는 목적격 관계대명사 who(m)[that]이 알맞다.

10 선행사 A man and his car가 사람과 사물의 혼합이므로 관계대명사 that이 알맞다.

11 관계대명사가 전치사의 목적어인 경우 전치사를 관계사절의

끝에 둘 수 있다.

12 관계사가 관계사절에서 선행사 a friend의 소유격 역할을 하므로 whose가 알맞다.

13 사람인 선행사를 포함하며 '~하는 사람은 누구나'라는 의미를 나타내는 주격 복합관계대명사 whoever가 알맞다.

14 계속적 용법으로 쓰였고 선행사가 사물이므로 주격 관계대명사 which가 알맞다.

15 선행사가 Atlanta가 장소이고 관계사절에서 부사 역할을 하므로 관계부사 where가 알맞다.

16 관계부사 how와 선행사 the way는 함께 쓰지 않고 하나만 써야 한다.

17 선행사가 없으므로 선행사를 포함하는 관계대명사 what이 와야 한다.

18 선행사 a freezer가 관계사절 안에서 주어 역할을 하므로 주격 관계대명사 which가 알맞다.

19 〈전치사+관계대명사〉의 어순일 때는 that을 쓸 수 없다.

20 ① 선행사가 사물이므로 whom을 that으로 고쳐 써야 옳다. ② 선행사 the present가 관계사절 안에서 목적어 역할을 하므로 what을 목적격 관계대명사 that 또는 which 로 고쳐 쓰거나 아예 생략해야 옳다. ③ 선행사 an important moment가 관계사절 안에서 소유격(its impact) 역할을 하므로 which를 소유격 관계대명사인 whose로 고쳐 써야 옳다. ④ 선행사가 없으므로 which를 선행사를 포함하는 관계대명사 what으로 고쳐 써야 옳다.

21 ① 주어가 Challenges이고 we face today가 목적격 관계대명사절이므로 동사 is를 are로 고쳐 써야 옳다. ② 〈전치사+관계대명사〉의 어순일 때는 who를 쓸 수 없으므로 who를 whom으로 고쳐 써야 옳다. ③ 접속사가 따로 없으므로 콤마 뒤에는 계속적 용법의 관계대명사가 이어져야 하고, 〈전치사+관계대명사〉의 어순일 때는 that을 쓸 수 없으므로 that을 which로 고쳐 써야 옳다. ⑤ 선행사 South Africa가 장소를 나타내는 말이며 관계사절 안에서 부사 역할을 하므로 which를 관계부사 where로 고쳐 써야 옳다.

22 (A) 선행사 many tents가 사물이고 계속적 용법의 관계사절 안에서 주어 역할을 하므로 주격 관계대명사 which가 알맞다. (B) 선행사 a family space가 관계사절 안에서 장소를 나타내는 부사 역할을 하므로 관계부사 where가 알맞다.

23 선행사 other options가 사물이고 관계사절 안에서 주어 역할을 하므로 주격 관계대명사 that[which]이 와야 한다.

24 (A), (B)에는 선행사를 포함하는 관계대명사 what이, (C)에는 information을 선행사로 하는 주격 관계대명사 that이 알맞다.

CHAPTER 11 명사 · 관사 · 대명사

★ POINT 01 셀 수 있는 명사 vs. 셀 수 없는 명사 p.134

A **1** chairs **2** water **3** a play
4 love **5** information

B **1** honesty **2** bread **3** trees **4** years

C **1** coins **2** dogs **3** money
4 milk **5** apples **6** luck

★ POINT 02 주의해야 하는 명사 p.135

A **1** is **2** have **3** are **4** glasses

B **1** are **2** pants **3** is **4** baggage is

C **1** committee is **2** Physics is
3 police are **4** scissors are

★ POINT 03 관사 p.136

A **1** The **2** the **3** a **4** The
5 an **6** X **7** X **8** the

B **1** go to bed **2** play the guitar **3** have lunch
4 once a month **5** a sense

★ POINT 04 소유대명사·재귀대명사 p.137

A **1** ourselves **2** yourself **3** hers
4 some friends of his

B **1** ours **2** yours **3** herself **4** himself

C **1** edit it myself **2** a student of mine
3 cut myself chopping

★ POINT 05 대명사 it의 쓰임 p.138

A **1** That → It **2** getting → get
3 think important → think it (is) important
4 They → It **5** does take → does it take

B **1** It is going to rain
2 How far is it from your house
3 made it possible to trade
4 it is already seven in the evening
5 it is great to have people
6 It is customary to give this

7 It will not be long before

★ **POINT 06** 부정대명사 I p.139

A 1 the other 2 the others 3 one, it 4 one
5 another 6 others

B 1 another → one 2 the others → the other
3 the other → another 4 the others → others

★ **POINT 07** 부정대명사 II p.140

A 1 Both 2 gives 3 Each 4 All

B 1 girl 2 has 3 men 4 go

C 1 Both of the actors 2 each product
3 Every park 4 all of the people

★ **POINT 08** 부정대명사 III p.141

A 1 either 2 none 3 Neither

B 1 Neither of my brothers 2 None of my friends
3 None of my money 4 either of the books

C 1 Neither of my cats 2 None of them
3 either of the dresses

REVIEW TEST 11 p.142

1 ③ 2 ③ 3 ③ 4 ① 5 ① 6 ③ 7 courage
8 Every student 9 is 10 others 11 Both
12 neither 13 ⑤ 14 ② 15 ③ 16 ⑤ 17 ⑤ 18 ⑤
19 ③ 20 ③ 21 ④ 22 ⑤ 23 (A) seem (B) another
(C) a 24 (A) both (B) one (C) the other

1 강조하는 말 Judy 뒤에 재귀대명사가 와야 하는데, 3인칭 단수 여자이므로 herself가 알맞다.
2 only가 붙은 말 앞에는 정관사 the가 와야 한다.
3 '또 다른 하나'라는 뜻의 부정대명사 another가 알맞다.
4 뒤에 오는 to부정사구를 대신하여 쓰이는 가주어 It이 알맞다.
5 '하나의'라는 뜻을 나타내는 부정관사 a가 알맞다.
6 '나의 것'이라는 뜻의 소유대명사 mine이 알맞다.
7 courage(용기)는 구체적 형태가 없는 추상적인 개념이므로 복수형으로 쓰지 않는다.
8 every(모든)는 뒤에 단수명사가 오며 항상 단수 취급한다.
9 학문 · 학과명은 단수 취급한다.
10 앞에 있는 some에 대응하여 정해지지 않은 '다른 학생들'이라는 뜻을 나타내므로 관사 the 없이 others를 써야 한다.
11 '둘 다'라는 뜻의 부정대명사 Both가 알맞다.
12 '둘 중 어느 쪽도 ~않다'라는 뜻의 부정대명사 neither가 알맞다.
13 식사를 나타내는 명사(breakfast, lunch, dinner) 앞에는 관사를 쓰지 않는다.
14 두 개 중 나머지 하나를 지칭할 때는 the other를 쓴다.
15 악기 이름 앞에는 정관사 the를 쓴다.
16 each는 항상 단수 취급하므로 단수동사 is가 와야 한다.
17 날씨를 나타낼 때는 비인칭 주어 it을 쓰므로, It이 되어야 한다.
18 water는 셀 수 없는 명사이므로 복수형으로 쓰지 않는다.
19 ① all 뒤에 복수명사인 shops가 왔으므로 was를 복수동사 were로 고쳐 써야 옳다. ② 시간을 나타내는 문장의 주어로 쓰이는 것은 비인칭대명사 it이므로, That을 It으로 고쳐 써야 옳다. ④ student는 가산명사이고 내용상 복수이므로 복수명사인 students로 고쳐 써야 옳다. ⑤ movie는 가산명사이고 단수형이므로 앞에 부정관사 a를 써야 옳다.
20 B의 대답에서 your는 your school을 가리키는 소유대명사 yours로 고쳐 써야 옳다.
21 앞에 나온 명사와 같은 종류의 불특정한 사물을 가리킬 때는 one을 쓴다.
22 서수 앞에는 정관사 the가 와야 한다.
23 (A) people은 단수형으로 쓰이지만 항상 복수 취급하는 명사이므로, seem이 알맞다. (B) 문맥상 '또 다른 하나의'라는 뜻의 another가 알맞다. (C) '~마다'라는 뜻을 나타내는 부정관사 a가 알맞다.
24 (A) '둘 다'라는 뜻의 both가 알맞다. (B) 둘 중 하나를 나타낼 때는 one을 쓴다. (C) 둘 중 하나를 뺀 그 나머지를 나타낼 때는 the other를 쓴다.

CHAPTER 12 형용사 · 부사

★ **POINT 01** 형용사의 쓰임 p.146

A 1 special 2 anything interesting 3 the
4 someone nice 5 hard 6 warm
7 cultural rules

B 1 The mistake made me nervous.

2 Is there anything wrong with your computer?
3 He found the shoes very comfortable.
4 happy to hear that she is alive.
5 This hospital is full of the wounded.
6 something special to do.

★ POINT 02 수량형용사 I p.147

A 1 a few 2 any 3 some 4 few
5 little 6 a little
B 1 any → some 2 a little → a few
3 some → any
C 1 Few 2 some[a few] 3 some[a little] 4 little

★ POINT 03 수량형용사 II p.148

A 1 a lot of 2 much 3 lots of 4 lots of
5 a lot of 6 many
B 1 much[a lot of, lots of] experience
2 much[a lot of, lots of] room
3 much blood 4 many[a lot of, lots of] reasons
5 a lot of museums
C 1 a lot of love 2 many calories
3 much information 4 Lots of fuel
5 are many interesting stories

★ POINT 04 부사의 쓰임 p.149

A 1 well 2 Strangely 3 actually 4 Unfortunately
B 1 hard 2 very 3 usually
4 loudly 5 quickly 6 too
C 1 easily가 lifted 수식 2 perfectly가 fits 수식
3 Suddenly가 she stopped to say hello to her friends 수식
4 so가 depressed 수식
5 yesterday가 bought 수식, well이 works 수식
6 much가 Thank 수식, very가 much 수식

★ POINT 05 부사의 위치 p.150

A 1 turn on it → turn it on
2 always will → will always
3 never would → would never
4 pretends sometimes → sometimes pretends
5 often are → are often
6 look up them → look them up
B 1 put out the campfire 또는 put the campfire out
2 is sometimes difficult to say
3 he often hurts others' feelings
4 managed to put it out
5 take off his dirty clothes 또는 take his dirty clothes off
6 decided to turn it down
7 Seaweed soup is usually cooked

★ POINT 06 주의해야 할 부사 p.151

A 1 lately 2 high 3 hardly 4 highly
B 1 weekly 2 daily 3 lovely 4 hardly 5 last
6 lately 7 Early

REVIEW TEST 12 p.152

1 ③ 2 ⑤ 3 ② 4 ⑤ 5 ③ 6 Put it on
7 sometimes shop 8 daily 9 late 10 few
11 is always busy 12 ① 13 ② 14 ⑤ 15 ⑤ 16 ⑤
17 ④ 18 ④ 19 ④ 20 ② 21 ③ 22 ④ 23 ④
24 (A) few (B) some (C) a few 25 (A) Many
(B) sometimes wish (C) can often

1 '약간의'라는 뜻으로 권유나 부탁을 나타내는 의문문에 쓰이는 것은 some이다.
2 '많은'이라는 뜻을 나타내며 셀 수 없는 명사 앞에 쓰이는 것은 much이다.
3 문맥상 '거의 ~않다'라는 뜻의 부사가 들어가야 하므로 hardly가 적절하다.
4 '약간의'라는 뜻으로 부정문에 쓰이는 것은 any이다.
5 '많은'이라는 뜻을 나타내며 셀 수 있는 명사 앞에 쓰이는 것은 a lot of이다.
6 〈타동사+부사〉로 된 동사구의 목적어가 대명사일 때 부사는 목적어 뒤에 와야 한다.
7 빈도부사 sometimes는 일반동사 앞에 쓰인다.
8 '매일'이라는 뜻의 부사 daily가 적절하다.
9 '늦게'라는 뜻의 부사 late이 적절하다.
10 '거의 없는'이라는 뜻을 나타내며 셀 수 있는 명사 앞에 쓰이는 것은 few이다.
11 빈도부사 always는 be동사 뒤에 쓰인다.
12 time은 셀 수 없는 명사이므로 앞에 few가 올 수 없다.

13 목적어의 상태나 성질을 나타내는 목적격 보어로 형용사가 와야 하는데, politely는 부사이다.

14 분사 affected를 수식하는 부사가 와야 하는데, heavy는 형용사이다.

15 주어의 상태나 성질을 나타내는 주격 보어로 형용사가 와야 하는데, terribly는 부사이다.

16 -thing, -body, -one으로 끝나는 대명사의 경우 형용사가 뒤에서 수식하므로 something exciting이 되어야 한다.

17 much는 셀 수 있는 명사 앞에 쓰일 수 없다.

18 '열심히'라는 뜻의 부사 hard가 되어야 한다.

19 experience는 셀 수 없는 명사이므로 few를 little로 고쳐 써야 옳다.

20 ① 〈타동사+부사〉로 된 동사구의 목적어가 대명사일 경우 부사는 목적어 뒤에 와야 하므로 try on it을 try it on으로 고쳐 써야 옳다. ③ sunshine은 셀 수 없는 명사이므로 few를 little로 고쳐 써야 옳다. ④ 긍정문이므로 any를 some으로 고쳐 써야 옳다. ⑤ babies는 셀 수 있는 명사이므로 Much를 Many 또는 A lot of[Lots of]로 고쳐 써야 옳다.

21 ① 문맥상 hard를 '거의 ~않다'라는 뜻의 부사인 hardly로 고쳐 써야 옳다. ② cookies는 셀 수 있는 명사이므로 much를 many로 고쳐 써야 옳다. ④ -thing, -body, -one으로 끝나는 대명사의 경우 형용사가 뒤에서 수식하므로 special something을 something special로 고쳐 써야 옳다. ⑤ days는 셀 수 있는 명사이므로 a little을 a few로 고쳐 써야 옳다.

22 조건문이므로 some을 any로 고쳐 써야 옳다.

23 time과 effort는 셀 수 없는 명사이므로 much 또는 a lot of, lots of가 알맞다.

24 (A) places는 셀 수 있는 명사이므로 few가 알맞다. (B) 긍정문이므로 some이 알맞다. (C) flights가 셀 수 있는 명사이므로 a few가 알맞다.

25 (A) people이 셀 수 있는 명사이므로 many가 알맞다. (B) 빈도부사는 일반동사 앞에 위치한다. (C) 빈도부사는 조동사 뒤, 일반동사 앞에 위치한다.

CHAPTER 13 비교

★ POINT 01 형용사·부사의 비교 변화 p.156

A **1** bigger **2** hardest **3** more careful **4** hotter
5 largest **6** safer **7** most popular

B **1** more **2** worse **3** most useful
4 more productive **5** easiest **6** better

★ POINT 02 원급 비교 p.157

A **1** more famous → famous **2** big as → as big as
3 so → as **4** hot → as[so] hot **5** than → as

B **1** not as[so] old as **2** not as[so] young as
3 as popular as **4** as ancient as
5 not as[so] cheap as **6** as much as

★ POINT 03 원급 비교 관용 표현 p.158

A **1** as much as possible
2 twice as much as Russia
3 as soon as you can
4 as much water as possible
5 three times thicker than

B **1** twice as heavy as **2** as much as possible
3 three times as big as **4** twice as hard as
5 as often as they can

★ POINT 04 비교급 비교 p.159

A **1** dangerously → more dangerously **2** than → to
3 very → much[even, far]

B **1** better than **2** more quickly than
3 was worse than

C **1** less comfortable than **2** far more efficient
3 even longer than **4** much larger than

★ POINT 05 비교급 비교 관용 표현 p.160

A **1** The more you are around the baby, the better it will be for her.
2 The less he spent, the more money he saved.
3 The drier the air is, the more water you need.

B **1** darker and darker
2 more and more crowded
3 The rarer, the more expensive
4 The more, the better
5 better and better **6** the paler, the cooler

★ POINT 06 최상급 비교 p.161

A **1** the coldest **2** (the) fastest

3 the most popular **4** the busiest

5 the hottest **6** the highest

B **1** most → the most **2** the bright → the brightest

3 far → by far

C **1** the tallest building **2** by far the best

3 lived the longest **4** the most diligent

★ POINT 07 최상급 비교 관용 표현 p.162

A **1** one of the scariest movies

2 the wisest person I've ever met

3 the best meeting we have ever had

4 one of the best authors in America

5 One of the most essential decisions

B **1** one of the most delicious dishes

2 one of the most learned people

3 one of the most successful companies

4 one of the worst movies (that) I've ever seen

5 the most beautiful city (that) I've ever been

6 one of the most popular garden flowers

★ POINT 08 원급 · 비교급을 이용한 최상급 표현 p.163

A **1** as[so] popular as **2** more comprehensive than

3 easier than **4** is larger than

5 your culture is the best

B **1** is more crowded than

2 as diverse as New York

3 faster than any other person

4 smarter than all the other students

5 more than any other game

6 better than all the other products

REVIEW TEST 13 p.164

1 ③ **2** ③ **3** ④ **4** ③ **5** ④ **6** the largest **7** better than **8** as[so] beautiful as **9** The younger, the more quickly **10** I can **11** more and more **12** twice as expensive as **13** the most talented actors **14** ④ **15** ① **16** ③ **17** ④ **18** ② **19** ③ **20** ⑤ **21** ① **22** ④ **23** ③ **24** ④

1 〈as+원급+as〉를 써서 '~만큼 …하게'라는 의미를 나타내므로 부사 well의 원급이 알맞다.

2 '가장 ~한'이라는 뜻의 〈the+최상급〉 형태가 와야 하므로 the longest가 알맞다.

3 〈비교급+than any other+단수명사〉로 최상급의 의미를 나타내므로 popular의 비교급 more popular가 와야 한다.

4 최상급의 의미를 나타내는데 뒤에 〈비교급+than〉이 있으므로 맨 앞에 No가 와야 한다.

5 '~하면 할수록 더 …하다'라는 뜻의 〈the+비교급, the+비교급〉 구문이므로 The older가 적절하다.

6 〈비교급+than any other+단수명사〉는 최상급의 의미를 나타내므로 the largest가 적절하다.

7 〈A ~ not as+원급+as B〉는 〈B ~ 비교급+than A〉로 바꾸어 쓸 수 있다.

8 최상급의 의미를 나타내는 〈no+명사+비교급+than〉은 〈no+명사+as[so]+원급+as〉로 바꾸어 쓸 수 있다.

9 '~하면 할수록 더 …하다'라는 뜻의 〈the+비교급, the+비교급〉 구문이 되어야 한다.

10 〈as+원급+as possible〉은 〈as+원급+as+주어+can〉으로 바꾸어 쓸 수 있다.

11 '점점 더 ~한'이라는 뜻의 〈비교급+and+비교급〉을 써야 하는데, more를 붙여 비교급을 만드는 형용사이므로 〈more and more+원급〉 형태가 알맞다.

12 '~보다 몇 배 …한[하게]'이라는 뜻의 〈배수사+as+원급+as〉를 쓴다.

13 '가장 ~한 것들 중 하나'라는 뜻의 〈one of the+최상급+복수명사〉를 쓴다.

14 very는 비교급을 강조할 때 쓸 수 없다.

15 big의 최상급은 biggest이다.

16 '가장 ~한'이라는 뜻의 〈the+최상급〉이 와야 하므로 the shortest가 적절하다.

17 〈the+최상급+(that)+주어+have ever p.p.〉는 '지금까지 ~한 것들 중 가장 …한'이라는 뜻이다.

18 〈배수사+비교급+than〉 구문이므로 비교급 older가 와야 한다.

19 비교급으로 최상급의 의미를 나타내는 구문으로 brave를 비교급 braver로 고쳐 써야 옳다.

20 〈as+원급+as〉를 써서 '~만큼 …하게'라는 의미를 나타내야 하므로 longest를 원급인 long으로 고쳐 써야 옳다.

21 (A) 문맥상 '~중에서 가장 …한'이라는 뜻을 나타내므로 최상급 the most popular가 적절하다. (B) 〈배수사+as+원급+as〉의 형태가 되어야 하므로 twice가 적절하다.

22 (A) 〈the+ 비교급, the+비교급〉을 써서 '~하면 할수록 더 …하다'라는 뜻을 나타내므로 the more가 알맞다. (B) 앞에 비교급 simpler가 있으므로 than이 알맞다.

23 '~보다 몇 배 …한[하게]'이라는 뜻의 〈배수사+as+원급+as〉가 와야 하므로 larger를 원급인 large로 고쳐 써야 옳다.

24 large의 비교급은 larger이다.

CHAPTER 14

전치사

★ POINT 01 전치사의 쓰임 p.168

A **1** me **2** reading **3** to my office
4 Instead of **5** danger

B **1** with themselves가 happy 수식
2 at midnight가 arrived 수식
3 from Seattle이 flight 수식
4 of February가 beginning 수식
at the beginning of February가 took place 수식
5 in socks가 holes 수식
in my family가 common 수식
6 To my surprise가 it turned out that he didn't commit the crime 수식

C **1** The leaves on the trees
2 is in his second year
3 From my point of view
4 on a quiet road in my hometown

★ POINT 02 장소·방향의 전치사 I p.169

A **1** up **2** in **3** from **4** around
5 between **6** into

B **1** by **2** behind **3** under **4** on
5 at **6** in front of **7** out of

★ POINT 03 장소·방향의 전치사 II p.170

A **1** on **2** above **3** at **4** in
5 in **6** above **7** at **8** on

B **1** above her head **2** on the ceiling
3 in the cage **4** at the station

★ POINT 04 시간의 전치사 I p.171

A **1** at **2** After **3** through **4** within
5 by **6** since **7** until **8** for

B **1** During **2** in **3** Since
4 after **5** from, until **6** before

★ POINT 05 시간의 전치사 II p.172

A **1** at **2** in **3** until **4** on
5 during **6** for **7** by

B **1** at midnight **2** until 1946 **3** in the afternoon
4 on Friday **5** for a week
6 by the end

★ POINT 06 원인·목적의 전치사 p.173

A **1** of **2** at **3** from **4** with
5 on **6** from **7** for **8** for

B **1** on **2** for **3** of **4** at **5** with

★ POINT 07 수단·도구의 전치사 p.174

A **1** without a pair of scissors
2 by reviewing the last chapter
3 in Spanish **4** with my headphones
5 by phone or e-mail
6 by credit card

B **1** with a pencil **2** by car **3** in Chinese
4 by bus **5** without, explanation
6 by listening to **7** without fuel

★ POINT 08 기타 전치사 p.175

A **1** about **2** for **3** on **4** against

B **1** against **2** for **3** on[about] **4** about[of]

C **1** for **2** against **3** of **4** on

REVIEW TEST 14 p.176

1 ② **2** ④ **3** ② **4** ① **5** ② **6** ② **7** ③ **8** ④
9 between **10** on **11** behind **12** until[till] **13** ⑤
14 ④ **15** ③ **16** ④ **17** ⑤ **18** ② **19** ③ **20** (A) at
(B) Through (C) between **21** ③ **22** ① **23** ② **24** ⑤
25 ②

1 계절과 같이 비교적 긴 시간 앞에는 전치사 in을 쓴다.
2 '~을 따라서'라는 뜻의 전치사 along이 알맞다.
3 구체적인 시간의 길이와 함께 쓰여 '~ 동안'이라는 뜻을 나타내는 전치사 for가 알맞다.
4 '~을 보고[듣고, 알고]'라는 뜻으로 감정의 원인을 나타내는 at이 알맞다.
5 완료의 기한을 나타내므로 by가 알맞다.
6 전치사 at은 어떤 한 지점을 나타내거나 구체적인 시각 또는 특정 시점을 나타낼 때 쓴다.
7 전치사 on은 '〈관련 · 주제〉 ~에 대하여, 〈장소〉 ~ 위에'라는 뜻으로 쓰인다.
8 전치사 for는 '~에 찬성하는, ~ 때문에'라는 뜻으로 쓰인다.
9 '〈둘〉 ~ 사이에'라는 뜻의 전치사 between이 알맞다.
10 특정한 날 앞에는 전치사 on을 쓴다.
11 '~ 뒤에'라는 뜻의 전치사 behind가 알맞다.
12 '~까지'라는 뜻으로 상태 · 상황이 계속됨을 나타내는 전치사 until이 알맞다.
13 '〈도구〉 ~을 가지고'라는 뜻의 전치사 with가 알맞다.
14 특정한 행사나 사건을 나타내는 말 앞에 쓰여 '~ 동안, ~ 중에'라는 뜻을 나타내는 전치사 during이 알맞다.
15 교통수단 앞에 쓰여 '~으로'라는 뜻을 나타내는 전치사 by가 알맞다.
16 어느 시점까지 동작 · 상태가 지속됨을 나타내는 전치사 until이 알맞다.
17 완료의 기한을 나타내는 전치사 by가 와야 한다.
18 '~의 용건으로, ~차'라는 뜻의 전치사 on이 알맞다.
19 요일 앞에는 전치사 on을 쓴다.
20 (A) at night, at noon 등과 같이 하루의 특정 시점을 나타낼 때 전치사 at을 쓴다. (B) '~을 관통하여'라는 뜻을 나타내는 전치사 Through가 알맞다. (C) '〈둘〉 ~사이에'라는 뜻을 나타내는 전치사 between이 알맞다.
21 시각 앞에는 전치사 at을 쓴다.
22 전치사의 목적어가 도시인 London이므로 in이 알맞다.
23 연도 앞에는 전치사 in을 쓴다.
24 (A) 어떤 것의 표면과 접촉해서 '~위에'라는 뜻을 나타내므로 on이 알맞다. (B) '~을 위해서'라는 뜻으로 목적을 나타내는 전치사 for가 알맞다.
25 (A) 셋 이상의 여럿 앞에 쓰여 '~ 사이에'라는 뜻을 나타내는 among이 알맞다. (B) '~에 대하여'라는 뜻의 about이 알맞다.

CHAPTER 15 일치 · 화법

★ POINT 01 수의 일치 I p.180

A 1 are 2 Is 3 needs 4 was
B 1 needs → need 2 live → lives
3 were → was 4 are → is
C 1 anybody[anyone] was coming
2 Not only, but also, am 3 has
4 Both, and, work

★ POINT 02 수의 일치 II p.181

A 1 are 2 is 3 is 4 were 5 is 6 looks
7 were
B 1 Playing games is 2 is limited to
3 Half of, is 4 Two thirds of, come
5 Families who eat, have

★ POINT 03 시제 일치의 원칙 p.182

A 1 we would be able to use electricity that day
2 had to do the job for him
3 meant to him 4 had found a job
5 had caught me cheating
B 1 found, had left 2 know, will return
3 don't understand, accepted
4 thought you wanted to study
5 said, had 6 think, is

★ POINT 04 시제 일치의 예외 p.183

A 1 sets 2 freezes 3 makes
4 were united 5 gained
B 1 isn't always helpful 2 are disappearing
3 moves around the Sun 4 broke out in 1789
5 is[was] going out with 6 works[worked]
7 was the thirty-fifth president

★ POINT 05 평서문의 화법 전환 p.184

A 1 it would be 2 I want to be
3 he had to study, that week

4 You should eat

B 1 (that) he felt better that day

2 (that) she would like to eat pizza

3 (that) he had hung out with his friends there

4 (that) she would participate in a volunteer program for the blind

5 Mike said (that) he had bought that book the day before[the previous day]

★ POINT 06 의문문·명령문의 화법 전환 p.185

A 1 was it → it was 2 has → had

3 don't → not to

B 1 Margo ordered him to stop smoking.

2 I asked Grandfather what he was looking at.

3 He told me not to play the violin after 7 p.m.

4 I tell my son to treat older people with respect.

5 She asked me if[whether] I had been to New York.

6 My teacher told me to finish the book by the next[following] day.

7 Susan asked me who had lent me the camera.

REVIEW TEST 15 p.186

1 ④ 2 ② 3 ① 4 ④ 5 ⑤ 6 ⑤ 7 ④ 8 ③ 9 what he had had for lunch 10 she didn't know what to do 11 not to eat too much chocolate 12 if[whether] I was single 13 want 14 had worked 15 are 16 have been 17 if[whether] I had, painted 18 ⑤ 19 ⑤ 20 ⑤ 21 ④ 22 (A) told (B) to give (C) had 23 ② 24 ①

1 〈most of+명사〉는 명사의 수에 동사의 수를 일치시킨다. / each는 항상 단수 취급한다.

2 every는 뒤에 단수명사가 오며 항상 단수 취급한다. / 학문 · 학과명은 단수 취급한다.

3 〈both A and B〉는 복수 취급한다. / 동명사구 주어는 단수 취급한다.

4 〈not only A but also B〉는 B에 동사의 수를 일치시킨다. / 〈a number of+복수명사〉는 복수 취급한다.

5 주절의 시제가 과거일 때 종속절에는 과거 또는 과거완료가 쓰이는데, 의미상 would be가 알맞다.

6 의문사가 없는 의문문(Sylvia said to me, "Can you help me?")을 간접화법으로 쓸 때 인용문은 〈if[whether]+주어+동사〉로 쓴다.

7 명령문(She said to her brother, "Clean your dirty car.")을 간접화법으로 쓸 때 인용문의 동사는 to부정사로 바꾼다.

8 주절의 시제가 현재일 때 종속절에는 시제의 제약이 없는데, 의미상 과거를 나타내므로 broke가 알맞다.

9 의문사가 있는 의문문을 간접화법으로 쓸 때 인용문은 〈의문사+주어+동사〉의 순서로 쓴다. 전달동사가 과거시제이므로 시제 일치의 원칙에 따라 직접인용문의 과거시제는 과거완료가 된다.

10 that절의 인칭대명사를 전달자의 입장에 맞게 바꾼다. 전달동사가 과거시제이므로 시제 일치의 원칙에 따라 직접인용문의 현재시제는 과거시제가 된다.

11 명령문을 간접화법으로 쓸 때 인용문의 동사는 to부정사로 쓰는데, 부정명령문이므로 to부정사 앞에 not을 붙인다.

12 의문사가 없는 의문문을 간접화법으로 쓸 때 인용문은 〈if[whether]+주어+동사〉로 쓴다. 전달동사가 과거시제이므로 시제 일치의 원칙에 따라 직접인용문의 현재시제는 과거시제가 된다.

13 〈the+형용사〉는 '~한 사람들'이라는 뜻으로 복수 취급하므로 복수형 동사를 쓴다.

14 주절의 시제가 과거이고 종속절의 시제가 주절보다 앞서므로 과거완료를 쓴다.

15 in your garden은 형용사구로, 수식을 받는 주어 The flowers에 동사의 수를 일치시킨다.

16 〈B as well as A〉는 B에 동사의 수를 일치시킨다.

17 의문사가 없는 의문문을 간접화법으로 쓸 때 인용문은 〈if[whether]+주어+동사〉의 순서로 쓴다.

18 who is carrying two bags는 형용사절로, 수식을 받는 주어 The man에 수를 일치시켜 동사는 is가 되어야 한다.

19 종속절이 역사적 사실을 나타내므로 과거시제(took)를 쓴다.

20 주어는 주격 관계대명사절의 수식을 받는 Most of the things이고 〈most of+명사〉는 명사의 수에 동사의 수를 일치시키므로 was를 were로 바꿔 써야 옳다.

21 동명사구 주어는 단수 취급하므로 make를 makes로 바꿔 써야 옳다.

22 (A) 말을 듣는 사람이 뒤에 나오므로 told가 알맞다. (B) 명령문을 간접화법으로 쓸 때 인용문의 동사는 to부정사로 바꾼다. (C) 주절의 시제가 과거이므로 종속절의 동사로는 과거형인 had가 알맞다.

23 (A) 주절의 시제가 과거이므로 종속절에는 과거 또는 과거완료를 쓴다. (B) 〈neither A nor B〉는 B에 동사의 수를 일치

시킨다.

24 (A) 동명사구 주어는 단수 취급한다. (B) -thing으로 끝나는 대명사는 단수 취급한다.

CHAPTER 16 특수 구문

★ POINT 01 부정 표현 p.190

A **1** hardly **2** Nobody **3** every

B **1** does not always go to bed

2 Neither of us wants

3 seldom match their sounds

C **1** Not all students **2** None of

3 have never heard

★ POINT 02 생략 p.191

A **1** (go out much) **2** Julie (is) **3** (I'll) return

4 (he was) **5** (gave) my sister

6 (they are important) to the individual company

B **1** Michael is a lot smarter than you (are smart).

2 I thought he was angry at me, but he wasn't (angry at me).

3 While (you are) doing the laundry, don't forget to add some soap.

4 Turn up the volume if you want to (turn up the volume).

5 Though (I was) hungry, I didn't eat anything after 6 p.m.

6 Anna plays the guitar better than Kate (plays the guitar).

7 The cost of 3D printing is getting lower and the quality (of 3D printing is getting) better.

★ POINT 03 동격 p.192

A **1** that Mike and Susan are getting married

2 exposing young children to computers

3 that tourists cause traffic congestion

4 the farthest known planet in our solar system

5 that human beings are essentially selfish

B **1** The fact **2** my boss

3 the world-famous photographer

4 Abraham Lincoln

5 The claim **6** the problem

C **1** 우리는 세계에서 가장 큰 대륙인 아시아에 산다.

2 그녀는 Brian을 만난다는 생각에 들떠 있다.

3 우리 수영 코치인 Sandy Brown이 지난달 은퇴했다.

4 Mike는 TV를 많이 보는 것이 십대 청소년들에게 나쁘다는 의견을 내놓았다.

5 그는 자기에게 경험이 없다는 사실로 인해 낙담하지 않았다.

6 아일랜드의 수도인 Dublin의 인구는 130만 명이다.

★ POINT 04 도치 I p.193

A **1** were rows of delicious-looking chocolate bars

2 stands an old castle

3 lay a small box wrapped in gold paper

B **1** do → am

2 So I will → So will I

3 So → Neither

C **1** neither is he **2** neither can I **3** so will I

4 so does my sister

★ POINT 05 도치 II p.194

A **1** could Max meet **2** did I imagine

3 had she seen a child

B **1** does John visit **2** has he watched

3 have humans created **4** did I dream

5 could he know

C **1** have they been to Canada

2 is it expensive **3** have I had

4 did she realize **5** did I realize

★ POINT 06 강조 p.195

A **1** does taste good

2 maps do reflect the world views

3 did look depressed yesterday

4 at 9 o'clock that we're supposed to leave

5 Sarah that[who] I met on the street by accident

6 a new skirt that Kate dropped by a store to buy

B **1** does have bad table manners

2 It is in this park that I take a walk

3 It was then that Andrew made a big mistake

4 It was Dean who crashed into the police car

REVIEW TEST 16

p.196

1 ④ **2** ⑤ **3** ⑤ **4** ③ **5** ④ **6** cannot[can't] always **7** It, that[who] **8** that **9** Neither **10** does **11** ④ **12** ① **13** ② **14** ① **15** I do want to have a great sense of humor. **16** It was Jake that[who] showed me how to swim. **17** Only after some time did he continue. **18** ① **19** ⑤ **20** ⑤ **21** ② **22** ⑤ **23** ③ **24** ④

1 부정어 never가 문두에 쓰였으므로 〈부정어+조동사+주어+본동사〉의 어순이 되어야 한다.

2 do동사를 이용하여 동사 wait를 강조하는데, 의미상 과거를 나타내므로 did가 알맞다.

3 일반동사가 쓰인 현재시제의 부정문 다음에 이어지고 주어가 I 이므로 neither do I가 알맞다.

4 Mark's wedding이 강조된 〈It was ~ that ...〉 강조 구문이다.

5 장소의 부사구가 문두에 쓰이면 주어와 동사가 도치된다.

6 '언제나 ~인 것은 아니다'라는 뜻의 부분 부정을 나타내므로 cannot[can't] always를 쓴다.

7 〈It was ~ that ...〉 강조 구문으로, 강조하는 대상이 사람이므로 that의 자리에 who를 쓸 수도 있다.

8 the news와 명사절 Peter broke his leg가 동격의 관계이므로 접속사 that이 들어가야 한다.

9 '둘 다 ~아니다'라는 뜻의 전체 부정을 나타내므로 Neither를 쓴다.

10 do동사를 이용하여 동사 have to를 강조하는데, 주어가 3인칭 단수이고 현재시제이므로 does가 알맞다.

11 A가 말한 문장이 현재시제의 부정문이고 be동사를 사용하고 있으므로 Neither am I.가 알맞다.

12 A가 말한 문장이 현재시제의 긍정문이고 조동사를 사용하고 있으므로 So can I.가 알맞다.

13 A가 말한 문장이 현재시제의 긍정문이고 일반동사를 사용하고 있으므로 So do I.가 알맞다.

14 do동사를 이용하여 동사 finish를 강조하는데, 주어가 1인칭 단수이고 과거시제이므로 I did finish it이 알맞다.

15 do동사를 동사 앞에 써서 문장의 내용이 사실임을 강조할 수 있는데, 주어가 1인칭 단수이고 현재시제이므로 do를 쓴다.

16 It was와 that 사이에 강조하는 말을 두고 나머지를 that 이하에 쓴다. 강조하는 대상이 사람이므로 that의 자리에 who를 쓸 수도 있다.

17 부정어 Only를 포함하는 부사구를 문장 앞으로 보내 강조할 수 있다. 이때 어순은 〈부정어+조동사+주어+본동사〉가 된다.

18 부정어가 강조되어 문장 앞에 오는 경우 〈부정어+조동사+주어+본동사〉의 어순이 되는데, 일반동사의 경우 do동사가 대신 앞으로 나가 Hardly did she eat이 되어야 한다.

19 〈It is ~ that ...〉 강조 구문이므로 that을 써야 한다.

20 Your guess와 명사절 Betty is from Canada가 동격의 관계이므로 which가 아닌 접속사 that이 와야 한다.

21 장소의 부사구가 문두에 쓰였으므로 〈부사구+동사+주어〉의 어순으로 써야 한다.

22 ① the idea 뒤에 동명사구가 이어지므로 that을 동격을 나타내는 of로 고쳐 써야 옳다. ② 장소의 부사구 There가 문두에 왔으므로 〈부사구+동사+주어〉의 어순으로 써야 한다. 즉, some dark clouds were를 were some dark clouds로 고쳐 써야 옳다. ③ 본동사 앞에 do를 써서 강조할 때 본동사는 동사원형으로 쓰므로, felt를 feel로 고쳐 써야 옳다. ④ 부정의 뜻이 있는 말이 문장 앞에 오는 경우 〈부정어+조동사+주어+본동사〉의 어순으로 쓰고 일반동사의 경우 do가 대신 앞으로 나가므로, have I를 do I have로 고쳐 써야 옳다.

23 (A) a rule과 뒤에 나오는 명사절이 동격의 관계이므로 접속사 that이 알맞다. (B) 〈It was ~ that ...〉 강조 구문으로, 강조하는 대상이 사람이므로 that의 자리에 who를 쓸 수도 있다.

24 (A) 장소의 부사구(At one ... restaurant)가 문두에 쓰였으므로 주어와 동사가 도치된다. (B) 부정어인 Not이 강조되어 문장 앞에 오는 경우 〈부정어+조동사+주어+본동사〉의 어순으로 쓴다.

www.nebooks.co.kr NE 능률

전국 **온오프 서점** 판매중

구문이 독해로 연결되는 해석 공식, 천문장

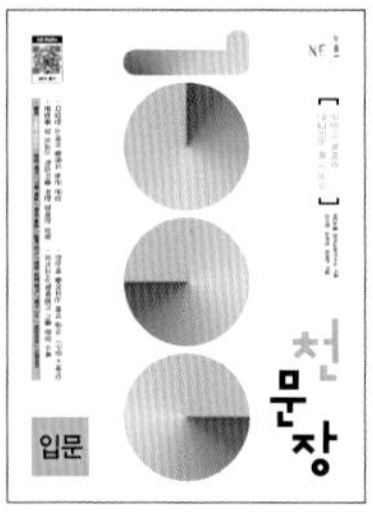

입문
(중2~중3)

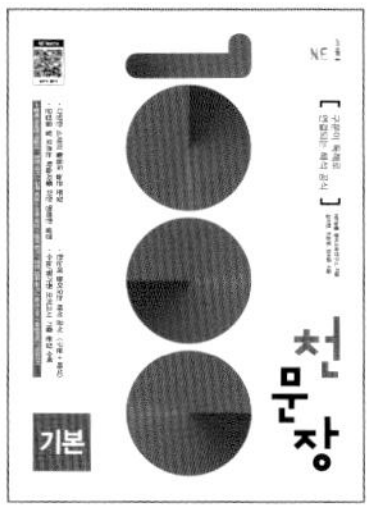

기본
(예비고~고1)

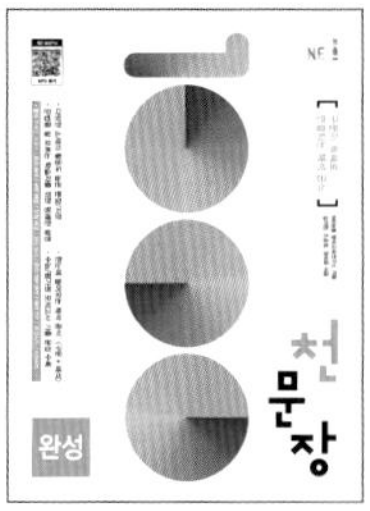

완성
(고2~고3)

한눈에 들어오는 해석 공식

· 도식화된 문법 설명과 <구문+해석>으로 제시되어 외우기 쉬운 해석 공식

다양한 소재의 활용도 높은 문장과 학교 시험 대비 서술형 문제 제공

· 구문/문법 적용 사례를 이해하기 쉬운 문장부터, 수능/평가원 모의고사 기출에 나오는 복잡한 문장까지 학습 가능

문법을 잘 모르는 학습자를 위한 명쾌한 설명

· 학생들이 독해 시 어려움을 겪는 포인트를 콕 집어 설명하는 해석 TIP 제공
· 확실한 개념 이해를 도와주는 삽화 제공(입문)